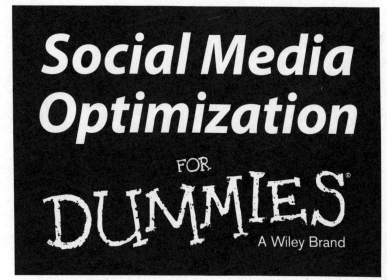

Social Media Optimization

FOR

DUMMIES®

A Wiley Brand

by Ric Shreves
with Michelle Krasniak

FOR
DUMMIES®
A Wiley Brand

Social Media Optimization For Dummies®

Published by: **John Wiley & Sons, Inc.,** 111 River Street, Hoboken, NJ 07030-5774, www.wiley.com

Copyright © 2015 by John Wiley & Sons, Inc., Hoboken, New Jersey

Published simultaneously in Canada

For general information on our other products and services, please contact our Customer Care Department within the U.S. at 877-762-2974, outside the U.S. at 317-572-3993, or fax 317-572-4002. For technical support, please visit www.wiley.com/techsupport.

Wiley publishes in a variety of print and electronic formats and by print-on-demand. Some material included with standard print versions of this book may not be included in e-books or in print-on-demand. If this book refers to media such as a CD or DVD that is not included in the version you purchased, you may download this material at http://booksupport.wiley.com. For more information about Wiley products, visit www.wiley.com.

Library of Congress Control Number: 2014958469

ISBN: 978-1-119-01609-0 (pbk); ISBN 978-1-119-01613-7 (ebk); ISBN 978-1-119-01612-0 (ebk)

Manufactured in the United States of America

10 9 8 7 6 5 4 3 2 1

Contents at a Glance

Table of Contents

Introduction

Over the past several years, social media has come to dominate conversations about digital marketing. The rise of social media as an online influencer has been dramatic and has happened quite quickly. In traditional media, the concept of word of mouth has always been respected as one of the most influential forms of marketing. In the Internet age, word of mouth now happens online, via social media. When your friends recommend things, you listen. When they share and like things, you notice. The concepts are as old as marketing itself, but the tools are new.

Social media optimization — or SMO, as it's often called in this book — is a marketing discipline that focuses on creating effective social media. This book starts with the assumption that you're already onboard with the idea of social media, but now you want to find out how to work with social media better, faster, and more effectively. Over the course of these pages, we share with you our experiences in managing social media, and try to communicate the lessons we've learned and explain the tools we've used. The goal of this book is to help you build a social media practice that gets results and doesn't make you nuts in the process.

The one given that you have to keep in mind is that social media is a fast-changing, fluid area. New tools will arise. New channels will take on importance. Books, by contrast, are largely static things. After you read this book, the burden is on you to make an attempt to stay abreast of things in this field and to keep your eyes open for new techniques and tools that you can fold into your practice.

About This Book

Social media has the potential to be rather overwhelming. The sheer volume of channels is daunting. After you pick your channels, the experience is still a bit like trying to drink from a fire hose; the amount of information pouring out can be phenomenal. This book is about taming the beast. It's about how to approach social media marketing, how to find the right channels and the right tools, and how to use them to your advantage.

As you read this book, you should be thinking about how the techniques and tools discussed can be integrated into your practice. Throughout the book, we make an effort to discuss different implementations, but every person has different priorities, abilities, and resources. This book can't be a one-size-fits-all text — and it doesn't try to be. Instead, the book highlights underlying principles and then shows how they can be implemented in various scenarios using a variety of tools. In other words, a philosophy is at work here, and you need to think about how it's relevant to your work. Don't get caught up in mechanical application of examples; rather, think about the underlying principles and how you can apply them to your needs.

Note the following text formatting conventions:

- ✔ Bolded text should be typed exactly as it appears in the book. The exception is when you're working through a step list: Because each step is bold, the text to type is not bold.

- ✔ Web addresses and programming code appear in monofont. If you're reading a digital version of this book on a device connected to the Internet, note that you can click the web address to visit that website, like this: `www.dummies.com`.

Foolish Assumptions

The world is full of assumptions, some foolish and some not. Here are ours:

- ✔ You're interested in social media marketing.

- ✔ You have some experience with things like Facebook and Twitter.

- ✔ You want to be an effective social media marketer.

- ✔ You're comfortable working with a browser and capable of executing common tasks.

Icons Used in This Book

The icons you see in the sidebar of the text signal important additional pieces of information.

The Tip icon marks tips (duh!) and shortcuts that you can use to make life easier.

Remember icons mark the information that's especially important to know. To siphon off the most important information in each chapter, just skim the text that has these icons.

The Technical Stuff icon marks information of a highly technical nature that you normally can skip.

The Warning icon tells you to watch out! It marks important information that may save you headaches or help you avoid disaster.

Beyond the Book

You can find more information than what's available in the pages of this book. On the Dummies.com website you can find a number of resources that supplement the book and provide you with more information about social media optimization:

- ✔ **Cheat Sheet:** The Cheat Sheet (www.dummies.com/cheatsheet/socialmediaoptimization) for this book includes at-a-glance references for common social media tasks.

- ✔ **Dummies.com online articles:** Visit Dummies.com for additional articles on social media optimization, including tips on how to add images to your tweets, how to put a Facebook Like Box on your web page, and how to get started with Hootsuite. You will also find a helpful list of free social media analytics tools. To read these articles, visit (www.dummies.com/extras/socialmediaoptimization).

Where to Go from Here

One of the neat things about *For Dummies* books is that they're not purely linear — that is, you're not expected to start on page 1 and read the book in sequence to understand things. *For Dummies* books are meant to be more like reference books, in the sense that you can start anywhere. If Chapter 8 looks interesting to you, great; start there. Everything you need to know about the things discussed in Chapter 8 is included in Chapter 8. The same is true of the other chapters, of course; each is self-contained.

That said, for those of you who are looking for a quick start, we've included a chapter especially for you. If you need to get a social media campaign up and running today, start with Chapter 3.

Part I
Getting Started with Social Media Optimization

Visit www.dummies.com/go/socialmediaoptimization for additional *For Dummies* content and resources.

In this part . . .

- ✔ Formulating a definition of SMO
- ✔ Understanding the connection between SEO and SMO
- ✔ Getting started with your social media campaigns

Chapter 1

Building the Foundations of Social Media Optimization

In This Chapter

▶ Formulating a definition of SMO

▶ Understanding the benefits of SMO

▶ Committing to SMO

▶ Finding an appropriate voice

Social media is now part of every digital marketer's tool kit. We're moving past the adolescent days of social media and moving into a more mature market. As social media has grown in importance and sophistication, a new discipline has emerged: social media optimization.

New tools and new techniques are great, but they bring with them increased complexity and risk of confusion. In an area that changes as quickly as digital marketing, it's easy to get sidetracked and distracted by new things and lose sight of the importance of the process behind social media. It requires effort to separate what really works from what is simply the hot new topic of the moment. Social media optimization emphasizes process and techniques and has proved its worth to brands worldwide. It delivers tangible benefits and can be reduced to a repeatable system that makes implementing social media optimization practical for digital marketing teams.

This book dives deep into the discipline of social media marketing and looks at the tools and techniques that have proved to be effective. This chapter explores the basics of social media optimization. It also looks at how social media optimization relates to other aspects of your marketing and, most important, how it relates to your website.

Defining SMO

Social media optimization — or *SMO,* as it is often called — is a marketing discipline that emphasizes a holistic approach to social media and website content management. Typically, SMO is used to drive traffic to a website or to raise awareness of a product, a promotion, or an event. Due to its close ties to websites and search engine optimization, SMO is often defined to include efforts to improve a website's social media effectiveness through the use of techniques such as content optimization and social sharing.

Social media optimization is a fairly recent concept in the world of digital marketing. Although the use of social media in digital marketing is well established, the concept of SMO is relatively new. In terms of distinguishing SMO from traditional social media marketing, SMO is more deliberate than traditional ad hoc social media marketing efforts and more closely integrated with efforts to market your website. SMO isn't purely about what you post in your social media profiles. SMO crosses boundaries. It's concerned with social media management, but it's also a philosophy of content management and website marketing, and it encompasses planning and executing a strategy designed to cross channels.

In terms of practice, SMO is an interesting mix of art and science. Although quantifiable concepts — such as page views, social shares, likes, and retweets — are key elements of SMO, so are less analytical skills. Important soft skills include social engagement — that is, the ability to interact directly with your audience via social media channels and the ability to craft creative and compelling content. The objective aspects of SMO are the subject of several great tools, such as Google Analytics and Facebook Insights, but the subjective skills are not only hard to quantify, but also hard to teach. In this regard, SMO values and rewards practitioners who have a mix of both practical analytic skills and soft skills that allows them to read an audience.

Many people find SMO to be rewarding. You get to work with a variety of dynamic channels, and you get to interact directly with the audience. If you're setting out to be an SMO practitioner, you need to cultivate both sides of your brain. Your analytical side needs to be able to create and justify a strategy, execute implementation of that strategy, read the analytics, and then feed that information into your plan. Your social side needs to be able to read an audience; anticipate their needs; and interact with them at an authentic, personal level.

Understanding the essential elements

SMO requires a mix of tools and skills. The good news is that you have a great deal of flexibility; there's no single definitive tool kit. Each SMO practitioner has his or her own favorite tools and pet techniques. If you ask a variety of people about the "essential elements" of SMO, you'll always get different opinions. That said, a few things are likely to be common to those opinions. Effective SMO requires the following things, at minimum:

- Social media profiles on the appropriate channels
- Access to the publishing controls for the social media channels
- Administrative access to your website
- Access to analytics data for your website
- Access to analytics data for your social media channels, such as Facebook Insights (shown in Figure 1-1)
- Willingness to make the effort needed to interact with your audience
- Time!

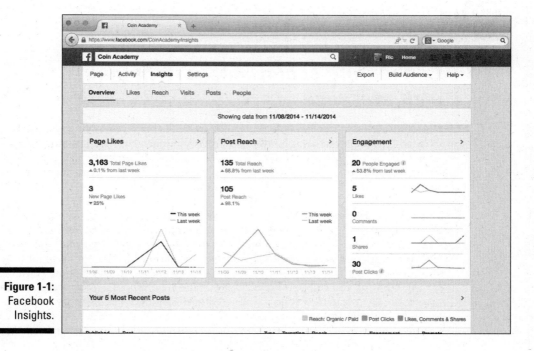

Figure 1-1:
Facebook
Insights.

As you can see, the list of essential elements is a mix of data tools and soft skills. The list is intentionally generic, because what is required for any particular campaign varies by the nature of the client, the audience, and the goals of the campaign.

Your social media tool kit is an area on which you can spend as much or as little as you want. An increasing number of commercial services are targeting SMO practitioners, and some of these services are quite attractive. Many practitioners use automated publishing tools or at least scheduling software that lets them prepare posts in advance for publication later; others add content and influencer discovery tools to their tool kits.

For most practitioners, the choice of tools largely depends on the following:

- ✔ Budget
- ✔ Personal preference
- ✔ Prioritization of needs
- ✔ Channel selection

Crafting the right tool kit is a personal decision. Many tools offer free trial periods. The best way to find what works for you is a hands-on trial. Be willing to experiment.

Connecting social media with your web presence

One of the most common uses for social media is as a means of strengthening your web presence. Social media can be very effective in both raising awareness of your website and driving traffic to the site. A properly cultivated SMO strategy can enhance what you're doing on your website and deliver tangible results.

The connection between your social media channels and your web presence goes in both directions. Social media can benefit your website, and your website can strengthen your social media efforts. Integration of your social media activity with your web strategy is a key component of SMO. Your website should be not only a focal point for social media activity, but also an outlet for the content you publish on your social media channels. Your website can also serve to create new followers for your social media profiles by pushing traffic to those profiles. You can even leverage the social networks of your site's visitors by implementing on your website popular sharing functionality from networks such as Facebook, Twitter, and Pinterest. Figure 1-2 shows how a site can integrate content from the social media channels and use sharing buttons to help promote the website's content.

The connection between your web presence and your social media constitutes a virtuous circle. Your web presence and your social media presence complement and strengthen each other. Through strategic use of your various publishing platforms, you can leverage your efforts across channels, reinforce your message, and provide a richer experience for your audience.

Social media widgets   Sharing buttons

Figure 1-2:
Website with sharing buttons and social media content widget.

Seeing What SMO Can Do for You

SMO can be tailored to a variety of tasks. To ask what SMO can do for you is to ask what social media can do for you. Indeed, anything you set out to do with social media, you can do more effectively through proper application of the principles of SMO. As its name implies, SMO is about optimizing your social media efforts, making them more efficient and more effective in achieving your goals.

Among the proven uses of social media are the following:

- Raising brand awareness
- Driving traffic to a website
- Improving search engine visibility
- Improving customer service
- Increasing brand loyalty
- Protecting and enhancing brand reputation
- Managing crises
- Generating leads

When you apply SMO tools and techniques to your social media efforts, you see the following benefits:

- Improved efficiency
- Time saving
- Better planning
- More structured execution of social media techniques
- Increased leverage of your efforts
- More comprehensive feedback and analysis of social media efforts
- Lower susceptibility to burnout

Put another way, SMO is a process improvement. It's largely about imposing on your existing ad hoc practice a more methodical, measured practice, with an emphasis on cost/benefit analysis and extending your reach without outrunning your ability to engage with the audience. By considering from the outset the need for integration of your social media marketing with your website content marketing, you can deliver more benefits with less effort.

Making a Commitment to SMO

Regardless of whether you're an individual looking to use social media for personal purposes or an employee of an organization that runs multiple social media profiles, successful SMO requires a commitment of time, budget, and human resources.

SMO also requires harmonization of your digital and physical marketing efforts. The SMO practitioner must not work in isolation or else opportunities are missed and true optimization is impossible. Your social media efforts need to work hand in hand with your web content efforts, your email marketing efforts, and any traditional media efforts; all your efforts are about consistency and the ability to get your message to the audience via the channels they prefer. To that end, a commitment to SMO means a commitment to working across channels to execute a comprehensive strategy and achieve agreed goals.

Finding Your Voice

One of the key attributes of success in social media is the creation of a human connection. Social media's strengths are in its personal character. People use the channels that suit them, and they like and share content that inspires them. When they decide to engage with an individual or a brand, they make a personal connection.

As a social media practitioner, you must keep the emphasis on the personal touch. You have to be the voice of your company or brand. You're the first point of contact — the one speaking for the brand. It's essential that you create and maintain an authentic and appropriate voice for the company or brand, which is key to positioning and key to generating meaningful interaction that speaks to your audience and shapes their perceptions.

Taking the time to define the voice of your brand is an important exercise that pays real dividends. If your firm hasn't already defined its voice, make that exercise a priority. Defining your brand has real advantages:

- ✔ It shows your audience the people behind the company.
- ✔ It makes it possible for individuals to make a personal connection with your company.
- ✔ It can separate your company from the competition.
- ✔ It builds trust.
- ✔ It makes it possible for you to be an influencer and a resource for your audience.

Put a face on your brand. People like to have something to talk about, but even more, they appreciate having someone to talk *to*.

In the field of social media, finding your voice is one of the most challenging topics, but it's not easily quantifiable. There's no statistic to track or feature to tweak. This classic soft skill requires the right person. The skill isn't easy to teach, but it's something you can practice. With planning and practice, you'll get better at speaking in an authentic voice that reflects your company values.

After you establish voice and tone guidelines, turn them into a set of guidelines for your practitioners.

Authenticity is key

Throughout this book, we say again and again that authenticity is key. Social media is personal, and people are very good at detecting fakes. When people ask questions, lodge complaints, or comment on specific items, you need to respond with genuine concern and willingness to listen.

On social media, you don't broadcast; you engage. Engaging means taking personal interest in what your users have to say.

No one wants to be talked to like he or she is merely a dollar waiting to be spent. Don't speak like a brand trying to sell. To succeed, make a human connection.

Creating a voice consistent with your brand

What's the personality of your brand? Playful? Authoritative? Maternal? Your brand personality should be reflected in your social media voice. If your brand is playful, your social media publishing and engagement should also be playful.

Whereas voice can usually be characterized by a simple adjective, tone is a different matter. The tone of your posts needs to reflect the audience being addressed and the matter being discussed. Although your brand voice may playful, if a customer has a complaint, your tone must not be frivolous. Your brand has one voice, but tone must vary as circumstances dictate. This concept is easy to grasp but hard to enforce. Your social media team needs to understand the importance of projecting a consistent presence for your audience.

Your voice doesn't change. Your tone adapts to respond to the audience and the circumstances.

In formulating the guidelines for your social media interaction, try looking at the issue from four angles:

✔ **Brand personality:** What feeling does your brand want to communicate? This feeling should be expressed as a simple adjective: playful, expert, helpful, and so on. This feeling is your overriding personality that influences all your communications.

✔ **Tone:** Define the tone to be used for various tasks. Your tone may be informative, sympathetic, or humble, depending on the circumstances.

✔ **Language used:** The words and phrases you use in your communications should reflect the words and phrases used by your audience. Although you want to set global parameters in this area, you also want to make an attempt to be flexible and mirror the language patterns of specific users when you're engaging one-on-one.

✔ **Purpose:** Always ask yourself "What is the purpose of this communication?" The answer will influence your choice of tone and language and help you communicate more effectively.

If you get your approach right, you'll find that people start to do some of your marketing for you. Sound too good to be true? It's not. When you speak to people in a voice that resonates with them, they're more likely to repeat what you say to others.

Chapter 2

SMO Is the New SEO

In This Chapter

▶ Building your case for SMO

▶ Exploring the relationship between SMO and SEO

▶ Planning for long-term social media growth

Social media optimization (SMO) is a key strategic component of digital marketing. Until recently, many firms focused their digital strategies on search engine marketing. In today's environment, social media has taken center stage.

As with any significant marketing initiative, the success of your social media strategy depends largely on good planning and effective execution. Before you get to the execution stage, however, you need to get the resources of your organization on board. You need to build a consensus for social media, and you need to get buy-in from management.

This chapter shows how to build a business case for SMO and explains how effective social media management can deliver significant benefits to your web marketing strategy.

Creating a Business Case

Although a number of companies have tried social media in some form, many have failed to commit the resources it takes to do it well. Often, the problem isn't a lack of awareness of social media; rather, it's lack of belief that a commitment of resources will deliver results. Facebook, Twitter, YouTube, Pinterest, Vine, Vimeo, Instagram — the list goes on and on and on, and it is easy to understand why the doubters have their doubts. The scope of the topic is a bit much to grasp, and it's natural to think that getting anything done is going to take a tremendous amount of time and resources.

The truth is that it does take time and resources to make a difference with social media, but that fact shouldn't stop you. The rewards can more than compensate for the effort required. What you need are a good plan and the resources to make it work. The first step for most people is making the business case that will motivate your firm to allocate the resources you need.

Selling social channels internally is best done in business terms. Define your vision and your goals; then map your goals to your firm's business strategy. You may find it tempting to talk in terms of the number of followers you'll gain or how many retweets you can get, but that approach is likely to meet with a lukewarm response. Instead, take out the social media jargon. The result you're seeking isn't about the channel. Draw attention to how your plan will advance the company's strategic business goals.

When you make your business case, focus on results, not on social media buzzwords.

For many decision-makers, a road map approach works well. Creating a visual road map for planning purposes is really quite easy. In short, you simply explain what you'll attack first, what comes next, and so on. Explain how long implementing your plan will take and what resources you need; always make the link back to the firm's business strategy. A visual road map lays things out in a fashion that reduces complexity and helps decision-makers see how the various elements of your strategy are connected. Moreover, a road map that lays things out on a timeline map helps manage expectations and gets people to think about the necessity for a consistent commitment over time.

If you look at creating a roadmap as a process, you could attack it like this:

1. **Use a software program to make a table.**

   You can use whatever program suits your work style best, such as Microsoft Word, Microsoft PowerPoint, or Microsoft Excel.

   We like to use Excel for this task. The default Excel columns/rows format works nicely for linear sequences. In most other programs, you have to create a table with as many rows and columns as you expect to use. Using Excel saves seconds!

2. **Create a Channel heading for the left column.**

3. **Add column headings for the time periods that make sense for your campaign.**

   In the example Excel road map shown in Figure 2-1, we lay out a 10-week campaign. Create ten columns labeled sequentially: Week 1, Week 2, Week 3, and so on, up to Week 10.

Channel	Week 1	Week 2	Week 3	Week 4	Week 5	Week 6	Week 7	Week 8	Week 9	Week 10
Facebook	Launch profile	Focus: videos	Focus: Contest	Focus: videos	Focus: Contest	Focus: videos	Focus: Contest Winners	Focus: videos		Focus: videos
Sponsored Posts	Push 1 post		Push Contest post	Push Contest post	Push Contest post		Push 1 post		Push 3 post	
Contest			Launch Contest			Contest Finishes				
Twitter	Launch profile	Focus: videos	Focus: Contest	Focus: videos	Focus: Contest	Focus: videos	Focus: Contest Winners	Focus: videos		Focus: videos
YouTube	Launch profile	2 new videos		2 new videos		2 new videos		2 new videos		2 new videos
Instagram	Launch profile	Set up Instagress	3-5 new images	3-5 new images	3-5 new images	3-5 new images	Focus: Contest Winners	3-5 new images	3-5 new images	3-5 new images

Figure 2-1:
A sample road map.

4. In the Channel column, add rows for each channel's activities in the campaign.

The example shown in Figure 2-1 has rows for Facebook, Twitter, YouTube, and Instagram. The Facebook channel includes two activities: Sponsored Posts and Content.

If you're running multiple activities on a channel simultaneously, you need multiple rows. If you want to run a contest on Facebook, for example, but also want to run a Facebook Sponsored Posts campaign, you need two rows.

5. In each activity row, enter the tasks planned for each week.

Include the start and stop dates of the initiatives, as well as periodic reviews. In Figure 2-1, the Facebook content launches in Week 3 and runs until Week 4. In that case you note the event across all the weeks in between.

6. Repeat Step 5 for each key task and periodic reviews.

You now have a visual timeline that communicates what you plan to do with each activity during each week of the campaign.

Come up with a coherent color-coding scheme for your timeline to make it more visual and easier to grasp at a glance. In the road map shown in Figure 2-1, the Facebook activities are blue, the Twitter activities are yellow, and so on.

When laying out your plan, don't forget to highlight the risks. No plan is without risks. Discuss the risks, show you grasp them, and explain how they can be minimized. Often, this part of your pitch is the key. Failing to acknowledge risk and have a plan to deal with it is often perceived by experienced management as being naïve and a sign of poor diligence.

Creating a solid business case can get you the resources you need and create the sort of internal consensus that gives you the flexibility to adapt and to execute your plan effectively in a fluid marketing environment. You have to know what resources to ask for, of course, as well as what you expect to come from your efforts.

Determining needed resources

Effective execution of a social media strategy requires time, effort and energy. Although the right tools can make life easier, there's no way around the fact that you need to set aside time for social media and that it requires personal commitment. Social media is personal media; it's about connecting with individuals in a manner that's genuine and true to your brand values. As such, it can't be automated. You can't set it and forget it.

The most important resource you need to create social media success is the human touch.

In the most basic terms, the resources you need can be grouped into three categories: time, creative resources, and software tools.

Time

Time is a valuable commodity and often the most expensive component of a social media initiative. You not only need to invest in planning, but also must remain available to manage the execution. A social media campaign isn't like an old-school media campaign, in which the job is largely done as soon as the artwork is off to the printer. Social media is fluid. It requires constant adjustment and the ability to respond both appropriately and in a timely fashion. It also requires a strong sense of engagement. You need to find the time and the focus to make it work. Start by setting aside an hour a day to find out what you can get done in that amount of time. Adjust your schedule, and be willing to spend additional time when you have a chance to engage with your audience.

Creative resources

Creative resources are next on your shopping list. A great social media campaign is backed up by great content. Your Facebook posts, your tweets, and your other text content should be planned and reviewed before you post them.

Although you must be flexible and willing to improvise, the key points of the content need to be planned in advance. If you're not a great writer, find one.

Visual media is also a highly effective social media asset. If you can tap artists who create great imagery — photos, charts, infographics, videos, and so on — you'll be one step ahead of the competition. Like creative text, imagery takes planning and time for execution. You should try to set aside budget for imagery if you aren't able to create it yourself.

Software tools

Software tools can help lighten the load and make your work more effective. Before you get started, you may want to build your tool kit. Here's a starter list of tools that can handle your basic needs:

- ✔ To help you manage multiple accounts and schedule your posts, try Hootsuite (`http://hootsuite.com`) (shown in Figure 2-2); it's a good choice with both free and subscription options. Hootsuite provides multiple-account management for both Twitter and Facebook. The premium version enables you to share account administration duties.

- ✔ To detect mentions of your brand or product on various social channels, use a tool like Google Alerts (`http://google.com/alerts`) or Social Mention (`http://socialmention.com`).

- ✔ To track the effect of your Facebook efforts, you need access to the Facebook Page Insights included with your Facebook Page.

- ✔ To track your success on Twitter, use the Twitter stats feature provided on Twitter.com.

- ✔ To assess the effect of your work on your website, you need access to your website analytics program. If you don't have one, try Google Analytics (`http://google.com/analytics`); it's free and easy to implement.

These suggestions are the minimum tools you need for your social media tool kit. You can add many more, though, assuming that it makes sense to take the time to learn the technologies and you have the budget for them.

Framing expectations

One of the keys to maintaining harmony on any team is managing expectations. Although a properly planned and executed social media campaign can work wonders, you don't want to overpromise. Social media isn't a wonder cure that can fix your business. Social media is better suited to some tasks than others.

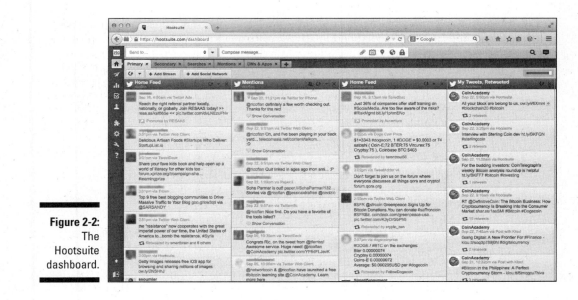

Figure 2-2:
The
Hootsuite
dashboard.

Here are 11 achievable goals you may want to consider when framing your next social media campaign:

- ✔ Raising brand awareness and increasing word-of-mouth marketing
- ✔ Expanding your audience
- ✔ Increasing the reach of your content
- ✔ Increasing knowledge of your customers and improving target marketing
- ✔ Obtaining timely competitive intelligence
- ✔ Generating leads
- ✔ Generating feedback
- ✔ Decreasing customer service response times
- ✔ Improving website traffic and search engine ranking
- ✔ Improving internal communication efficiency
- ✔ Building expert status and managing reputation

Structure your expectations with respect to your business goals and with consideration for your resources. Although the points we outline can be achieved with social media, no single campaign initiative can achieve all goals, and you should never set out to achieve all your goals in a single campaign. Be selective. Don't overpromise, and don't spread yourself too thin. Focus on what you can do, given the limitations of your work environment.

Whenever possible, start by setting baselines against which you can measure your efforts. Take some time before you begin to get a candid snapshot of where you are right now. This method gives you a chance not only to see clearly where you stand, but also to identify areas that would benefit most from additional efforts. You may just find that with a small bit of effort in one area, you can achieve big gains — an opportunity that you never want to miss.

If you're about to embark on an extended campaign, it's best to set interim benchmarks. You know where you are now and where you want to be in six months, so also set goals for where you want be in two months and in four months. Breaking the campaign into manageable bits is one of the easiest ways to keep things from overwhelming you and the surest way to make sure that you don't discover a problem until it's too late to fix it.

Whatever you do, you can never go wrong if you remember the mantra of success marketers: Under promise, over deliver.

Creating a Connection between SMO and SEO

One of the most common justifications for embarking on a concerted effort in social media is improvement in website traffic and in search engine ranking — areas in which social media is a proven winner. There is a direct positive relationship between success in social media and the health of a website. The big question is whether the relationship between social media mentions and search engine position is the result of cause and effect or mere coincidence. The search engines vehemently claim that there is only a corre-lation between mentions and search engine rank, whereas a number of practi-cal studies find indications that there's more to it than mere coincidence.

To appreciate the issue fully, it helps to understand how search technology has evolved over the past few years. As social media rose in prominence, search engines began to look to the social channels for clues about which content was important. The search engines viewed social activity as an indi-cator of the relative value of the content that was being liked and shared. Think of likes and shares as votes; the search engines believed that if more people voted for Article A than for Article B, Article A was more significant and more likely to rank above Article B in the search results. This simplified analogy explains what is known in search engine circles as *social signals*.

In 2010, a Google insider indicated that social signals played a direct role in Google rankings (see `http://searchengineland.com/what-social-signals-do-google-bing-really-count-55389`). Recently, Google backed away from that statement, saying that it doesn't factor Facebook likes and Twitter tweets into its rankings. Google says that the relationship between social signals and search rank is a mere correlation rather than a cause-and-effect relationship. Put another way, if a lot of people are sharing your content and tweeting about it, that content is likely to be awesome, which means that it will show up in other measured areas. If the content is awesome, people will be linking to it and creating solid traffic: two factors that Google considers in its ranking algorithms.

Microsoft's search engine, Bing, has made similar statements. Back in 2010, Bing seemed to indicate that social signals were important, but recently, it backed away from that statement.

The search engines' apparent shift away from using likes and shares as a direct ranking factor makes good sense. After the disclosure in 2010 that social signals influenced search engine ranking, a flurry of activity arose, designed to game the system. People were creating phony accounts to create likes and shares, and purchasing likes and shares on sites such as Fiverr (`www.fiverr.com`). The search engines have always been sensitive to attempts to manipulate their rankings, so it should come as no surprise that they've removed this weapon from the search engine spammers' arsenal.

The current role of social signals

Search engine optimization strategy is a moving target. The search engines are constantly refining their methodology. With regard to social signals, the emphasis in today's ranking algorithms seems to be on a mix of popularity and authority metrics. The search engines strive to link specific items of content to specific content creators. The goal is to determine the influence and expertise of the content creator. The search engines rightly believe that content from a respected authority should carry more weight than content from an unknown person or organization.

What can you take away from this fact? Here are two things you should integrate into your strategy:

✔ As the old saying goes, there's no substitute for great content. The better the content you create, the more likely it is to be liked and shared across social channels, and the more likely it is to rise to the attention of the search engines.

If you want to succeed in social media, create content that inspires.

✔ Social participation is key. You need to be active in social channels to help establish your presence and to build a case that your content is influential and should be prioritized above your competitors' content.

Although the search engines deny that social signals have a direct effect on ranking, that's not a reason to back off on your attempts to secure likes, shares, and other social mentions. Social signals clearly have value and indirect effect. Here's why:

✔ A social share exposes your content to more people, which increases the likelihood that someone will create a link to your content. Backlinks have direct positive effects on your search engine ranking.

✔ More exposure can also translate into more traffic, a wider audience for your content, and an increase in brand mentions.

✔ More mentions translate into increased recognition and increased trust.

✔ Your social activity often appears in search results, in addition to the links to the actual content itself. Social activity gives you another bite at the apple — another chance for someone to discover your content.

Even if the social activity itself isn't directly influential, what happens as a result of the social activity is very influential.

Quality versus quantity

Not all social mentions are created equal. Here's a question for you. Which of the following mentions is more influential: a mention from your buddy who has 10 followers, or a mention from an industry expert who has 10,000 followers? The answer should be pretty obvious: The mention from the industry expert is more useful to you, because the expert is the more influential user. In this situation, the search engines give more weight to a social mention from the industry expert.

The analysis does get a bit more complex, but only a bit. Here's that same question one more time: Who's more influential? An industry expert with 10,000 followers, of whom 10 percent publish online regularly, or an industry expert with 10,000 followers, of whom 2 percent publish? Again, the answer is probably pretty obvious, it's the user who has a large following of publishers. You want to get your content in front of influential users with large followings, and your chances of extending your reach are increased significantly if the followers are also publishers.

You need to make an effort to target influential users. To determine who your most influential users are, try the following:

- ✔ Look up the user on Twitter. How many followers does he or she have?

- ✔ Look up the user on Facebook. How many friends does he or she have? How many Facebook followers does he or she have?

- ✔ Check out the user's LinkedIn profile. How many recommendations does he or she have, and are those recommendations in areas that are useful to you?

- ✔ Look up the user's score on Klout.com. The higher the user's Klout score, the more influential the user. Figure 2-3 shows how Klout can help identify an influencer.

- ✔ Search for the user online. See how many hits his or her name generates and the nature of those hits. Are the items that show up relevant to your areas of interest?

- ✔ If you want to go further, look at the list of the user's followers on Twitter and Facebook and do a quick analysis of them. How many of the followers are actively publishing online?

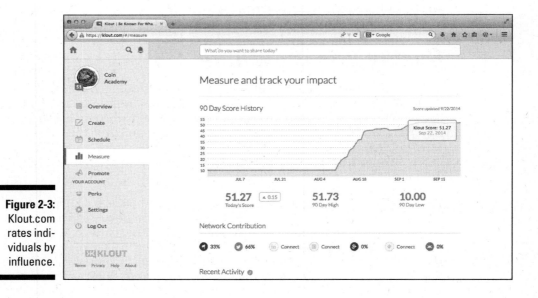

Figure 2-3: Klout.com rates individuals by influence.

After you have these bits of critical intelligence at your disposal, you can tailor messages to the most influential users and thereby leverage their networks to your advantage. Although conducting this research takes some effort, targeted content aimed at influential users can deliver significant benefits.

Connections between Google+ and SEO

In all the discussions of the role social signals play in the Google rankings, one thing is missing: Google never indicates how it treats social media activity inside Google+. Google's failure to take a position one way or the other has left open the question of whether Google+ content is considered in the Google search engine.

When the Google experts explain why they can't rely on Twitter and Facebook as reliable indicators of the importance of content, they tend to emphasize that the Google search engine spiders aren't always able to access the information on Twitter and Facebook. Google doesn't control those channels, so it would be risky for the company to rely on them. Google+, on the other hand, is a Google property. No obstacles prevent the Google search engine from mining Google+ activity; it's all one big family.

The SEO experts are divided on whether Google+ influences Google search results. Some respected authorities find no clear connection between Google+ and Google search rank. Other studies show that large numbers of +1s (the Google+ equivalent of a "like" on Facebook) have a meaningful effect on a site's rank in the Google search index. Still other research indicates that although Google+ activity may not help with ranking, it does drive indexing — that is, the Google search engine uses a Google +1 to help it discover and index content.

This matter is unlikely to get a definitive answer from Google, which tends to keep this sort of information quiet. A reasonable deduction seems to be that Google+ activity is more likely to have an effect than activity on outside channels such as Facebook and Twitter.

Your best course of action is to make sure that Google+ is part of your SMO activities and to make a consistent, concerted effort to have your content appear in Google+.

Google+ and personalized search

One area where a +1 has a clear positive effect is personalized search results. If a Google+ user stays logged into Google while he browses the web (and many users do), when he uses Google to search for something, the search results he sees are subtly different from the results that someone else sees.

Google personalizes the search results of logged-in users to reflect the user's personal preferences and browsing habits. If that user has given a piece of content a +1, that content ranks higher in the search results displayed to the user.

This insight translates into a social media strategy. You want to engage on Google+. The goal is to generate +1s for your content. As those +1s ripple outward through the network of Google+ users, your content influences more and more personalized search results.

Reaping the Benefits of SMO

A firm that's just starting down the path of professional-level social media marketing can look forward to a reasonable period of harvesting the low-hanging fruit. Your first efforts are likely to meet success and deliver clear benefits.

For firms that have engaged in social media successfully in the past, the landscape is different. Fast growth is characteristic of the early days of any new technological trends, and eventually the pace of growth slackens. Don't worry. This pattern is normal. Also, don't be surprised if activity levels vary by season. Summer can be slow, and holiday seasons can be slow. After you're past the initial high-growth period, you should think of your progress in terms of year-to-year growth rather than month-to-month patterns.

Many firms that have mature social media efforts reach a plateau, and they must adjust their strategies to push through the plateau. At this stage, if you really need to push for more followers, you need additional resources and perhaps even a fresh approach. Following are some possible responses:

✓ Increase your activity on your existing channels. Tweet more. Blog more. Post more on Facebook.

✓ Add to your team. More resources can mean more reach and more chances to engage simultaneously.

✓ Change your approach. Has your audience plateaued, or have you?

✔ Revisit your creative collateral. A fresh look may do wonders.

✔ Narrow your focus. Find your niche, and go deep. Be the subject-matter expert instead of the jack of all trades.

✔ If you've maxed out your activity on a particular platform, maybe it's time to find a new platform to engage with users.

At a certain point in time, the balance of your focus will shift from building a network to getting more out of your existing network. Although you'll certainly continue efforts to expand your reach, you want to tap into the potential of the network you've already created. The odd thing about social networks is that they can stagnate. Fans and followers lose passion and interest over time if you fail to stay relevant to their changing needs. The dynamic between you and your audience is akin to a personal relationship, and it requires a personal touch to keep your network engaged with your brand.

Chapter 3

Starting Your SMO Journey

In This Chapter

▶ Establishing a presence on social media

▶ Finding the right networks

▶ Setting up profiles on Facebook and Twitter

▶ Customizing content to channels

*T*his chapter is for those of you who are new to social media or have been tasked with setting up new profiles for a new venture. The chapter's focus is on getting up and running quickly by creating profiles on the two most popular services: Facebook and Twitter.

This chapter covers how to build new profiles for Facebook and Twitter and explains how to get your profiles ready for the world of social media fans who are just waiting for you to appear on the scene. Along the way, you get some tips on creating effective profiles and getting basic housekeeping matters in place to facilitate tracking your progress in social media.

Establishing Your Presence in the Social Media World

If you want people to find you on social media, you have to *be* on social media. Your first step down the road to social media fame and fortune is creating your profiles on various social media sites. There are some obvious sites where you really should be, regardless of your business or your goals, but there's a whole world of other social media sites you should also consider as time and resources permit.

There are some differences between using social media for promoting yourself and using it for promoting a business. Some channels, such as Facebook, have rules about how you can use the service for commercial purposes. Generally, sites are a little more restrictive with regard to businesses, so make sure you investigate the terms and conditions before you invest a bunch of time in a business promotion effort.

Finding the networks that are right for you

In today's social media world, everyone should maintain a presence on two sites: Facebook and Twitter. Both sites have very large user bases and a proven track record of generating engagement and of driving traffic and brand affinity.

Not very far behind, in terms of influence, is a group of brand-name sites that can add significantly to your efforts, including Google+, LinkedIn, YouTube, and Pinterest. That said, beyond the two biggies (Facebook and Twitter), any additional social channels you choose should be selected on the basis of whether time permits you to do a good job with them and whether they're suited to the nature of your site, product, or brand. If you produce no video content and have neither the time nor the budget to start, being on YouTube is of very limited use. Your limited time and resources are best spent working in channels where your efforts are likely to bear fruit.

In order to decide where you want to engage, we think it's useful to take a look at the biggest players in social networking and online communities. Table 3-1 lists the top 15 social networking sites as of October 2014, according to eBiz MBA (http://ebizmba.com).

Table 3-1	The 15 Largest Social Networking Sites
Name	*Monthly Visits, as of October, 2014*
Facebook	900,000,000
Twitter	310,000,000
LinkedIn	255,000,000
Pinterest	250,000,000
Google+	120,000,000
Tumblr	110,000,000
Instagram	100,000,000
VK	80,000,000

Name	Monthly Visits, as of October, 2014
Flickr	65,000,000
Vine	42,000,000
Meetup	40,000,000
Tagged	38,000,000
Ask.fm	37,000,000
MeetMe	15,500,000
Classmates	15,000,000

There are a couple of interesting points worth noting about the data in Table 3-1.

- ✔ Note the relative sizes of the communities. Although Facebook enjoys a huge lead over everyone else, there are a number of other very substantial players in this field.

- ✔ Most of the sites listed have a very clear and unique focus, but three of the top 15 have substantial overlap: Pinterest, Instagram, and Flickr are all concerned with photo sharing. That said, each is slightly different in terms of features and their suitability for purpose. When selecting where to engage, choose wisely.

- ✔ Most of the sites are global in their reach, but VK has a distinctly European focus and audience.

- ✔ Note that Classmates is unique on the list, because it is more of a community of communities. People join Classmates to find their school alumni, hence the site is essentially a very large collection of smaller communities, each built around a particular school. Within each of those schools are even smaller communities focused on a particular year or range of years. It is very difficult to leverage Classmates for any purpose other than personal marketing.

The point to take away from the list of the top 15 is that you have choices and that you need to make decisions about where to engage and how to allocate your time. The top 15 are all very broad in terms of their appeal; these are not specialty sites or niche communities appealing to only one type of user.

Each community has its own set of rules regarding behavior and commercial promotion. Make sure you are aware of these rules and obey them. Nothing will spoil your community reputation faster than running afoul of the local rules of conduct.

Going even further, there's an entire world of specialty and niche communities online. If you're serious about expanding your reach, you want to identify which communities are aligned with your offering and then make an effort to become visible in those communities.

By way of example, if you sell vintage watches, you want to have a Facebook Page and a Twitter profile for your business, and you may want to consider prioritizing the following:

- ✔ **Google+ (`https://plus.google.com`):** Your Google+ profile can help drive traffic to your site and give you access to topical communities you can join. Google+ also helps you boost your YouTube channel's visibility.

- ✔ **Pinterest (`https://www.pinterest.com`):** Pinterest is focused on images, so use it to display photos of your cool vintage watches. Pinterest is a good way to tap into the style and fashion communities, and you can also follow people with similar interests.

- ✔ **YouTube (`https://www.youtube.com`):** Open a YouTube channel and use it to create a collection of vintage watch advertisements and industrial films. You may even want to create original videos showcasing the coolest items in your collection or showing people the restoration process. Link the channel to your Google+ account for more exposure.

- ✔ **Vintage Watch Forums (`http://vintagewatchforums.com`):** A community of watch collectors and enthusiasts, this forum cannot only generate traffic and raise awareness of your brand with a sympathetic target audience, but also can provide a sales forum where you can list your products.

- ✔ **Watch Talk Forums (`http://watchtalkforums.info`):** This site is similar to Vintage Watch Forums but has a broader focus on watches in general. Again, with the forums, you tap into a community of like-minded individuals and can feature your inventory in the sales forum.

- ✔ **NAWCC (`http://nawcc.org`):** The National Association of Watch and Clock Collectors is a membership site that also includes a forum and a sales area. Joining this site gives you access to educational information, possible news content for your social media channels, access to other watch specialists, and another potential sales outlet.

Finding specialty communities is simple: Just spend some time with Google. Join a few sites, watch their activity levels, and verify that they're a good match for you.

When you join niche community sites, make sure to check out their rules regarding promotional activity on the site. You want to make an effort to become a valued member of the community, rather than simply someone who shows up to post promotional messages.

Promoting yourself

Social media is a very effective way of building your personal brand. To get a quick start at social media stardom, open accounts on Twitter and Facebook. When you have things moving along nicely on those channels, start looking further. Logical next steps include Google+ and LinkedIn.

Creating a Facebook personal profile

When you sign up for Facebook, the system automatically gives you a personal profile. No further action is needed; Facebook creates everything. All you need to do is customize your profile to suit your personality.

Facebook intends for personal profiles to be used by people, not by businesses. Facebook Pages are for businesses. Facebook Terms & Conditions specifically prohibit the use of a personal profile for commercial promotion.

Your personal profile is a place for you to connect with your personal network: your friends and family. If you're a public personality, the proper course is to keep your personal profile for friends and family and to set up a Page for your public persona. The next section discusses how to set up a Page.

Facebook strictly controls personal-profile creation. You have very few options for affecting the appearance of your profile. Figure 3-1 shows the default Facebook personal profile.

Figure 3-1:
A Facebook personal profile.

Your profile should reflect your personality. Although there's not much you can do to customize the page, you can control the following images:

✔ **Cover photo**: That's the big picture at the top.

✔ **Profile picture**: That's typically used for an avatar or a photo of you.

The profile picture appears in multiple places on the page and will also be shown on all your posts, both on your page and elsewhere. Choose this image carefully!

Figure 3-2 shows were each of these images appears with the ideal dimensions of each.

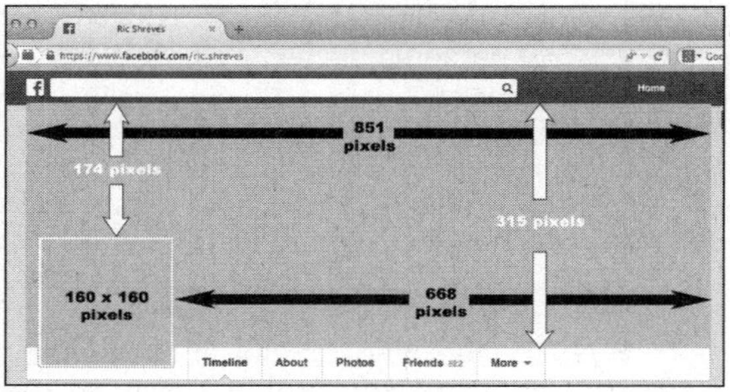

Figure 3-2:
Facebook
image
options.

Here's how to add a cover photo.

1. **Log in to Facebook.**

2. **Go to your profile.**

3. **Click the camera icon at the top left of the cover photo.**

   When you click, you will see a set of options:

   • *Choose from My Photos:* Click this to select an image from the photos already associated with your Facebook account. If you click this, you see a new pop-up window asking you to select from the photos already on your Facebook account. Just click the image you want to use.

   • *Add Synced Photo:* You may, or may not see this option; it's only available if you have installed the Facebook application on your smartphone. If this option is available, you can use it to automatically change your timeline image to a photo you have on your smartphone.

- *Upload Photo:* Click this to upload a new photo from your computer. If you choose this option, you see a pop-up window that lets you find and select a file from your local computer. When you select it, you need to click again to upload it.

- *Reposition:* Click this to reposition the existing cover photo.

- *Remove:* Click this to delete the existing cover photo.

Given the limited options for editing images inside of Facebook, it's best to create your Cover Photo first, outside of Facebook. Although you can upload any image wider than 720 pixels, the optimal image size is 851 pixels wide and 315 pixels tall. Facebook also recommends JPG format. The file size needs to be less than 100KB.

4. **When you see the image on the page, you can click and drag it to position exactly where you want it.**

5. **Click Save Changes.**

To change your profile picture, follow these steps.

1. **Log in to Facebook.**

2. **Go to your Personal Profile.**

3. **Click the camera icon at the bottom left of the profile picture.**

   When you click, you see a gallery of the photos already on your Facebook account and two links you can click:

   - *+Upload Photo:* Click this to upload a new photo from your computer. When you choose this option, you see a pop-up window that enables you to find and select a file from your local computer. After you select it, you need to click again to upload it.

   - *Take Photo:* Click this and Facebook attempts to use the camera on your computer to capture a photo. If you don't have a camera, this option is not available to you.

4. **Click and drag the cropping frame to select the portion of the image you want to use.**

5. **Click Save Profile Picture.**

Creating your Twitter profile

Setting up a new profile on Twitter is fast and easy. Like Facebook, Twitter controls most of the formatting and design of the profile page, but there are some things you can control. Unlike Facebook, there is no difference between a Twitter profile for a person and a profile for a business.

To create a new personal or business profile, simply visit Twitter.com, then follow these steps.

1. **In the fields provided on the Twitter home page, enter your name, your email address, and the password you want to use with your new account.**

2. **Click the Sign Up for Twitter button.**

3. **On the next screen you can choose a username.**

   Twitter makes suggestions for your username, but you can select whatever you want. Enter your preferred username, and the system tells you if it is available.

4. **Click the button labeled Create My Account.**

5. **If the system prompts you for a phone verification, enter your phone number and click Verify Phone Number.**

   After the SMS arrives to your phone, enter the code in the Twitter verification screen and click the Verify the Code button.

6. **Twitter prompts you to log in and then steps you through a new account wizard.**

   The wizard asks you about your interests and recommends some accounts for you to follow. The recommended accounts are just a suggestion, and you can skip them for now.

Somewhere along the line you will receive a confirmation email from Twitter. When you receive that email, click on the link in it to get full access to your account.

After all the account setup tasks are complete, you customize the appearance of your Twitter profile. You can control few elements, but you're able to add a header and customize your profile photo. Figure 3-3 shows a Twitter profile with a custom header and a custom profile photo.

It's time to give your Twitter profile some personality by adding a header image and a profile photo.

1. **Log in to your Twitter account.**

2. **Access your Twitter profile page by moving the mouse over your icon on the top, then selecting the View Profile option.**

Figure 3-3:
A Twitter
profile.

3. **Click Edit Profile on the right side of the page, underneath the header image.**

4. **To add a profile photo, click Change Your Profile photo, as shown in Figure 3-4 on the left side of the page.**

Figure 3-4:
Changing your
Twitter profile
photo.

5. **Select the Upload Photo option.**

   When the pop-up appears, navigate to the location of the photo you want to use, click it, and then click the Open button.

   The system uploads the image and then shows you an editing window where you can position the image. After you have the image positioned where you want, click Apply.

6. **To add a header image, click Change Your Header Photo, as shown in Figure 3-4 at the top of the page.**

7. **Select the Upload Photo option.**

   When the pop-up appears, navigate to the location of the photo you want to use, click it, and then click the Open button.

   The system uploads the image and then shows you an editing window where you can position the image. After you have the image where you want it, click Apply.

Image-editing options are limited in Twitter. It's better if you edit your images before you move them on to Twitter. For the header images, the recommended dimensions are 1500 pixels × 500 pixels. The file cannot be more than 5MB in size. For the profile photo, the best size is 70 pixels × 70 pixels.

While you are on the Profile page, it's also a good idea to go ahead and populate the rest of the account info. Make sure to add your personal or business website URL in the field provided and use the Bio field to add some copy about yourself or your company.

Promoting your business on Facebook

If you're looking to get a quick start in social media for your business, the essential recommendation we make is the same as the one we make for individuals: Start with Facebook and Twitter. Getting set up on Twitter is essentially the same for individuals or businesses. Facebook, however, is different. Facebook requires commercial enterprises to use Facebook Pages, not profiles. Profiles are for individuals and have fewer business-friendly features. Pages are tailored to business needs and are a better choice.

Facebook Profiles versus Pages

Here's a quick rundown on the differences between a Facebook Personal Profile and a Facebook Page.

Personal Profiles

- ✔ Optimized for people and provide a way to connect and interact with friends
- ✔ Can be friended or followed
- ✔ Can't be used for commercial activity
- ✔ Can have unlimited followers but only 5,000 friends
- ✔ Can send unlimited messages to friends
- ✔ Limited advertising (you can only boost a post with no targeting)
- ✔ Unable to install apps to extend functionality
- ✔ Limited to one person (administrator)
- ✔ No statistics

Pages

- ✔ Optimized for businesses to showcase their work and their location
- ✔ People connect with the Page via likes; no friends or followers exist
- ✔ Can conduct commercial activity
- ✔ Can have an unlimited number of likes
- ✔ Can't send messages to a person who likes the Page unless that person sent a message first
- ✔ Can purchase targeted advertising
- ✔ Can install apps to extend Page functionality
- ✔ Can have multiple administrators
- ✔ Provide statistics (in Facebook-speak, Insights) on Page activity

Facebook Pages for businesses

A Page has to be created by someone who already has a personal profile on Facebook. After you're a member of Facebook, you can create and manage multiple Pages. After you create the Page, you can add other administrators, but all administrators must already be active on Facebook. Figure 3-5 shows a typical Facebook Page built for a business.

Assume that you already have a personal profile and want to create a new Facebook Page for a local business. Here's how you do that:

1. **Log in to Facebook.**

2. **In the left column of the Facebook home page, find the PAGES section.**

Figure 3-5:
A Facebook
Page for a
business.

3. **Move your mouse over the Pages label and then click the More link.**

   You may have to hover over the Pages label to see the More link. Conversely, you may be able to see the Create a Page link from Step 4 without needing to use the More link. If that's the case, skip directly to Step 4.

4. **On the page that loads, click the + Create a Page button.**

5. **On the next page, select Local Business or Place.**

   Each of the choices shown on the page has slightly different options. You need to select the choice that matches most closely the nature of your business. For most companies, the right choice is one of the six options for the type of page you're creating.

6. **Fill in the details about the business, as follows:**

   • Select a category that matches your business.

   • Provide the business name in the field provided.

   • Add the address and the telephone.

   • Click the Get Started button.

7. **Fill in the details on the Set Up (name of your business) page, as follows:**

   - Add one or more categories that best fit your business.

   - Add a description in the field provided.

   - Add your website URL.

   - Choose the Facebook web address you want for the Page.

   - If the business has a physical address, select the Yes check box and confirm whether this page is the official page for the business.

   - Click the Save Info button.

8. **Add a profile picture, and click Next.**

   See the "Creating a Facebook Personal Profile" earlier in this chapter for information on adding a profile picture.

9. **Click the Add to Favorites button.**

   Though this step is optional, if you click Add to Favorites, a link to the Page is displayed in the left sidebar of the Facebook home page, making it easier to locate your Page in the future.

10. **Set up and pay for advertising for your page.**

    You're not required to pay for advertising for your page. Click Skip to go immediately to your new Page.

Pages, like Profiles, offer only limited options for customization of the appearance of the Page. You can, and should, control the following images in order to reinforce your branding:

- ✔ **Cover photo:** That's the big picture at the top.
- ✔ **Profile picture:** That's typically your logo or other brand mark.

The cover photo is by far the largest image on the page and really defines the character of the page. You should select the image used here with your company brand identity and the personality you want the page to project in mind.

You can change the cover photo as often as you like, making it a great place for promotions and seasonal messages.

Here's how to add a cover photo:

1. **Log in to Facebook.**

2. **Go to your profile.**

3. **Move your mouse over the cover photo, and click Change Cover.**

   When you click, you see a set of options:

   - *Choose from Photos:* Click this option to select an image from the photos already associated with your Facebook account. You see a new pop-up window asking you to select a photo that's already in your Facebook account. Just click the image you want to use.

   - *Upload Photo:* Click this option to upload a new photo from your computer. You see a pop-up window that lets you find and select a file on your computer. After you select the file, click the Open button to upload it.

   - *Reposition:* Click this option to reposition the existing image.

   - *Remove:* Click this option to delete the existing image.

 Given the limited options for editing images inside Facebook, it's best to create your cover photo first, outside Facebook. Although you can upload any image wider than 720 pixels, optimal image size is 851 pixels × 315 pixels. Facebook also recommends JPEG format. File size needs to be less than 100KB.

4. **After the image appears on the page, click and drag it to position exactly where you want it.**

5. **Click Save Changes.**

To change your profile picture, follow these steps:

1. **Log in to Facebook.**

2. **Go to your profile.**

3. **Click the camera icon in the bottom-left corner of the Profile Picture box.**

   You see a gallery of the photos already in your Facebook account and four options you can click:

   - *Choose from Photos:* Click this option to select a photo from the images you have already added to your Facebook Page. Simply click to select the photo, then the system prompts you to drag it into position.

   - *Upload Photo:* Click this option to upload a new photo from your computer. You see a pop-up window that lets you find and select a file from your computer. After you select the file, click the Open button to upload it.

- *Take Photo:* Click this option, and Facebook attempts to use the camera on your computer to capture a photo. If your computer doesn't have a camera, this option isn't available.

- *Remove:* Click to delete your existing Profile Picture.

4. **After the image appears on the page, click and drag the cropping frame to select the portion of the image you want to use.**

5. **Click Save Profile Picture.**

Your profile photo appears in numerous places, including all posts that you make. Select an image that's suitable in shape and content, and make sure it remains legible in small thumbnail size. Check your brand guidelines about permitted uses!

Getting Off to a Painless Start

Starting a new social media campaign is one of the easiest, and most rewarding, parts of the process. Setting up the accounts is relatively easy, and your first push for fans and followers will yield fast results. With a small bit of effort, you can reap some solid rewards and get things off to a good start.

Before you get started promoting your profile, however, you need to take care of a bit of housekeeping.

Adding analytics

The first item on the list is making sure you have are systems in place for measuring the impact of your social media activities. Both Twitter and Facebook have analytics built in, so you're all ready to go on those channels, but what about your website? Do you have a web analytics program set up for your site? If you don't, stop right now and get one set up; you need to know whether your efforts to push people to your site are working.

Several good web analytics programs are available, and one of the best is also available free of charge: Google Analytics. We recommend that you stick with Google Analytics absent a strong preference for another product. Google Analytics provides great value and likely provides most people more data than they'll ever use. Go to www.google.com/analytics to sign up for a free account. Follow the steps to get it integrated with your website.

Setting a baseline

The second housekeeping matter you need to attend to is recording a baseline against which to measure your progress. This process is simple. Open your favorite spreadsheet program, and follow these steps:

1. **Create five columns, and give them the following labels:**

   • Channel

   • Start (and today's date)

   • 30 Days

   • 60 Days

   • 90 Days

2. **In the first row, type** Facebook **in the first column.**

3. **Enter the following information in the second row:**

   • In the first column, type **Likes**.

   • In the second column, put the appropriate number of likes as of today (your starting date).

4. **Enter the following information in the third row:**

   • Type **Reach** in the first column if you're dealing with a Page for a business; type **Followers** if you're dealing with a Personal Profile.

   • In the second column, put the appropriate number as of today (your starting date).

5. **Enter the following information in the fourth row:**

   • In the first column, type **Shares**.

   • In the second column, put the total number of shares received as of today (your starting date).

If you're managing a Facebook page, you can get accurate data easily from Facebook's Insights, a free analytics service provided to all Pages. If you're managing a Personal Profile, and you want to track engagement, you have to do the calculations manually.

6. **In the fifth row, type** Twitter **in the first column.**

7. **Enter the following information in the sixth row:**

   • In the first column, type **Followers**.

   • In the second column, put the number of followers as of today (your starting date).

8. **Enter the following information in the seventh row:**

   - In the first column, type **Engagements**.

   - In the second column, put the number of engagements recorded as of today (your starting date).

   You can find data on your success in generating engagement on Twitter on your Twitter Analytics page. Key actions, such as retweets and replies, indicate success at engaging with your audience.

9. **Save the spreadsheet.**

   Figure 3-6 shows how a simple social media tracking sheet might look.

   Keep the spreadsheet safe; you'll want to update it as you move forward and keep track of these key items.

Figure 3-6:
A sample tracking sheet.

Channel	Start	30 days	60 days	90 days	
Facebook					
Likes	389				
Reach	1,988				
Shares	22				
Twitter					
Followers	77				
Engagements	14				

Picking the Low-Hanging Fruit

Both Facebook and Twitter make it easy to get off to a good start by helping you find people you already know who are on the service. But before you rush off and start telling people to visit your profile, you need to make sure that there's something for them to see when they arrive. There's no sense in driving people to an empty page!

Building your Facebook following

Your initial approach with Facebook needs to focus on content creation, followed by efforts to drive people to your Page.

Create content on your Page by creating timeline posts. Follow these steps to post the first item to your timeline:

1. **Log in to Facebook.**

2. **Go to the page you're managing.**

3. **Create a post welcoming people to your Page.**

   In your post, include a bit about your business or organization. Be welcoming; be human.

4. **Create a timeline post introducing your primary website.**

   Make sure you include the URL.

5. **Create a timeline post inviting followers to follow you on Twitter.**

   Include the URL.

6. **Create additional timeline posts directing followers to each of your other social media profiles, if any.**

7. **If you have a blog or new content of any kind on your website, create a post telling people about it.**

   Include the URL.

 Visual content makes for great posts. Have photos of your place of business? Create a gallery, and upload them. Nice office photos help establish credibility, and photos of your location and building exterior can also help people locate your place of business.

When you have some content for your visitors to see, invite people to like your Page by following these steps:

1. **Like the Page you manage by clicking the Like button.**

2. **Click the Build Audience link in the top-right corner of the Page.**

3. **Select the Invite Friends option.**

4. **In the pop-up window that appears, scroll through your list of friends, and click the Invite button next to those you want to invite to like your Page.**

5. **When you finish, click the Close button.**

Promoting your Twitter profile

The initial steps for adding content and growing an audience on Twitter are the same for businesses and individuals. After logging in to Twitter, follow these steps:

1. **Create a new tweet welcoming people to the page.**

2. **Create a tweet introducing your primary website.**

   Include the URL.

3. **Create a tweet telling people about your Facebook page.**

   Make sure to include the URL.

4. **Create additional tweets to introduce each of your other social media profiles (if any).**

5. **Perform a quick Twitter search on a topic that would be of interest to your followers, and retweet that topic.**

To find some followers, follow these steps:

1. **In the Who to Follow box in the right column of your Twitter profile, click the Follow button next to anyone who seems relevant.**

   If you're not sure that a person is a good match, click the name to view the details of the account owner.

2. **Click the View All button next to Who to Follow to see a complete list of Twitter's suggestions.**

3. **Click the Popular Accounts link (which is below the Who to Follow box) to see a list of the most popular accounts on Twitter.**

   You can follow any of these people as well.

4. **Click the Find People You Know link to open a new window that lets you import contact lists from popular applications, such as Gmail, AOL, Microsoft Outlook, and Yahoo!.**

   The People You Know page also gives you the option to invite friends directly by entering their email addresses.

Build an audience for a Personal Profile

If you're working with a Personal Profile and want to build an audience, follow these steps:

1. **Click the Friends link.**

2. **On the page that loads, click the + Find Friends button.**

3. **When the new page loads, use the search form to find specific people by name, or** use the Add Personal Contacts function to import your contact lists.

   You can import contacts from a variety of services, including Skype, Yahoo! Mail, and iCloud.

Matching Content to Channels

Some channels are better suited to particular types of content than others. Twitter, for example, with its 140-character limit, is a poor place to try to publish large amounts of information. A better course would be to publish a long piece as a Facebook post, create a tweet about it, and link to the Facebook post on Twitter. In some cases, an even better place to post is your blog. After you've published the blog post, you can create a short note about it on Facebook and create a tweet to promote it on Twitter, in each case adding the URL of the blog post.

Facebook is appropriate for the following types of content:

- Short to medium-length text posts
- Links to pages off Facebook
- Galleries of images
- Polls asking questions of your followers
- Video content

Twitter is good for these things:

- Posting links to other resources
- Posting single images
- Sharing (retweeting) other tweets
- Sending direct messages to followers
- Making announcements

Part II
The Push and Pull of SMO

Find us on Facebook

 Coin Academy

✔ Like You like this.

 Coin Academy
Yesterday at 4:23pm

While it's true that Bitcoin risk increases when we start talking about investment, this report, from the Pennsylvania Dept. of Banking might be a bit extreme...

http://cointelegraph.com/.../pennsylvanias-department-of-bank...

You and 3,162 others like Coin Academy.

For instructions on adding a Facebook Like box to your website, visit
www.dummies.com/go/socialmediaoptimization.

In this part . . .

- ✔ Driving traffic to your website with SMO
- ✔ Increasing the audience for your content
- ✔ Letting people know about your social media profiles

Chapter 4

Driving Traffic to Your Website

In This Chapter

▶ Finding the right content mix

▶ Getting the most out of likes and shares

▶ Connecting with new fans

Many people believe the primary task of social media optimization (SMO) is driving traffic to your website. Although it is true that SMO can do a lot of things for you, perhaps nothing is as important as the effect it can have on your website traffic. SMO's ability to raise awareness of your content and inspire people to visit your site to view what you offer makes it a key tool in the digital marketer's toolkit.

The ubiquity of social sharing on the web today is the mechanism that enables SMO to have a tremendous impact on your website. By placing your content in social channels and encouraging people to like and share your content with others, you extend your reach far beyond what is possible with a website alone. A fundamental prerequisite, however, is having compelling content to promote through your social channels. When that content is in place, the social media practitioner can use the social channels to leverage visibility and drive people to interact with the content.

Blending the Right Mix for SMO Success

An old saying is worth repeating: Content is king. That simple phrase is still kicked around the web for a very solid reason: It's fundamentally correct. Content is what people search for. It's what people share. It's what people come to your site to see. If your goal is to attract people to your site, you have to start by building great content. If you don't create great content, you can't be very surprised if people aren't drawn to it. But is great content alone sufficient for success in the noisy, crowded world of social media? No, it isn't. If you want to stand out from the crowd, you have to engage with your audience.

Your content strategy needs to take into account the target audience and also allow for a certain amount of variety. If you expect people to come back after they read the first piece, you must engage them and offer them a reason to return. *Engaging content* is content that people find compelling in some fashion; it is content that speaks to them. In order to create engaging content you need to understand you audience and write in a voice that your audience can identify with. If you want people to visit your site again, you must also allow for a certain amount of variety in your content planning. You can't simply produce the same sort of content over and over again and expect people to keep coming back for more. The right blend of content will speak to and engage your audience and will provide sufficient variety to motivate them to make repeat visits.

Creating compelling content

If you want people to get excited about your content, you have to give them content worth being excited about. Compelling content can take many forms, such as the following examples:

- A wonderful image
- A useful infographic
- A funny story
- A timely piece of news
- Useful advice
- A time-saving tip
- An inspirational story

What is "compelling" is largely situational. No firm rule says that a particular type of content is always compelling. The trick is to know your audience and match your content to their interests. We're strong believers in devoting part of your energies to the creation of content that's commercially neutral — that is, content that's not created as a direct selling tool but created to be helpful to the audience.

Our philosophy on content creation is simple: Pushing commercial messages on people all the time doesn't work. Although you can get away with pursuing a commercial agenda some of the time, you need to have an appropriate blend of neutral content and commercial content. This may sound counterintuitive, but trust us: Repeatedly broadcasting commercial content to the exclusion of other types of content will kill your social media audience in no time at all.

In the context of using social media to drive website traffic, success depends largely on your ability to do two things:

- ✔ Attract people to the site.
- ✔ Turn one-time visitors into repeat visitors.

Both these goals are best achieved through the publication of content that people find useful or entertaining. Sometimes, useful and entertaining content may have a direct sales benefit; other times, it doesn't. That said, it's not a difficult task to keep your neutral content in line with your commercial offering. By way of example, if you sell golf clubs, you should offer practical golf tips. Although your golf tips may not be repeatedly encouraging the purchase of your golf equipment, your content creates a connection with your audience that familiarizes them to the benefit of your brand, making it more likely they'll trust you when they need to make a decision about which product to purchase. Moreover, the odds of your site visitors' becoming evangelists and sharing your content with others increase dramatically with the publication of useful content items.

Be giving. Although no one can afford to provide freebies and run contests all the time, you can afford to be generous in sharing your knowledge and experience.

Great neutral content ideas include

- ✔ Expert advice
- ✔ Industry-related news
- ✔ How-to articles
- ✔ Republished posts from related blogs (with permission, of course!)

There are no hard-and-fast rules about what content works best. One type of content, however, seems to work well consistently: great images. Strong pictures (or illustrations) tend to generate a disproportionate number of shares compared with pure text content. Images can be grasped quickly, and they lend themselves to spur-of-the-moment sharing. But the trick is matching the content to the audience. Write about topics your visitors care about. Funny cat photos may be a big hit in your personal Facebook News Feed, but they may not do so well on your FOREX.com investors' advice portal. On the other hand, a nice infographic showing trends in swap volume and spreads on different exchanges might work exceptionally well with traders.

Images account for 87 percent of the Shares on Facebook and comprise 75 percent of all content posted on Facebook Pages worldwide!

You also need to consider the frequency of updates to your website. If you rarely posts new content to your website, it's hard to raise the site's visibility and nearly impossible to build repeat visits. Fresh content is important; it gives you ammunition for your social media efforts, and it keeps the search engines happy. Frequency of change is also a search-engine ranking factor, so try some of these ideas to keep your content fresh:

- ✔ Post email interviews with industry players. These interviews are easy to create, and a steady stream of them will keep your blog ticking over with new material. If reaching out to external sources is problematic, try interviewing the key people at your company. Key personnel interviews tend to humanize a company and are appreciated by vendors and major clients.

- ✔ Post weekly tips.

- ✔ Periodically write a summary of press and media coverage of your company, with outbound links to all the mentions.

- ✔ Create photo essays on local or industry events. Essays work surprisingly well.

- ✔ Include old photos of team members (from their school days, for example) or vintage photos of your business or industry.

- ✔ Write "top ten" lists related to your industry. They're perennial favorites and relatively easy to create.

Don't forget that your website needs to exhibit good usability. People need to be able to find things easily, and the site needs to load quickly. Without ease of use and speed, visitors will simply go somewhere else. To get the most from your great content, you have to make it shareable. Make sure you have social sharing tools implemented on your website. See Chapter 7 for information on those tools.

Creating engagement

The whole point of social media is to connect with people. If you're using your social media accounts only to broadcast, you're missing the point. It's often said that effective social media is a conversation. There's a lot of truth to that statement. Effective social media practitioners share many attributes with good conversationalists. You can't have a good conversation if all you do is talk about whatever pops into your head; you have to listen, and you have to respond appropriately to what other people say. Online engagement in social media works exactly the same way. You need to select your topics in light of your audience, and you need to listen to your audience, both to understand better what they want to hear from you and to respond appropriately when they address you directly.

Measuring engagement

All this talk about increasing engagement on your website presupposes that you have some way to measure engagement. Your web analytics program is a good place to start; it gives you good data for assessing the relative success of your efforts to keep users engaged on your website. Start by looking at the average time spent by visitors on your website. You want to track this average for trends. Next, look at the average number of page views per visit, and be prepared to track this figure over time. Finally, take a look at your ratio of new visitors to returning visitors; over time, you want to see the proportion of returning visitors grow.

Don't stop with web analytics. Also analyze the number of Shares and Likes generated over specific periods. If your site permits comments, track the number of comments received. Similarly, if you provide video content, track the number of views. If you provide file downloads, track downloads. If your site allows users to create accounts, track the number of new accounts created. Put another way, the mix of metrics you use to measure engagement on your site depends on the nature of your site. Regardless, the emphasis should always be on the frequency and depth with which people actually interact with your content. The more interaction, the better the engagement.

Chapter 19 takes a deeper look at key social media metrics.

If content is king, engagement is divine.

Following are some effective techniques for generating engagement:

- ✔ Ask questions.
- ✔ Post photos and encouraging people to provide captions for them.
- ✔ Share behind-the-scenes photos of a product in development or part of a process people normally don't see.
- ✔ Use polls or surveys. Head-to-head battles ("choose one") work particularly well.
- ✔ Retweet Twitter posts.
- ✔ Share content created by others.
- ✔ Add comments to content created by others.
- ✔ Reply to comments about your content.
- ✔ Reach out to thank people who retweet and share your content.
- ✔ Follow those who follow you.
- ✔ Respond quickly when direct questions are asked or when problems are reported.

  ✔ Set up a monitoring tool, such as Google Alerts, to monitor for mentions of your brand. When mentions are spotted, link to the stories and, where possible, add comments to the comment thread.

Engagement is more art than science. It's the one area where gifted social media practitioners clearly stand out from the crowd. It's very difficult to teach engagement, but even when you struggle with it, persevere; you'll only get better with practice.

Everyone has bad days (some of us, weeks!), and at times, generating engagement feels like an uphill struggle. When that happens, try some of the following techniques to open new avenues, and you may just find that things get a little easier:

  ✔ Run a Google News (http://news.google.com) search for mentions of your brand or product and then engage the users who mentioned you. Comment on the posts, tweet the URLs, and so on.

  ✔ Visit a forum where your users are active to find out what people are talking about. Engage in the forum, or draw inspiration from a discussion on the forum for a blog article that you post back into the forum.

  ✔ Run a Twitter search for mentions of your brand or product. Follow the users and retweet the mentions, where appropriate.

  ✔ Search Facebook and Google+ for new groups and communities where your target markets might hang out. Get involved.

  ✔ Try engaging on a new social media channel. If you have the resources to do get involved on a new channel, it can be worthwhile. Sometimes, being the fresh new face on a channel creates new opportunities and a new audience. New channels can also put life into your efforts and break up monotony.

Leveraging Likes and Shares on Facebook

Facebook provides two primary mechanisms for users to interact with the content of others: Likes and Shares. Figure 4-1 shows the Like and Share buttons that you can embed in your website.

Although both Likes and Shares are desirable, they communicate slightly different things, which may affect your approach to integrating these options into your content or your web page.

Current number
of Likes

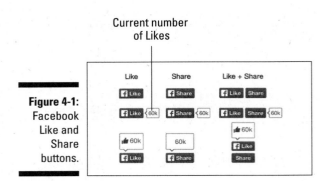

Figure 4-1:
Facebook
Like and
Share
buttons.

According to Facebook, users see Like and Share buttons 22 billion times daily across more than 7.5 million sites.

Understanding Facebook Likes

Confusing terminology seems to be a minor specialty at Facebook. It turns out that there are two types of Likes: You can Like content or you can Like a Page. Page in this case means a Facebook Page, as opposed to a web page or a Facebook Personal Profile. Despite the identical names, Liking a content item and Liking a Page have different effects.

When you click the Like button on a web page somewhere, two things happen:

- ✔ A link to that content shows up on your Facebook Timeline.
- ✔ The web page registers another Like, which you can often see on the web page as a Like counter. Figure 4-1 shows how this Like mechanism is typically deployed on a website.

The same thing happens when you see someone else's post on Facebook and click the Like link. The fact that you liked the post shows up in your Activity Feed, and the post's Like count goes up by one.

The consequences of Liking a Facebook Page are slightly different. If you go to a Facebook Page (say, the Page of some business) and click the Like button on that Page, three things happen:

- ✔ A link to the Page shows up in your Activity Feed.
- ✔ The Page gets to show a new Like.
- ✔ When things are posted to that Page, those items also show up in your News Feed.

Likes (of either sort) have another, less obvious, effect: Facebook factors the user's history of Liking particular things into the algorithm it uses to select items to display to that user. Every time a user Likes something, Facebook pays attention and assumes that it means the user wants to see more items of a similar nature.

What you Like on Facebook shapes what you see in the future on Facebook.

Understanding Facebook Shares

Sharing is a very different mechanism from Liking. Shares offer the user more options than Likes do and have several unique features:

✔ When a user clicks the Share button, she gets the chance to add her own message to the item that's being Shared.

✔ The Facebook Sharing mechanism tries to include not only the title and a bit of the text from the page being shared, but also an image that's grabbed from the page. The item appears in the user's Timeline and is much more noticeable and more compelling than what results from a simple Like. Figure 4-2 shows a Facebook Share pop-up window. You can see that the user has the option to add a comment and that the system also grabs the article title, image, and text intro.

✔ With shares, users can select where the information will be shared: in their own Timelines, on Pages they manage, in Groups where they have the ability to post items to the Group Timeline, in private messages to other users, or even on a friend's Timeline.

Figure 4-2: A Facebook share pop-up window.

What's better: A Like or a Share?

The short answer: It depends on whether you're talking about a content item or a Facebook Page.

For specific content items, shares are preferable to likes. When a Facebook user clicks a Like button, the item liked appears in her Facebook Activity Feed. The link won't be very prominent and won't include any images; as a result, Likes aren't terribly effective at driving traffic to a web page. Although content Likes aren't quite as desirable to publishers as Shares, they're definitely worth having. A visitor to your site who sees that your page has a large number of Likes is more likely to trust the page and give it credence. Think of Likes as votes for your content.

By contrast, if you're managing a Facebook Page, you want to be making a serious and concerted effort to get people to Like your Facebook Page. Likes of a Page create an ongoing relationship between a user and the Page and make it much more likely that you'll see future traffic from that user. Indeed, in the context of a Facebook Page, getting Likes is arguably more important than getting Shares, as a Like opens a channel for connecting with the user in the future.

When it comes to deciding whether to put a Like button or a Share button on a web page you control, the best course is to use both!

Some publishers prefer that their content get shares, as shares typically involve more engagement than likes. A user who goes to the effort of clicking Share and then adding his own thoughts to the post has shown significantly greater commitment and is essentially curating content in his timeline. Friends tend to pay more attention to shared links, and shared links typically produce more inbound traffic to the content being shared.

Liking is easier for users, but a share, accompanied by a positive comment, is more compelling.

Sharing on other channels

Sharing of content is ubiquitous in the social media world. A large number of social media sites offer some sort of sharing functionality. You should consider one simple factor as you pick the right channels for promoting your website: Where is your target market active? To the extent resources permit, you should be engaged in the same channels as your target audience. When that isn't possible, give your audience a choice of channels for sharing. By watching where your audience shares your website content, you can identify new channels and prioritize the expansion of your social media presence.

If you're using a website powered by WordPress, Joomla! or Drupal, you'll find social sharing plug-ins that cover a vast majority of services. You can configure those plug-ins to display the channels you want. It's worth your while to periodically try new and emerging channels to see whether they get a reaction from your audience.

Balance the desire to experiment with the need to reduce complexity for your visitors. Social psychologists have long stated that too many choices can result in people's simply not making a decision. The same principle applies to your choice of social sharing tools. Too many choices isn't better. Don't clutter the screen with a huge number of sharing buttons on the off chance that someone, somewhere will want to use an obscure service!

Most people don't know it, but every social sharing button you add to your website slows the page's loading speed. Social sharing buttons typically use JavaScript to load the information on shares and to activate their functionality, which means more scripts for your page to load. Slower pages are bad for search engine rankings and bad for business. Amazon.com research shared publicly stated that every 100 milliseconds added to page loading speed resulted in a 1 percent drop in sales!

Finding New Fans and Creating New Mavens

Your audience is out there — somewhere! Take heart; your audience does exist, and you just need to figure out how to reach it. It doesn't seem to matter what your opinions are or whether your message has objective merit. The Internet is a big place, and there's an audience for everything. The trick is how to get out the word to those people — how to reach beyond your website to let them know you exist and have something they want to hear.

Before you get started, you need to have a good idea of exactly who you're trying to reach. There's value in taking the time to create a persona of your target audience. After you have a persona you believe in, you can use it to inform and frame your efforts to create content that appeals to the sort of person described in the persona. If you haven't already created a persona of your ideal audience member, take 30 minutes and put some thought into building a persona of your target market. With a typical audience member in mind, answer the following questions:

- How old is the person?
- Is the person male or female?

- ✔ What sort of a job does he or she have?

- ✔ Do this person have a family?

- ✔ Where does this person live?

- ✔ What are his or her interests?

- ✔ How far did this person get in school?

- ✔ How does this person speak? Does he or she use slang, for example?

- ✔ What does this person do with free time?

- ✔ What sort of things would this person find interesting?

- ✔ Where does this person hang out online?

- ✔ What devices does he or she use to surf the web?

- ✔ In general, what does this person care about?

If you can't answer these questions with any confidence, it's time to embark on some research. Following are some easy ways to build up this persona:

- ✔ Ask your customers directly about their preferences. If that's not possible, set up and run a simple online or email survey of your customers.

- ✔ Look at how your competitors are positioning their messages. What sites are your competitors on?

- ✔ Run a Google search for any specialty blogs or other publications that targeting the same group of users. Forums in particular are very helpful for building up persona information.

- ✔ If you're using Google Analytics for your site, view the Audience section of your analytics dashboard for demographics data about your website visitors. Information available can include age, gender, interests, and device use.

- ✔ If you have a Facebook Page, use Facebook Insights to find out more about your audience. Follow these steps to see the Facebook Insights report:

    1. *Click the Insights tab on your Facebook Page.*

    2. *Click the People tab.*

    3. *Review the age, gender, location, and preferred language of people who like your Facebook Page.*

    Figure 4-3 shows some of the demographics data you can find in Insights for a Facebook Page.

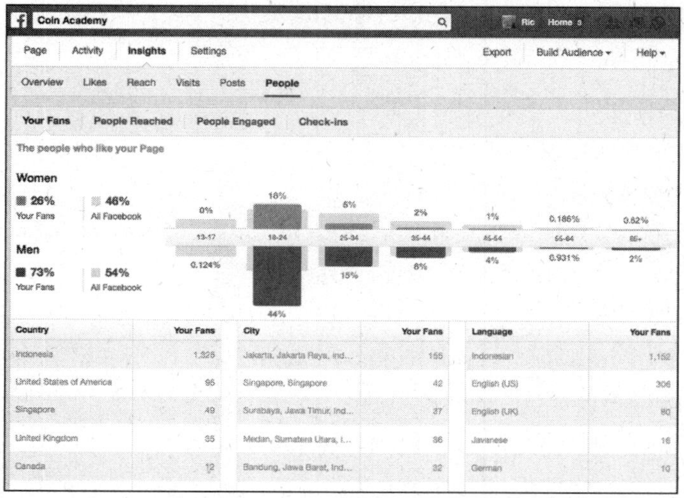

Figure 4-3:
Facebook
Page
Insights.

After you have a picture of who's in your target market and where you can find those people, the process of expanding your reach becomes much easier.

Social media provides one of the most effective ways to extend your reach beyond the boundaries of your website. If your goal is to increase traffic to your website, one of your primary goals should be to grow the audience for your website. By raising awareness of your website and what you have to offer, you create demand.

Engaging in online communities

Facebook, Twitter, Pinterest, Instagram, and LinkedIn are some of the biggest and most influential sites in the social media world. The sites are described in various ways. Some are called social networking sites, some are called microblogging sites, and others are called photo blogging sites, but they have one thing in common: They're communities bound by a common platform and often by common interests.

Membership and participation in online communities should be a key component of your social media strategy. Your success as a community member often defines the success of your overall efforts. Active participation in the community raises your visibility, attracts fans and followers, and lets you stay in touch with your target markets.

Optimizing for mobile

Statistics released by Nielsen in 2014 indicate that people spend more time using the Internet on their smartphones than they do on their computers. Of the group using their mobile devices for Internet access, Nielsen found that 47 percent use social media daily. Given these numbers, it's extremely important that you make sure that your website is optimized for mobile devices. The ability to display content consistently and effectively across devices is known as *responsive design,* which should be considered a requirement in today's society. The wide variety of devices on the market, from tablets to smartphones, makes it challenging to provide an interface that's usable and friendly for everyone. It's easy to test your website for device compatibility, however.

To check your website, visit the W3C mobileOK Checker (`http://validator.w3.org/mobile`), which is a website development tool. Type your URL, and click the Check button. The tool analyzes your website and scores it for compatibility, listing any issues it finds. If you want to use a tool that lets you see what your site looks like on various devices, you may prefer to use Mobile Emulator (`www.mobilephoneemulator.com`) for phones or Screenfly (`http://quirktools.com/screenfly`) for a variety of mobile devices.

Facebook and Twitter are two of the most obvious examples of how success within the community can translate into success outside the community. It's increasingly common to see a company's Facebook or Twitter profile rank higher than the company's website in Google search results. With that kind of visibility, don't be surprised if people searching for your company or brand start by clicking your social media profile to find out more or to find your website URL. Given this trend, it's essential that you make an effort to have an effective and active profile on the social media channels for the following reasons:

- To capture visitors who start with your Page or use the internal search function of the social media channels.

- To take advantage of Google's propensity to rank social media profiles highly in search results. (You want to use this feature to your advantage; it's a second chance to rank ahead of your competitors.)

You have many ways to use communities to your advantage in creating traffic for your website, such as the following:

- Monitor the channel for discussions about topics relevant to your content, and join the discussion. Contribute to the discussion, and offer links to relevant content.

✔ Listen for recommendation requests, and respond with advice and, where appropriate, with links.

✔ Share relevant content from any source.

✔ Follow active members, and see whether they have blogs; if so, ask for backlinks to your website.

✔ Make sure that your email signature file has links to your site and social media profiles.

✔ Be responsive; answer all questions you're asked.

✔ Start a LinkedIn group if your niche currently isn't being served by one (or you feel that you can run a better group).

✔ Start a group on Facebook.

✔ Target Facebook interest groups with Facebook ads.

✔ Run Twitter ads.

✔ Take advantage of the Google+ Communities feature, which is largely underused by brands. This feature is fertile ground for creating your own community of like-minded individuals.

✔ Use hashtags to connect your content with trending topics.

Exploring the wide world of niche communities

Beyond the top 15 online communities is a wide world of smaller niche communities. These communities make up for their lack of size with passion. The people who engage in these communities are your future evangelists. If you can position yourself as a valuable community member, you can reap significant rewards.

As the web grows, the ability to hypertarget niche communities becomes increasingly important. There's a very good argument that your future success on the Internet lies in your ability to be highly targeted. It's better to have a highly engaged audience of 1,000 than an indifferent audience of 100,000.

Start by searching for the niche communities that are relevant to your brand or product. A quick Google search is a great way to begin. For example, if you are looking to identify potential community sites to reach watch collectors, you might run a search for *watch collector forum*. If you're already involved in a forum where your target markets hang out, don't underestimate the power of asking for recommendations. After you find appropriate communities, read the rules, set up your profile, and begin to engage. It's usually good to start slow. Get a feel for how things are done and how people interact. Niche communities are often more idiosyncratic (and more judgmental!) than major sites such as Facebook and Twitter.

Niche communities tend to be very cost-effective and very high-contact. You can easily reach people who are passionate about a topic to make your voice heard by engaging directly with the users in the forum. If the group offers advertising on the site, niche sites typically are good places to invest a bit of your display advertising budget.

You should also investigate whether the site has a blog and, if so, whether it accepts guest bloggers. Guest blogging on a niche site delivers visibility to your target audience and backlinks to your primary site, making it a valuable partner in your efforts to build reputation and to increase organic search engine rankings.

Chapter 5

Widening Your Reach

• •

In This Chapter

▶ Getting a wider audience for your audience

▶ Creating effective content

• •

*O*ne of the most common goals for social media practitioners is increasing traffic to a website. For others, however, it isn't so much about driving traffic to the website as it is about getting your content seen. If your goal is to get the content in front of as many people as possible, you need to broaden your thinking beyond your website. Indeed, even if your goal is driving traffic to your site, getting eyes on your content has an indirect value.

The web is increasingly about sharing and repurposing content. So many sites are willing — even eager — to publish your content that it's very easy to get your content in front of people, assuming that you're willing put your content on sites other than your own. If you're willing to release your content under generous licensing terms, you also open the possibility for your content to be reused and mashed up.

This chapter looks at the opportunities for extending the reach of your content beyond your website and discusses how to create content that travels well.

Taking Your Content to the World

So you're creating some awesome content. That's great, but why are you publishing it only on your site?

If you want to raise awareness of your content efforts, publish your content on a variety of channels. Don't put all your content only on your website and hope you can drive viewers there. The goal is to get eyeballs on the content, so part of your strategy should involve taking the content to the viewers. Get the content out there where it can be seen, creating awareness of all the great things you're doing. After people discover that you have desirable content, they'll come to you.

Expanding your reach beyond your site visitors

When it comes to increasing distribution of your web pages themselves, you use the various sharing services discussed in Chapter 4, such as Facebook and Google+. But when your website also includes media files, you have additional opportunities to extend your reach beyond your website. Indeed, the creation of alternative media for use on your website is a very effective technique that opens new possibilities for extending your reach. Popular media choices include PDFs, Microsoft PowerPoint files, and videos.

Finding places to publish your content isn't difficult at all; you can find a large number of sites designed to republish your content. The trick is finding sites that offer the following:

- Access to your target markets
- Opportunities for sharing
- Branding and licensing controls

Additionally, it would be really nice if the site provides backlinks to your site and has high search engine ranking, both of which help with your own search engine optimization (SEO) efforts.

Although it's easy to identify sites that meet the first three criteria, it's hard to find a site with good page rank that also provides backlinks. Many of the highly ranked sites use *nofollow* links, meaning that although you can input links to your site, those links are not followed by the search engines, and you do not receive credit for them as backlinks.

There are several ways to find out whether a site uses nofollow links, including looking at the source code. The easiest way is to simply visit www.feedthebot.com/tools/linkcount/ and enter the URL. The Feed the Bot Link Count tool gives you a summary of the links on the page and tells you which links on the page use the nofollow attribute.

Getting started with file sharing sites

All the sites discussed in this chapter work in a similar fashion. You open an account on one of these sites and then create your own channel, where you can insert your branding and post some basic information about your website, including a backlink.

After you create and customize your account, you can begin to upload files. When you add a new file to the system, you're given the chance to write a description and can include a link to the article on your site. Make sure that your description not only reflects the content of the document, but also includes your target keywords.

For example, if you were publishing a sample chapter from an ebook about WordPress, your description might look something like this: "This complete sample chapter is from *HowTo: WordPress 4*, a new title published by water&stone. This 350+ page ebook covers all the tasks you need to set up and own a WordPress CMS website. This excerpt is Chapter 7, 'Managing Menus.' Learn more by visiting the book's website, `http://WordPressHowToBook.com`."

In this example, the description is written to target keywords associated with the product — in this case:

- ✔ WordPress 4
- ✔ WordPress
- ✔ WordPress CMS
- ✔ HowTo:WordPress 4 (the book title)

The description also includes a hyperlink back to the official website for the book.

You can choose to allow or disallow downloads and embeds on other sites. If you want your content to travel and get more visibility, allow both. Another option relates to the license for the item. As a general rule, give your content the most generous license possible, but always require attribution.

When you've added content to the sharing site, you have the option to embed the document in your website by using the other site's file viewer. The embedded viewer interface allows you to show your files directly inside your web page — a nice feature that has the added benefit of promoting your presence on the channel. Additionally, for video content, allowing a third party to host the video and then using that site's embedded player to display it on your site decreases load on your server and often delivers better performance for viewers.

Shareable licenses

Before you put your content on sites such as YouTube (http://youtube.com) or SlideShare (http://slideshare.net) (see "Document-sharing sites" later in this chapter), you need to make decisions about the license associated with the content. The license you select determines how other people can use the content. The options typically range from the strict terms of traditional copyright to a variety of more liberal choices, often under the auspices of Creative Commons (CC) (http://creativecommons.org).

The Creative Commons licenses arose in 2001, when Lawrence Lessig set up a not-for-profit organization dedicated to formulating alternatives to traditional copyright. The group sought to create content use licenses more suitable to modern technology. Today, six Creative Common licenses are available. You need to select a license that lets your content travel but ensures that you're given credit for it.

✔ **Attribution** (sometimes abbreviated CC BY): Allows others to distribute, remix, edit, and incorporate the licensed work as long as the creator is given credit. Attribution is the broadest of the CC licenses.

✔ **Attribution-NoDerivs** (sometimes abbreviated CC BY-ND): Allows others to redistribute the licensed work both commercially and noncommercially as long as the creator is credited and the work is distributed unchanged.

✔ **Attribution-NonCommercial-ShareAlike** (sometimes abbreviated CC BY-NC-SA): Allows others to edit and incorporate the licensed work noncommercially as long as the creator is credited and the new work is licensed under the same terms as the original.

✔ **Attribution-ShareAlike** (sometimes abbreviated CC BY-SA): Allows the same uses as the CC BY-NC-SA license but allows commercial use as well.

✔ **Attribution-NonCommercial** (sometimes abbreviated CC BY-NC): Allows the same uses as the CC BY-NC-SA license, but the new work doesn't have to be licensed under the same terms as the original.

✔ **Attribution-NonCommercial-NoDerivs** (sometimes abbreviated CC BY-NC-ND): Allows others to download and share the licensed work as long as the creator is credited, but doesn't allow others to change the licensed work in any way or to use it commercially. This license is the most restrictive CC license.

Some sites offer their own flavors of licenses. On YouTube, for example, the default license is the YouTube Standard License. Make sure that you understand the terms of any license you associate with your content. Although you can often change the license terms later, stricter changes aren't applied retroactively, meaning that if you release a document under an open license, any files downloaded according to those terms won't be restricted by your subsequent selection of a more restrictive license.

Document-sharing sites

For sharing PDF and PowerPoint files, definitely consider using these four sites:

✔ SlideShare (www.slideshare.net)

✔ Issuu (http://issuu.com)

✔ Google Drive (`https://drive.google.com`)

✔ Scribd (`https://www.scribd.com`)

SlideShare, Issuu, and Scribd are similar services. All three sites allow you to share a variety of document formats. Technically, SlideShare focuses on presentations, Scribd focuses on books, and Issuu pushes a magazine format, but you can use them all for several common document formats. Of the three sites, SlideShare receives the most traffic and has the greatest reach.

For all three services, you should create a branded profile to use for your publishing activities. Accounts are free on all three, and all three offer the option to embed very nice media players that let you display your content on your site while publicizing your account on the service. Figure 5-1 shows how a PDF uploaded to SlideShare can be displayed on your website via the embedded file viewer provided by SlideShare.

SlideShare is owned by LinkedIn and as a result gives you very good integration with LinkedIn — a bonus. SlideShare now supports logging in with your LinkedIn ID. When you're logged into SlideShare with your LinkedIn credentials, you can easily display your SlideShare presentations on your LinkedIn profile.

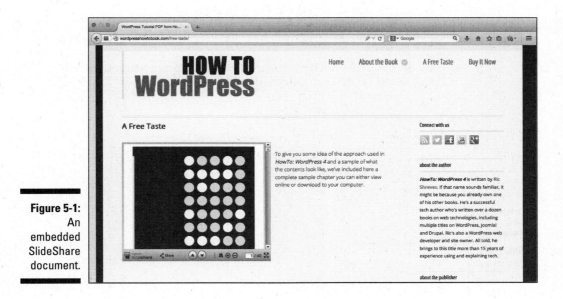

Figure 5-1: An embedded SlideShare document.

Google Drive normally isn't thought of as a file-publishing service, but you can use it to publish documents publicly. Here's how to publish a file publicly on Google Drive:

1. **Go to `https://drive.google.com`, and log in to your Google account.**

   If you don't already have a Google account, you need to create one to use Google Drive.

2. **Create a new folder, and name it `Public Files`.**

   The `Public Files` folder is where you'll store all your publicly visible files.

3. **Right-click the Public Files folder and choose Share from the context menu.**

   You see a pop-up menu.

4. **Click the Advanced link (see Figure 5-2).**

   After you click the Advanced link, a new set of options appears in the pop-up window (see Figure 5-3).

5. **In the Who Has Access section, click the Change link next to the padlock marked Private.**

   You see a window with the privacy options.

6. **Select the On - Public on the Web option and then click the Save button.**

   Any files you add to the `Public Files` folder are marked as Public and shared on the web automatically.

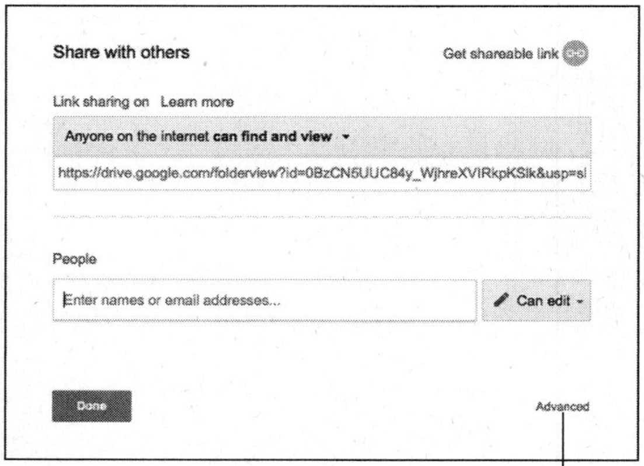

Share with others

Get shareable link

Link sharing on   Learn more

Anyone on the internet **can find and view** ▾

https://drive.google.com/folderview?id=0BzCN5UUC84y_WjhreXVIRkpKSlk&usp=sl

People

Enter names or email addresses...

✎ Can edit ▾

Done

Advanced

Figure 5-2: The Share pop-up menu.

Advanced link

7. Upload the file you want to share.

Make sure to upload it to the `Public Files` folder.

Figure 5-3:
The
Advanced
Share
options.

An added benefit of using Google Drive is that files published publicly tend to get indexed quickly in the Google search engine.

Video-sharing sites

Video content travels really well and has great viral potential. If you're producing video content for public consumption, you really need to publish it as widely as possible. You should always post public video content on YouTube (`https://www.youtube.com`). If you have the time to manage accounts on other video-sharing sites, you should also consider using Vimeo (`https://vimeo.com`),Vine (`https://vine.co`), or Instagram (`http://instagram.com`). (Note that both Vine and Instagram support only very short videos.)

YouTube should be your first choice for video content because it receives the majority of the video traffic on the web and is also part of the Google empire. Videos uploaded to YouTube tend to rank well in the Google search engine, and YouTube content integrates easily with Google+.

Hosting your videos on YouTube has the added advantage of saving you bandwidth and storage space. Put the videos on YouTube and then embed them in your site — the best of both worlds.

YouTube also allows you to create your own channel, which gives you the option to upload your videos and to curate content from others. YouTube provides an easy-to-use embedded video player that you can use to display the videos on your site. Figure 5-4 shows an embedded YouTube video player on a website.

For more information about working with YouTube channels, check out *YouTube Channels For Dummies* by Rob Ciampa, Theresa Moore, John Carucci, and Stan Muller (2015).

Vimeo is an interesting alternative to YouTube. Like YouTube, Vimeo lets you host videos and embed them in your site. Although Vimeo sees less traffic than YouTube does, you may prefer Vimeo if you're concerned about having more control of the video interface and the quality of the videos you post.

Vine and Instagram are totally different types of video sites. Both emphasize very short videos, and both are tailored to mobile users. Vine videos

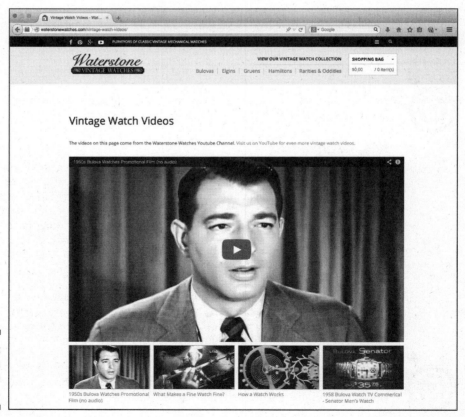

Figure 5-4: Embedding a YouTube video.

are limited to 6 seconds; Instagram videos, to 15 seconds. If your content is suitable for these channels, you should consider them. With the short format, there's no room for fluff; these sites force you to produce tight, to-the-point video content. Some brands have been achieving good results with well-produced, punchy videos.

Twitter owns Vine, and as a result, it's easy to embed Vine videos in your Twitter feed.

Making RSS work for you

RSS, which stands for *Really Simple Syndication,* is a long-standing Internet protocol that enables people to subscribe to content sources and see the results inside their RSS newsreaders. Figure 5-5 shows a typical newsreader interface.

If your website uses a popular content management system such as WordPress, Joomla!, or Drupal, you're certain to have RSS functionality; it's already built into the systems. If not, the functionality is easy to add, and it's worth the effort.

If you have a static HTML website, or you are using a CMS that does not include RSS functionality, you can easily add the feature with Google Feedburner (`http://feedburner.google.com`), a free Google service that converts your content into standard RSS feeds.

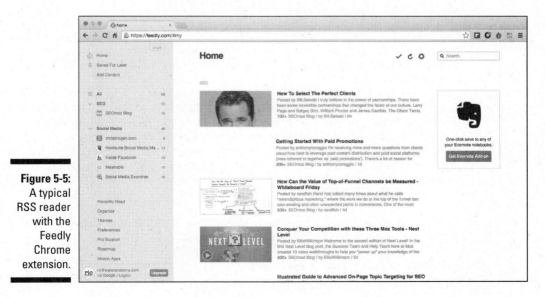

Figure 5-5: A typical RSS reader with the Feedly Chrome extension.

Different systems handle RSS in different ways. Some give you significant control of what is broadcast; others, not so much. Where possible, make sure that your RSS output includes the following:

- ✔ Site name
- ✔ Article title
- ✔ Author
- ✔ Synopsis
- ✔ Link back to the complete article

If your goal is to generate additional traffic to your site, it really is best to publish only a simple excerpt via RSS; don't publish the entire article. Let the excerpt act as a teaser to whet the readers' appetites and inspire them to click the link to read the rest of the article on your site. Requiring readers to visit your website to read the full article provides the opportunity for additional page views and further engagement.

RSS is waning somewhat in popularity. It's being challenged by sharing on platforms such as Facebook, which has turned into a news source for many users. Also, an increasing number of mobile applications address the same needs as RSS in more elegant fashion. That said, RSS remains a useful protocol, and for the near future, it should be part of your content distribution strategy.

Setting up email subscriptions

Offering people the option to receive your content via email is another useful strategy for increasing your content distribution. You have two ways to harness the power of email for content distribution: email notifications and newsletters.

Giving users the chance to receive email notifications when you publish new articles is useful but limited in purpose and in reach. Essentially, email notifications are convenient tools for reaching people who are already aware of your site. A well-designed newsletter can be much more effective in extending your reach. Although notification subscriptions tend to be automatic and communicate only the most recent post, a newsletter gives you more control of what is published and when.

For most people, creating a periodic newsletter that publicizes new content is the better approach, for the following reasons:

- ✔ You control when it's published.
- ✔ You control how much content is displayed.

✔ You can publish or publicize content that's not on your website.

✔ You can add social sharing tools to your newsletters, extending their reach.

✔ You have better control of branding.

Using email for content distribution has its own overhead. If you're using a newsletter approach, you not only have to build the newsletters, but also have to handle your mailing lists and deal with distributing the newsletter. Although you can do everything by yourself, several services make the tasks associated with newsletter publication significantly easier. Among the most popular solutions are

✔ Constant Contact (www.constantcontact.com)

✔ HubSpot (www.hubspot.com)

✔ Infusionsoft (www.infusionsoft.com)

✔ MailChimp (http://mailchimp.com)

✔ VerticalResponse (www.verticalresponse.com)

If you use WordPress, you have a built-in email notification system. All you need to do is turn it on!

Making Content That Travels Well

A content distribution strategy is nothing without appropriate content. That said, coming up with appropriate content doesn't have to be difficult. Although you can always create content specifically for use on specific channels, odds are that you already have suitable content that you can use with just a little additional effort.

When you're preparing content for use on third-party sites or in your newsletter, keep a few things in mind:

✔ **Write short, snappy titles that pose a question or plant a seed.** The title "Content Management Techniques," for example, isn't nearly as compelling as "Ten Easy Tips for Creating Great Content."

✔ **Write a strong intro teaser that can be used independently.** If you keep your teaser to a reasonable length, you can use it without editing when you post the content to Facebook or social bookmarking sites. (See the "Creating teasers" section later in this chapter for more information.)

✔ **Make sure you include links inside the article.** Help people find this content on your site, and help them discover other content on your site.

✔ **Use images.** If you're creating text content, make sure that you also use images. Effective image use increases sharing dramatically.

Repurposing content for use on other sites

Don't have any PDFs, PowerPoint slideshows, or videos to publish? No problem. Just make some out of your old content! It's perfectly acceptable to recycle your old content by freshening it and formatting it for a different type of media.

Repurposing your old content can give it new life. You can go about this task in several ways. The simplest approach is to take one of your old articles and freshen it with new data. Bring the article back to life by updating the underlying research or by folding in changes that have occurred since the original article was written. Publicize the updated post as you would a new post. Here are other ideas for bringing your old content to life:

✔ Break an old article into smaller pieces and dive deeper into the details.

✔ Use an old article as the basis for a presentation. Put the slides you create on SlideShare.

✔ Use an old article as the basis for a video. Share the video on YouTube.

✔ Create an e-book, and give it away on your site or sell it on Amazon. Either way, pull out samples and post them to your favorite document-sharing sites.

When you're refreshing existing content, try to keep the original URL intact. The original URL is already indexed by various services and may even be bookmarked by some people. If you absolutely have to create a new article, make sure that you link the old and new articles.

Creating teasers

A *teaser* is a short excerpt from a content item designed to achieve two goals:

✔ Tweak the interest of the reader

✔ Promote your key phrases

The ability to create great teasers is an essential content marketing skill. A good teaser should inspire the reader to click through to read the entire article. Writing great teasers is more art than science, and developing the skill can take some time, but it's not hard to do. You'll quickly discover that crafting a purpose-built teaser saves you a ton of time as you promote your content on various channels.

A good teaser

- Is short (no more than one paragraph)
- Arouses curiosity
- Makes a connection that inspires action
- Doesn't give away the punch line
- Doesn't overpromise
- Avoids clichés
- Calls for action

Use your teasers in the following locations:

- Facebook when you post a link to the content
- The entry page of your blog (assuming that your blog entry page shows only excerpts rather than full articles)
- Description content on YouTube, SlideShare, Issuu, and similar sites

Chapter 6

Raising Awareness of Your Social Media Presence

....

In This Chapter

▶ Creating awareness of your profiles

▶ Integrating social media updates into your website

....

*I*f you build it, they will come. More likely, they won't come unless you take steps to promote your social media presence. Although we can talk all day about how social media optimization can do this or do that, at the most fundamental level, everything depends on your having a solid presence on social media. You have to have followers. You have to have activity on your social media profiles if you want your profiles to deliver benefits.

Managing the growth of your social media profiles is one of the most under-discussed topics in the field of social media optimization. Most discussion focuses on how social media profiles can benefit your website, but a more accurate view is that social media and your website are intimately connected. You need to think about how your social media presence and your website can help each other.

As a social media practitioner, you need to focus part of your efforts on culti-vating the growth of your social media profiles. This chapter looks at tools and techniques that you can use to directly promote your social media presence.

Publicizing the Existence of Your Social Media Presence

Raising awareness of your social media profiles requires a flexible approach. The challenges new profiles face are very different from the challenges faced by more mature profiles. The techniques you used when you started your profile have to change as your presence on the channel grows.

For new profiles, a chicken-and-egg kind of dilemma exists. You want more followers for social media profiles, but you struggle to extend your reach because you lack followers. For more mature profiles, the challenge is to keep reaching new people and to continue to inspire loyalty from your existing followers. Although your reach will improve as your audience increases, new challenges move to the forefront and will shape your efforts.

If you're in a hurry — if you need to ramp up your social media profile reach quickly — some paid alternatives can help. One of the most effective tools is Facebook's Ads program. Facebook Ads are paid display ads shown to Facebook users depending on the conditions you set when you create the ad. The system allows you to promote posts, Pages, or your website. The system is flexible and can deliver very good results. You can manage the budget on a daily basis and turn the ads on or off as needed. The best feature lets you target the ads to a specific audience. You can choose who sees the ads based on location, language, age, interests, and a variety of other factors.

Twitter also offers a paid advertising program that allows you to promote tweets. The Twitter program has a less direct approach to generating followers, but it's still effective.

You should never take some shortcuts. One of strategies we always advise against is "buying" followers. Although running pay-per-click ads to promote your social media profiles is perfectly acceptable, using a commercial service that promises to deliver a specific number of followers is not. Remember, effective SMO is never just about reach; it's about reaching the right people. Organic growth and targeted advertising deliver better results than buying followers.

Publicizing your profiles

Employ multiple tools to get the word out about your social media profiles. First and foremost, integrate your social media profiles into your normal communications flow so that every time you connect with someone, you also tell them about your social media presence. Make sure you do all the following things:

- Display links to your social media profiles on your website.
- Add your social media profiles to your business cards.
- Add links to your profiles in your customer service emails.
- Include links to your profiles in your newsletter template.
- Include links to your social media profiles on your email signature file. Figure 6-1 shows one way to integrate social media links in an email signature file.

Figure 6-1:
An email
signature
file with
social
media links.

Ric Shreves I Co-Founder
Coin Academy
CoinAcademy.co

P: (+62) 8 179 333 444

✔ On each of your social media profiles, add links to your profiles on the other channels you use.

✔ If you have a physical location, such as an office or a store, announce your social media profiles where they're visible to employees and visitors.

Promoting cross-channel

Strength in one channel should always be leveraged to raise awareness of your presence on other channels. There's no reason why you can't talk about your Google+ profile in your Facebook account; indeed, you should. Tell people where they can find you on other channels. Help point them in the right direction to find you elsewhere. Some systems make it very easy for you to automatically promote your content on other channels; others require you to copy and paste items you want to be seen.

Twitter allows you to link your profile with other services. One option, for example, lets you post your tweets to your Facebook profile automatically. To tap this time-saving feature, follow these steps:

1. **Log in to your Twitter profile.**

2. **Click the Settings link.**

   The Settings link is below the menu that appears when you move your mouse over your avatar on the top bar. Figure 6-2 shows what that link looks like.

3. **Click Apps on the Settings page.**

4. **Find Facebook in the list of Apps and then click Connect to Facebook.**

5. **The system prompts you to log in to your Facebook account to confirm the connection.**

After you complete these steps, every post you make to your Twitter account is also posted to your Facebook timeline.

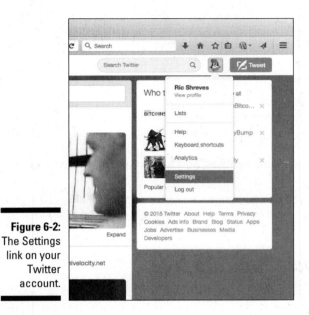

Figure 6-2:
The Settings
link on your
Twitter
account.

YouTube also makes it very easy to cross-promote your YouTube presence on other channels. You can set up automatic notifications that announce your YouTube actions on Twitter or Facebook. You can set up the automatic posting by following these steps:

1. **Log in to your YouTube channel.**

2. **Go to the Account Settings page by moving your mouse over your avatar on the top bar and then clicking the gear icon.**

3. **Click Connected Accounts.**

4. **Click the Connect button next to the Facebook or Twitter logo.**

5. **Follow the onscreen directions to confirm the connection.**

Other channels don't have cross-promotion tools like Twitter's and YouTube's, but there's no reason why you can't make manual cross-posts.

Several third-party tools are designed to handle cross-posting for you. Typically, posting on multiple channels simultaneously is just one of the features these services offer. If you're interested in exploring what those tools can do for you, try out Buffer (https://bufferapp.com), Hootsuite (https://hootsuite.com), or Sprout Social (http://sproutsocial.com), which all offer free trials.

Here are some easy-to-manage ideas for cross-posting social media content:

✔ If you're on Pinterest (`http://pinterest.com`), add the Pinterest extension to Google's Chrome browser. With the extension in place, it's very easy to pin content from your other profiles and maintain links to the original source.

✔ Pinterest, SlideShare (`www.slideshare.net`), Scribd (`https://www.scribd.com`), and several other services include a share feature for posts. After you create something new on the channel, use the share feature to push the content out to Twitter, Facebook, or elsewhere.

✔ You can connect SlideShare to your Facebook, LinkedIn, and Google+ profiles. The configuration controls are located on the Account Settings page.

✔ If your Google+ page and your YouTube profile share the same Google login, your Google+ page includes a tab marked YouTube. Click that tab to publish your YouTube video content on Google+.

✔ Where appropriate, always cross-post your Facebook Page content to your Facebook Profile. Similarly, cross-post your Google+ Business Page contents to your Profile and display it publicly.

✔ You can configure LinkedIn to display your Twitter posts in your LinkedIn Profile automatically. You can find these controls in the Privacy & Settings section — one of the links underneath your profile.

Displaying Social Media Content to Your Website Visitors

Virtually all the major social media sites provide a way for you to display content from that site on your website. Often, the display is handled by an easy-to-use widget provided by the social media site. Facebook, Twitter, YouTube, SlideShare, Vimeo, and many other sites use this approach.

Integrating Facebook

Widgets are small bits of code that you can copy and paste into your website. The widgets display content or enable limited functionality. Facebook provides several ready-to-use widgets that you can display on your website. The widgets display content from your Facebook Page or Profile and add Like or Share functionality. In Facebook terminology, two broad categories of widgets are available: Plugins and Badges.

Facebook has 11 Plugins. Some of the Plugins are merely buttons; others display lists of your followers, your most recent posts, or a combination of these things.

You can find the fill list of Facebook Plugins at `https://developers.facebook.com/docs/plugins`.

Four Plugins display buttons on your website content:

- **Like button:** Displays the Facebook Like button and how many likes the page has received. When a user clicks the button, a new Like is registered, and the content is promoted on the user's Facebook profile. Facebook provides Like buttons tailored to the web and to Android and iOS mobile devices.

- **Share button:** Displays the Facebook Share button and how many likes the page has received. When a user clicks the button, he can enter a comment about the content and then share that content on Facebook.

   The Like and Share buttons are often used together.

- **Send button:** When a user clicks the Send button on your website, she's prompted to send the content privately via a Facebook message or an email. The button also enables her to post to a Facebook Group. The Send button isn't implemented as frequently as the Like and Share buttons.

- **Follow Button:** Displays a Follow button as well as the number of followers and (optionally) a selection of pictures of existing followers. When a user clicks this button, he subscribes to updates from the Facebook account.

The other seven Facebook Plugins are designed to display content from your account on your website:

- **Activity Feed:** Displays a box containing a list of actions taken by Facebook users, such as Likes or recommends for the page. This Plugin doesn't show specific content items — just user actions.

- **Comments:** Allows users to make comments on your content. The comments made appear both on the content page and on the user's timeline.

- **Embedded Posts:** Allows you to embed a single story in a web page. You normally use this feature to promote a specific post on your Facebook page. The box also includes a Like button to prompt users to like the content on Facebook.

- **Facepile:** Displays a list of profile photos of people who liked the content.

- **Feed Dialog:** Works the same way as the Share button. This old Facebook Plugin has largely been superseded by the Share button.

✔ **Like Box:** Combines three useful functionalities into one Plugin. Use this Plugin on your web page to display content from your Facebook time-line, to provide a list of followers, and to display a Like button. Figure 6-3 shows a typical implementation of the Like Box.

✔ **Recommendations Feed:** This Plugin is similar to the Activity Feed Plugin. The difference is that the Activity Feed shows the most recent user likes and recommendations, whereas the Recommendations Feed shows a list of the content that has the most likes and recommendations.

Figure 6-3: A Facebook Like Box.

Facebook Badges are similar to Plugins, in the sense that they're prepared bits of code you can drop into a web page. Badges are easier to use than Plugins but offer fewer options.

Badges are available to anyone. Plugins require you to be registered on the Facebook Developer site. Registration is free. Find out more at `https://developers.facebook.com`.

Facebook has four types of Badges:

- ✔ **Like Badge:** Used to promote Facebook Pages, the Like Badge displays on your web page a box containing the name of one of the Facebook Pages you like, along with a button that enables others to like the page. To compare this feature with the Facebook Like Box, compare the image in Figure 6-4 with Figure 6-3.

- ✔ **Page Badge:** Select one of the Facebook Pages you manage and create a Page Badge. The Badge displays a box containing the name of the Page, the profile photo, the page status, and the number of followers. When a user clicks the box, he's taken to the Facebook Page.

- ✔ **Photo Badge:** This Badge shows a list of the most recent photos from your Facebook profile. When a user clicks the photo, she sees the photo on Facebook.

- ✔ **Profile Badge:** This Badge is used to promote your Personal Profile on Facebook. It displays your name, your profile photo, your profile status, and (if made public) your email address. When a user clicks the box, she sees your Facebook profile.

Figure 6-4:
A Facebook
Like Badge.

Badges are simple to create, and you can use a few options you can use to tailor the display. To get badges for your profile or your Page, visit `https://www.facebook.com/badges`.

Integrating Twitter

Twitter offers multiple options for integrating Twitter content and functionality into your website. The options are

- ✔ **Tweet button:** Prompts users to click to tweet the page on which the button appears. The button also displays the count of total tweets received. There's even an option to specify a hashtag for use with the tweet. You can see these two variations in Figure 6-5.

- ✔ **Follow button:** Displays a Follow button on a web page. When a user clicks the button, he subscribes to the updates from your Twitter account (assuming that he has a Twitter account!).

- ✔ **Mention button:** Displays a Mention button that enables the user to send a public message to another Twitter user at a specific account.

- ✔ **Embedded Tweet:** Embeds a single tweet in a box on your website. The Embed function includes multiple options for tailoring the output.

  The Embedded Tweet widget is typically most effective when your tweet includes an image or a Vine video.

- ✔ **Embedded Timeline:** Displays a list of the most recent tweets from a particular Twitter account, along with the name of the account, the profile photo, and a prompt to follow the account. Figure 6-6 shows this widget in action.

  The Embedded Timeline widget can do a lot more. Using the configuration options for the widget, you can tailor it to display a list of favorite tweets or tweets from a specific list or collection. You can even set it up to dynamically display Twitter search results by configuring it to display all tweets that use a particular hashtag.

Figure 6-5:
The various
Twitter
buttons.

Figure 6-6:
An embedded Twitter
timeline.

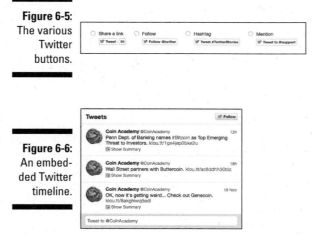

You can easily build Twitter buttons by visiting
`https://about.twitter.com/resources/buttons`.

To find the best interface for building the Embedded Timeline widget, log in to your Twitter account, go to the Settings page, and select the Widgets option.

Part III
Leveraging Social Media with Your Website

Find out how to add images to your tweets by visiting
www.dummies.com/go/socialmediaoptimization.

In this part . . .

- ✔ Integrating social media into your website
- ✔ Inspiring more user interaction
- ✔ Understanding and implementing ocial media standards

Chapter 7

Integrating Social Media Tools

Your website lies at the heart of your social media optimization (SMO) efforts. Accordingly, one of the basic tasks you need to accomplish is integrating key social media tools into your website. Several tools help you accomplish tasks that are important for your efforts, from promoting the sharing of your website content to publicizing your social profiles to improving user registration.

Integrating social media into your website is a valuable exercise. With only a small bit of work, you can advance several of your social media optimization goals, including improving the visibility of your social media channels, making it easier for people to share your content and increasing you engagement with users. The beauty of it all is that many of the tools covered in this chapter come ready to use from the vendors, most of them free of charge. All you need to do is identify the tools you want to use, grab the code, then integrate with your web pages.

Improving Your Visibility

You may get tired of reading this, but we'll write it again just the same: Your social media profiles and your website are parts of a virtuous circle. You always want to cross-promote your website content on your social media channels while promoting your social media presence on your website. The relationships among your various channels should be symbiotic; each helps and promotes the others.

People at the companies behind all the big social media sites understand the importance of connecting to website content and provide a wide variety of social sharing and promotional tools for you to use. All the major social media sites offer ready-to-use sharing tools such as promotional badges and buttons. The tools are free to use and often include a fair number of customization options. In addition, some third-party services offer plug-ins for the most common content management systems. These plug-ins aren't tied to a single service; they allow you to connect with many of the most popular social platforms.

 If you're using WordPress or one of the other popular content management systems to manage your website, you may find that some social media tools are built into your website theme or template. Although these tools are often limited, they're extremely easy to implement. If you need richer functionality, add a plug-in or widget to your site.

Integrating social media tools with your website allows you to achieve three goals:

✔ Raise awareness of your social media profiles.

✔ Enable sharing of your website content.

✔ Display social media content on your web pages.

When it comes to publicizing the existence of your profiles and giving users the chance to share your content, you have plenty of choices. Which tools you use is up to you, but there are some clear winners. Channels such as Facebook and Twitter have so many users and are so commonly used that you certainly want to make it easy to connect with those platforms. You should look beyond the obvious choices, however. Although the other services may not deliver as much (or as frequently) as the biggest sites, those other services' contributions to your traffic and your visibility can still add up.

Sharing content from your site to social media

Integrate social sharing tools with an eye to achieving maximum effect. The goal isn't simply to make it possible for users to share your content; the goal is to encourage sharing. Effective promotion of sharing is largely the byproduct of two factors: placement and selection of sharing tools.

Placement of sharing tools is one of the keys to success. You want the tools to be visible at the right time, which is an issue that crosses the line between psychology and usability. Will users want to share an article before or after they read it? We argue that it's more logical to assume that people need a prompt to share at the end of an article, after they've read it and decided that it's worth sharing. Placing the social sharing prompt at the end of the content also means that the user doesn't have to scroll to the top of the page to find the sharing tools. If you want to play it safe, place sharing prompts at both the top and the bottom of the article.

Some third-party systems, such as Shareaholic, offer a floating toolbar that remains visible alongside the page contents as the user scrolls up and down the page. Figure 7-1 shows a floating toolbar.

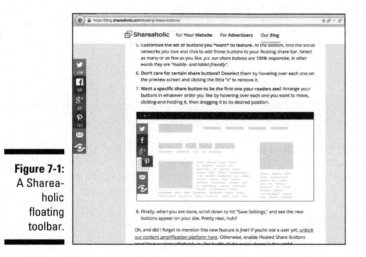

Figure 7-1:
A Shareaholic floating toolbar.

Regardless of which approach you take to the placement of your sharing tools, it's important to provide easy access to the channels that suit your content and your users. For most sites, you should integrate at least Facebook and Twitter. For other sites, the choice of sharing options depends largely on the nature of your content and the proclivities of your target audience.

Table 7-1 gives you some ideas to get you started with the selection of basic sharing tools for your site.

Table 7-1	Matching Content to Channels
Type of Website	*Social Media Channels*
News and articles	Facebook
	Twitter
	Google+
	LinkedIn
	WordPress
	Digg
Visual content	Facebook
	Twitter
	Google+
	Pinterest
	Instagram
	Reddit
	Flickr
Product sales	Facebook
	Twitter
	Google+
	Pinterest
Content for professional and career-focused audiences	Facebook
	Twitter
	Google+
	LinkedIn

The easiest solution to the dilemma of implementing tools for multiple social media sites may be to use a third-party sharing widget that provides links to multiple services. A service such as ShareThis is one solution, though it does add a bit of complexity for your visitors. The ShareThis plug-in provides a wide range of options for sharing your content, and this means the user has to click the content and then find the service to which he or she wants to share; it's a bit more complex than just having a simple button someone can click for an instant share to a specific service such as Facebook or Twitter. You can get the ShareThis plug-in at `http://sharethis.com`. Figure 7-2 shows the ShareThis plug-in.

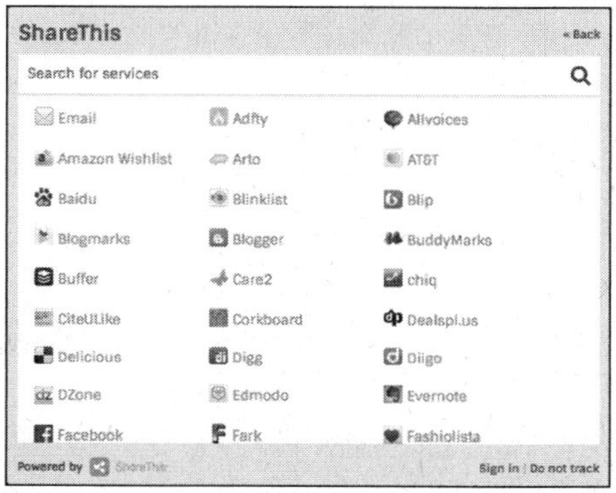

Figure 7-2:
ShareThis in
action.

Sharing social media content on your site

If your goal is to display content from your social media channels on your web pages, you have fewer choices than you do for connecting your page content to your social media channels. However, all the major players provide ready-to-use widgets that satisfy most people's needs. The question of what social media content to integrate is a byproduct of three factors:

- ✔ Where you have profiles
- ✔ Which channels you're active on
- ✔ Whether the content from the social media channels can be integrated smoothly into your site

Integrating social media content into your site not only promotes the social media profiles, but also provides a richer experience for site visitors.

Facebook and Twitter content-sharing widgets are widely used on the web, but other services (including Pinterest, YouTube, and SlideShare) have widgets that are free and easy to implement, and you shouldn't neglect these alternatives. By displaying photos, videos, or external documents, you provide your visitors a richer content experience that's likely to translate into longer time on the page and better engagement. Figure 7-3 shows how you can use a Pinterest widget to showcase products.

Figure 7-3:
A Pinterest content widget.

Using Facebook Tools

Facebook offers a variety of options for website owners. The tools fall into three categories:

- ✔ **Badges** to let people know you have a Facebook profile and to give them to option to follow you directly from your web page
- ✔ **Sharing tools** to share your website content on Facebook
- ✔ **Content display widgets** to display on your website posts from your Facebook Timeline or to embed specific posts from Facebook in a web page

For most people, the right mix of tools is a combination of the Facebook Like and Share options. If you're promoting a Facebook Page, you should also consider implementing the Like Box, which provides both content from your Facebook Page and prompts for the viewer to like the Page. If you're promoting a Facebook Personal Profile as opposed to a Page, the Like Box isn't an option, but you can still display specific posts from your Personal Profile by using the Embedded Posts widget. The Embedded Posts widget has one unique advantage: You can use it to display any public content from Facebook, not just content from your own Personal Profile or Page.

Although Facebook provides an assortment of buttons, badges, and widgets, not all are widely used, and frankly, not all are terribly useful from an SMO perspective. The Facebook Activity Feed, for example, lists all the Facebook activity related to your site by showing a list of all the Likes and Recommends given to the site. This feature takes up a lot of space and doesn't add much to the promotion of your site (and does nothing for the promotion of your presence on Facebook). Similarly, the Facebook Badges are of limited use, as they provide little in the way of functionality. The one exception worth noting is the Facepile Badge, which enables you to display photos from your Facebook Personal Profile on your website. The Facepile Badge, however, isn't available for Pages.

For details on Facebook Badges, see `https://www.facebook.com/badges`. You can find the other Facebook buttons and widgets on the Facebook Developer website at `https://developers.facebook.com`. Chapter 6 provides more information about each of the badges and widgets.

Working with Facepile

One widget used on many sites, Facepile, bears mention here. The Facepile widget shows the number of likes your site has received and thumbnail profile photos of the people who Liked it. This widget is interesting not only because it shows like behavior (which is often viewed as an endorsement of your content), but also because it selects the profile photos that are relevant to the viewer. In other words, it lists Facebook users who are friends of the visitor who is viewing the page. This feature personalizes the experience and strengthens the endorsement. If your friends like something, odds are that you'll like it too.

The Like Box and the Follow button can also be configured to show the profile photos of the viewer's friends.

Integrating Google+

For many, integrating Google+ will be a second-tier priority because of the perception that it has less impact than sites like Facebook or Twitter. We encourage you, however, to make it a top-tier priority. Google+ visibility often brings with it search engine optimization (SEO) benefits, particularly with regard to getting your content picked up quickly by Google's spiders. Give visitors the chance to +1 your content items, and you'll see benefits — at least on Google.

The Google +1 feature is the Google+ equivalent of a Facebook Like.

Google+ integration tools fall into three categories:

- ✔ **Buttons** to encourage people to follow your profile, or to share or +1 content
- ✔ **Badges** to promote your Google+ presence
- ✔ **Widgets** to display content and functionality

Google's version of the Facebook Like functionality is the +1. You can add a button to your site to encourage people to +1 a particular content item and, essentially, give their vote of endorsement. +1 buttons are easy to implement and should be part of your social media integration strategy.

Sharing on Google+ is viewed differently from sharing on Facebook. Google considers sharing to be a "lightweight endorsement" that carries less weight than a +1. Google provides a button for sharing to enable this functionality. When a visitor clicks the Google+ share button, the content is shown on the visitor's Google+ profile, but it's not given a +1 endorsement.

The Google+ share function is more limited than the Facebook share function. Users who click the Google+ share button can't add comments to the post.

If your goal is to promote your Google+ profile, you can use either the Follow button or a badge. The Follow button informs visitors that you have a Google+ profile and gives them the option to follow you from the web page. Google+ badges are interesting options with more functionality than their Facebook counterparts. Badges are available for your profile, your company pages, or a Google+ community. Badges inform visitors that you're active on Google+ and also allow them to click to follow or +1 the profile, page, or community. Figure 7-4 shows a typical Google+ badge.

Figure 7-4:
A Google+
badge.

Google+ content widgets are quite different from those provided by Facebook. There's no equivalent to the Facebook Like Box, for example. Google doesn't provide a widget that shows the stream of posts from your profile; it only allows you to embed specific posts in your web page. Although it's unfortunate that you can't show the stream, the embedding tools for specific posts are very good. You can embed articles, images, and videos, as well as songs and movies from Google Play. One interesting feature is what Google+ calls *interactive posting* — that is, displaying a post and associating with it a unique link with a call to action, which enables you to do some neat things. If you have a post about an event, you can display the post and add a button that users can click to RSVP to the event. When a user clicks the button, he goes to your RSVP page.

Find out more about the various Google+ integration options for your web pages by visiting `https://developers.google.com/+/web`.

Tapping Into the WordPress Community

WordPress users have a secret advantage: They can publish and share their content in the large WordPress community. By default, all users of the WordPress blogging platform are part of the WordPress network. Users with WordPress accounts can easily comment on other WordPress blogs and can set up alerts to keep them advised of new content in their areas of interest. As users view content, they can vote for it by clicking the Like link (which sometimes appears as a heart-shaped icon rather than a text link). WordPress Likes help raise the visibility of the content by highlighting it to other members to the WordPress community.

Users of WordPress.com — that is, the hosted blogging service — are already members of the WordPress community. Users of WordPress.org — the open source content management system — can connect their publishing to the WordPress community by creating an account at WordPress.com. After you connect to the WordPress community, you can add the WordPress Like function to your WordPress-powered website. Figure 7-5 shows a typical WordPress Like button.

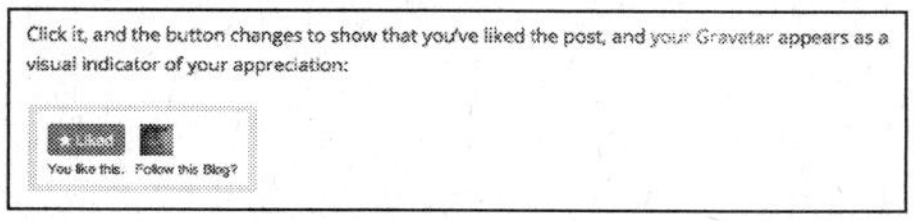

Figure 7-5:
A Word-
Press Like
button.

> Click it, and the button changes to show that you've liked the post, and your Gravatar appears as a visual indicator of your appreciation:
>
> ★ Liked
> You like this.   Follow this Blog?

The WordPress Like function works similarly to a Facebook Like or a Google +1. Visitors to your site who are also members of the WordPress community can click a Like button to vote for a post and can follow your site to receive notifications when new posts are published. When a post is liked, a counter showing the total number of likes is shown on your site and the post may also be displayed in the user's WordPress account.

Several WordPress plug-ins enable you to add the Like functionality to your site. Visit the WordPress plug-in directory at `https://wordpress.org/plugins`.

Implementing Social Login

Social login, sometimes called *social sign-in,* is an increasingly popular approach to website user authentication. A site that provides social login gives its users a way to log in to the website through the use of an existing social media profile. If you use social login, a new user who wants to create an account on your website doesn't need to remember yet another user-name and password; she can simply connect by using her credentials from one of the common social networks, such as Facebook, Twitter, Google+, or LinkedIn. Figure 7-6 shows an implementation of social login with options for the visitor to log in via Facebook, OpenID, Twitter, or WordPress.

Social login delivers several benefits for website owners:

- ✔ **Decreased barrier to user registration:** Users no longer have to remember separate usernames and passwords for all the sites they visit, thereby removing a disincentive for them to create new accounts on your site.

  A case study from Janrain has shown that social login increases registration rates by as much as 50 percent. (See `http://janrain.com/resources/case-studies/interscope-records/` for more information.)

- ✔ **No need to manage support and security:** All issues related to the username and password are no longer your problem; with social login, the username and password and all the related issues reside with the social media channel. If users forget their passwords or have other problems, they deal with the social media channel to sort it out.

- ✔ **Access to user demographic data:** Social login can give the site owner access to a wide variety of information about the user. The information is automatically extracted from the social media profile used for the login. Although users' information varies from system to system, some services produce an incredible amount of information — far more than you'd normally obtain through your own user registration process.

If you're in a jurisdiction that imposes limits on the information you can gather from users, you can still use social login, though your ability to gather the richer demographic data may be limited. Facebook, for example, offers an anonymous login product, and some systems, such as OpenID, don't disclose user demographic data at all.

✔ **Access to the social media channel:** If you use a social media ID for authentication, it's easy to integrate additional features from that social media channel. If your site uses Facebook Login, for example, using Facebook Comments for your site's commenting functionality is super easy.

✔ **Mobile friendliness:** Social login makes it easier for users to log in on mobile devices. Traditional authentication on a mobile device typically takes more time and effort for users than social login does.

✔ **Multiple-site login:** Social login is all about decreasing complexity for users, which translates into better conversion rates for site owners. This concept, known as Single Sign On (SSO), is increasingly seen as a step forward in website usability.

In response to the rise in the number of social login options, several companies have released all-in-one solutions that allow you to tap into power of multiple social login systems through one platform. Among the players are OneAll, Janrain, Gigya, and LoginRadius. The aggregated solutions are convenient, but often require some sort of subscription fee. OneAll (www.oneall.com) is the most affordable of the bunch and one of the easiest to use. OneAll offers a free basic plan as well as plug-ins that simplify setup for users of common systems such as WordPress, Drupal, Joomla!, and PhpBB.

Facebook Login

Facebook Login, previously known as Facebook Connect, is the free authentication option that websites and apps can use to enable their users to log in by using their Facebook credentials. Facebook Login is one of the most popular social login protocols. Given the wide adoption of Facebook by users, offering Facebook Login makes sense for many site owners.

Although it's best to offer users their choice of logins, if you're going to implement only one type of social login, it should be Facebook Login.

Setting up Facebook Login can be very simple. If you're running a site powered by WordPress, Joomla!, Drupal, or another popular content management systems, you can install plug-ins to implement Facebook Login. Even if you use a prebuilt plug-in, you still need to do some of the work yourself. Using

Facebook Login requires you to register on the Facebook Developers site (`https://developers.facebook.com`) and create a Facebook app.

Users in countries that block Facebook, such as China, can't use Facebook Login.

If you can't find a plug-in that works with your site, or if you're simply a do-it-yourselfer, you can implement Facebook Login manually by using the JavaScript Software Development Kit (SDK). Manual implementation is a bit of a chore, as it requires integration with your website's existing authentication system. Still, if someone on your team has programming skills, the job isn't terribly difficult, and the documentation is good.

You can find instructions for manual implementation at `https://developers.facebook.com/docs/facebook-login/v2.2.`

Twitter login

The second most popular social login protocol, offered by Twitter, is Sign In with Twitter.

If you're running a site powered by a content management system such as WordPress, Joomla!, or Drupal, you can install plug-ins that implement Sign In with Twitter. If you prefer, you can implement Sign In with Twitter manually. Visit `https://dev.twitter.com/web/sign-in` for instructions on manual implementation.

Sign In with Twitter plugins for the various common content management systems can be found on the extensions sites for each CMS.

Google+ login

If you use Gmail, Google+, Google Drive, Google Docs, or YouTube, you have a Google username and password that enables you to use Google+ Sign-In. Given the large number of people who have Google credentials, it's not surprising that many sites are allowing people to log in with their Google usernames and passwords, and, for the same reason, you might want to consider including the feature on your own website.

Google+ Sign-In offers smooth integration with the functionality of the underlying Google+ social network. Plug-ins for all the popular content management systems are available and can be downloaded from the various official CMS extensions websites. If you prefer the do-it-yourself approach, you have a wide variety of options for manual implementation of Google+ Sign-In, including implementing it client side, server side, hybrid, or cross platform.

You can find out more about implementing Google+ Sign-In at `https://developers.google.com/+/web/signin`.

Other login alternatives

An increasing number of social networks are offering authentication options to their users. The platform you implement should reflect your user base. If you're uncertain, stay with the big players, or implement a solution that brings multiple systems to your site. In addition to the options discussed earlier in this chapter, social login options are available from the following networks:

- ✔ LinkedIn
- ✔ PayPal
- ✔ Microsoft
- ✔ Foursquare

Open standards in authentication

Two other names you're likely to hear in any discussion about social login are OAuth and OpenID. Here's what you need to know about them:

- ✔ **OAuth** is an open authorization protocol. It underlies most of the popular authentication systems, including those of Facebook, Twitter, Google+, LinkedIn, Microsoft, and PayPal. Learn more at `http://oauth.net`.

- ✔ **OpenID** is an open authentication system based on OAuth. Unlike OAuth, which is mostly the province of developers, OpenID

is a consumer-oriented service that's likely to be used by at least some of your website's visitors. If you want to accommodate OpenID users, you should include OpenID in your list of authentication options. Learn more at `http://openid.net`.

From an SMO point of view, neither OAuth nor OpenID offers any direct value for your efforts. These services do nothing to improve your users' ability to share content or your ability to gather demographic data, so consider whether the effort of implementing them is worthwhile.

Chapter 8

Inspiring User Engagement

*G*etting people to engage with you on your site is one of the holy grails of digital marketing. Two of the easiest ways to do this are to offer website comments and discussion forums.

Remember when websites had guestbooks? Online commenting and discussion have come a long way since then, growing into powerful channels for engaging with website visitors. Widespread adoption by big brands and publishers shows the effectiveness of providing discussion tools for site visitors. These features are so common now that if you find a major website without a comments box, it seems a little odd.

Tapping into the engagement potential of comments and discussions can be a challenge, however, with technical and management issues. This chapter explains how you can approach engagement and how providing a place where people can discuss your content can enhance your social media optimization (SMO).

Inviting Comments and Discussion

Providing users a way to voice their opinions and add their thoughts to your content items is a valuable and effective way of creating engagement right on the pages of your website. Although comments are most often thought of in the context of a blog, the effectiveness of the functionality merits a much broader implementation. Users who are willing to take time to add a comment are much more likely to engage with you in other ways. In other words, commenting is a way to build a connection with people.

People who care enough to comment are the kind of visitors you want to make a connection with. People who comment have the potential to become evangelists.

The manner in which you implement commenting affects its effectiveness. If you're going to set up commenting on your site, do it right and feature it prominently; don't add it as a second thought and bury it. The fastest way to fail at implementing a commenting feature is to simply tack it on and wait to see whether anyone uses it. Commenting should be part of your web design strategy, and inspiring comments should be one of your goals. The number of comments should be one of your success metrics.

You should consider two other factors when making the decision whether to include commenting or discussions on your site:

> ✔ **The amount of traffic your site receives:** If your site receives very little traffic, commenting and discussions are likely to underperform. You need to have an active site with at least reasonable amounts of traffic. In the absence of visible activity, you wind up in kind of a vicious circle: No one wants to post unless people are posting.

> Nothing is worse than a barren discussion forum, which is like a ghost town with tumbleweeds blowing down the streets — unwelcoming and just a bit creepy.

> ✔ **Your ability to moderate the comments and discussions:** Commenting and discussion forums require added management overhead. Never forget that someone has to be reading the posted comments to moderate them. An active comments or discussion system can take up a significant amount of your time. You have to stay on top of activity on the forum, not only to respond and engage people, but also to police the activity for inappropriate posts and abusive individuals. Spammers in particular love unmoderated comment systems and forums. Ignore moderation at your peril!

Understanding website comment functionality

Adding a comments feature to your website gives you another route for engaging with your visitors and brings the added advantage of generating that engagement right on your web page. Comments can also generate new content on your pages and create a richer experience for site visitors, which can translate into more time spent on the site and SEO benefits. The BBC News website provides a great example of how commenting can enrich the pages of a website. Figure 8-1 shows a typical web comments feature on that site.

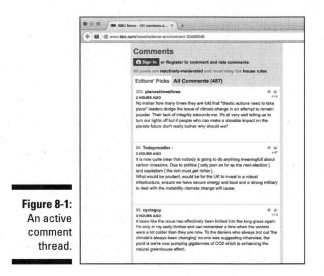

Figure 8-1:
An active
comment
thread.

Setting up comments is very easy. All the popular content management systems include comment functionality, either in their core packages or through the use of a plug-in. Additionally, you can implement several commenting platforms simply by cutting and pasting a bit of code; no programming skill is needed. Some of the popular standalone commenting platforms include

- Facebook Comments (`https://developers.facebook.com/docs/plugins/comments`)
- Google+ Comments (`https://support.google.com/blogger/answer/2981015?hl=en`)
- Disqus (`https://disqus.com`)
- Livefyre (`http://web.livefyre.com/comments/`)
- Echo (`www.echostudio.co/`)

When deciding which commenting system to implement on your site, look for one that offers visitors a chance to subscribe to the comment thread. That way, as other comments are posted, visitors who previously commented are notified by email about new comments. Comment subscriptions are extremely effective in generating repeat visits and also appreciated by users.

Although most people are used to seeing comments in the context of blog or news sites, don't let that fact limit your thinking. You can implement comments with virtually any type of content, and they work as well for images and videos as they do for text.

The keys to creating effective commenting are common-sense:

- **Make commenting prominent.** Don't bury the commenting feature. Keep the form visible, and make the posted comments stand out on the page.

- **Make it easy.** The fewer steps it takes to post a comment, the better.

- **Make it immediate.** If you want to moderate comments, make sure that you turn them around quickly.

Comment spam can be a problem. Whenever you open up a comment thread, you will get a certain number of spammers; it's just a by-product of the Internet activity. Although you should always moderate your comment threads to watch out for and delete spam, you might find a system like Akismet (`http://akismet.com`) useful. Akismet is from the makers of WordPress. It is a hosted antispam service you can use to protect your site from spammers. Akismet works on a variety of platforms (not just WordPress!). The system is free for personal websites. Business plans start at just $5 a month.

Building your own discussion forum

If you want to move beyond simple comment functionality, consider discussion forums. Although discussion forums aren't technically forms of social media, they generate compelling engagement. A successful forum creates a community of users who come to your site to interact with you and with one another. Nothing builds brand affinity like repeat visits and a personal stake in content creation; forums deliver both of those items.

Discussion forums are powerful tools when harnessed properly. Given the right setup and management, discussion forums can help you achieve some lofty goals:

- Build a sense of community.

- Provide a space for knowledge sharing.

- Elevate customer service and support.

- Create brand affinity.

- Provide an SEO boost by adding more content to your site.

If you're thinking that "lofty goals" implies a steep climb, you're right. Discussion forums also have significant overhead in terms of technology and time management, particularly the latter.

Start small, and grow organically. Launch with a limited number of forum topics, focusing on major topics most likely to be of interest to your visitors. As activity grows, your users will tell you what new topics you need to open.

You can implement discussion forums on your site in several ways. Several stand-alone systems have good reputations and power many of the forums you see today on the web. Following are some frequently used tools:

- phpBB (`https://www.phpbb.com`) (see Figure 8-2)
- Simple Machines Forum (`www.simplemachines.org`) (SMF)
- Invision Power Board (`www.invisionpower.com`) (IPB)
- bbPress (`https://bbpress.org`)
- vBulletin (`www.vbulletin.com`)

Although the systems in the preceding list require you to download and set up the forum on your own server, other hosted alternatives require little technical skill. The route you choose is up to you, but open-source packages (that is, the free packages!) invariably require you to have some technical knowledge and to do some of the setup and maintenance yourself. Some of the popular hosted forum options include

- Vanilla Forums (`http://vanillaforums.com`)
- Quick Topic (`www.quicktopic.com`)
- ProBoards (`https://www.proboards.com`)

Figure 8-2:
A phpBB forum implementation.

Hamilton Watch Forum

Topics	Author	Replies	Views	Last post
Announcements				
Forum Terms of Service: All Members Please Read	TechGuy	0	1733	Tue Jun 14, 2011 9:10 pm TechGuy
Topics				
Around The World Hamilton [Go to page: 1 ... 15, 16, 17]	stales	161	18883	Sat Dec 06, 2014 8:21 pm vintagehamiltons
Case design patents	vintagehamiltons	4	1886	Sat Mar 29, 2014 4:54 pm salsaku
Hamilton Resource Center	Dave	2	3461	Sun Mar 04, 2012 10:25 am Dave
What's wrong with this picture? [Go to page: 1, 2]	hamiltonelectric	10	135	Sat Dec 13, 2014 7:04 pm retroworx
1960 Montclair dial variation	Namespetra	1	46	Sat Dec 13, 2014 6:58 pm Dave
There are still good watches out there: Hamilton Oval 14K	coronado	3	110	Sat Dec 13, 2014 10:42 am vintagehamiltomt
International Dial Abilities [Go to page: 1, 2]	MPassaro	17	344	Sat Dec 13, 2014 10:08 am n-theory
Question of interchanging hands	GreenBayStamps	0	40	Sat Dec 13, 2014 8:54 am GreenBayStamps
My favorite Electric Ladies model... The Bagley?!?	cj415	0	58	Fri Dec 12, 2014 4:38 pm cj415
Resource for Custom Cut Crystals	retroworx	3	84	Fri Dec 12, 2014 4:34 pm gatorcpa
Ventura Case Back	retroworx	2	70	Fri Dec 12, 2014 9:12 am retroworx

Many hosting companies provide turnkey installation of the most common forum systems, streamlining setup.

Forum management is an issue you absolutely must consider. Forum startup can be hard work that takes effort over time. Moderating a forum can be a hugely time-consuming, and often frustrating, endeavor. This area is one in which you can be a victim of your own success. If your forum takes off, you may find yourself facing long nights in front of a computer dealing with argumentative users, spammers, and trolls! Forums can also be a lot of fun and are very likely to create new personal relationships, however, so you simply have to weigh the pros against the cons before you decide to implement a forum on your site.

Lay down clear rules for forum participation, and keep the rules short and to the point. Complex terms and conditions don't get read and fail to achieve their goals.

Implementing a forum alternative

Over the past several years, forums have been supplanted by the emergence of group functionality on Facebook and LinkedIn. Because Facebook and LinkedIn Groups are free and incredibly easy to set up, many smaller companies may favor creating a group over building their own forum functionality. Groups are useful if you're looking to build a specialty discussion for a specific demographic or for a short-lived event, situations where implementing a full forum system would be impractical. Figure 8-3 shows an active Facebook Group.

Figure 8-3:
A Facebook
Group.

Both Facebook Groups and LinkedIn Groups tap into the social sharing functionality of their platforms. Comments posted to a group often wind up on the user's timeline, where they're visible to the user's friends. Social visibility drives further membership in the group and, in turn, more activity. Using the group functionality has drawbacks, however:

- ✔ Not all your potential users may be active on Facebook or LinkedIn.
- ✔ The content is no longer under your control; it's controlled by the provider. If Facebook or LinkedIn changes its terms and conditions, the change may affect your group. At some point, these services may phase out the group functionality, and if that happens, what happens to the content you worked so hard to create?
- ✔ Because the content isn't hosted on your site, you gain little SEO benefit.
- ✔ Groups offer limited branding opportunities.
- ✔ Groups don't allow you to monetize them via advertising or sponsorship.
- ✔ Groups give you limited ability to gather data and engage in direct marketing with group members.

Given the limitations of groups, the question is "What do you want to get out of a forum?" If your goal is simply added engagement and relationship building, LinkedIn and Facebook Groups are great choices. If, on the other hand, you're looking to monetize your forum or to achieve maximum leverage for your site or your brand, building a dedicated forum on your domain is a better choice.

Follow these steps to add a Facebook Group:

1. **Log in to Facebook.**

2. **In the Groups section in the left column, click the Create Group option.**

3. **Enter the necessary information in the following fields of the pop-up box:**

   - *Group Name:* Give your group a useful and easy-to-find name.

   - *Members:* Type the names of the people you want to invite to the group. You have to invite at least one person; you can invite more later.

   - *Privacy:* Choose the privacy option you want for the group: Public, Closed, or Secret. Public groups allow anyone to join. Private groups are by invitation only. Secret groups are private and don't appear in search results.

Secret groups are useful for small workgroups and project teams.

4. **On the next screen, select an icon for the group.**

   The icon appears in the Groups column, next to the name.

5. **Click OK to finish.**

Follow these steps to create a LinkedIn Group:

1. **Log in to LinkedIn.**

2. **Under the Interests choice on the main navigation, select the Groups option.**

3. **At the bottom of the right column on the Groups page, click the Create a Group button.**

   You see a page where you enter the details of the Group.

4. **Complete the required fields on the form and then click either Create an Open Group or Create a Members-Only Group.**

   - *Open Group:* Anyone can join this type of Group.

   - *Members-Only Group:* Basically a private Group. This type of Group is useful for internal use or for projects.

5. **When you're prompted to add people to the Group, you can add people immediate or skip this step.**

   After you complete the steps, the LinkedIn Group is immediately ready for use.

Implementing Social Discussion Tools

Social discussion tools are essentially commenting and discussion systems that you can add to your site. These systems are platform-independent, so you can include them in your website regardless of the programming language or content management system you're using.

All discussion systems are simple to implement; you just plug them in and go. The downside of any discussion system is the uncertainty about which tools and companies will be around in the next year, the year after that, or five years from now. If you implement a tool, and support for that tool is discontinued or the company that offers it goes under, what happens to the content in all your comments? Although these systems offer attractive, easy-to-implement functionality, you have to weigh the benefits against the business risk of putting your content (or, in this case, comments on your content) in someone else's hands.

Using Facebook Comments to build audience

The most social-media-savvy of the social discussion tools comes from one of the leaders in the field: Facebook. Facebook Comments is a free commenting plug-in that enables you to leverage your site visitors' connections with Facebook. When you implement the Facebook Comments plug-in, a comments box appears on your website. Users with Facebook accounts can post comments by using their Facebook credentials. Activity on the comments plug-in is visible to the users' friends through the Facebook News Feed. Figure 8-4 shows Facebook Comments.

Facebook Comments does three things for you:

✔ Handles display of the comment form and comments

✔ Allows people to leave comments without having to create a new account or log in to your website

✔ Provides social media visibility via the posting of the comment activity on the user's Facebook Timeline

The combination of utility and boosted visibility on a key channel makes Facebook Comments a winner for many people.

Though a lot of people seem to overlook this feature, Facebook Comments includes a moderation option. The plug-in allows you to review comments before they're posted, and you can also create blacklists of prohibited words and even ban users. Get the code for Facebook Comments at https://developers.facebook.com/docs/plugins/comments.

Figure 8-4:
Facebook
Comments.

> 1,901 comments ▾
>
> Add a comment...
>
> ☑ Post to Profile   Posting as Ric Shreves (Change) [Comment]
>
> **Waloo**
> kima dima
> Reply · Like · Follow Post · 22 seconds ago
>
> **William**
> me passa o telefone dele
> Reply · Like · Follow Post · 11 minutes ago
>
> **Ram**
> best and useful for fb. users.
> Reply · Like · Follow Post · 15 minutes ago
>
> **Prince Ar**
> please give me cd key.
> Reply · Like · Follow Post · 38 minutes ago
>
> **Santiago Zeg**
> Aplica a todos y en cualquier circunstancia
> Reply · Like · Follow Post · 39 minutes ago
>
> View 1,877 more ▾

Exploring alternative systems

Facebook Comments isn't the only social commenting platform in the market today. Others are Disqus (https://disqus.com), Livefyre (http://web.livefyre.com), and Viafoura (http://viafoura.com). All three platforms have a similar approach to commenting, in that they strive to give website owners access to a community of users. After a user uses one of these systems to make a comment on a site, he can easily comment on other sites that employ the same system. Users are often able to follow other users, and some systems even provide ratings for users. Each of these platforms also integrates with the most common social media channels to enable users to share their comments on their preferred social network.

Disqus is the most mature of these solutions and the one with the largest user base. It's the only one of the solutions mentioned here that has a free option for website owners. You can use the basic Disqus commenting system free of charge, but if you want additional features, such as single sign-on or other enhancements, you have to pay a subscription fee. Disqus offers ready-to-use widgets for common content management systems such as WordPress, and you can configure it to match your site's look and feel.

Disqus enables you to export your comments in XML format at any time, thereby giving you control of your content and allowing you to move to another system if you so desire.

Although Disqus focuses on creating a broad-based commenting platform, Livefyre and Viafoura have more functionality. Livefyre and Viafoura offer commercial products that bring a range of functionality designed to generate user engagement and enrich your website content. Each includes commenting, social sharing, and aspects of gamification — including user ratings and rewards systems — to help motivate users to engage on your site. The products allow you to integrate a wide range of user-generated content into your site easily and then enhance it with your own content.

If your budget is robust enough to support commercial solutions, you may want to consider a solution like Livefyre or Viafoura. They provide high-level functionality that may help your brand create more compelling social engagement.

Chapter 9

Implementing Social Media Standards and Protocols

*H*ave you ever shared something on Facebook and found that the share displays some bizarre image unrelated to the content or that the description looks like nonsense? Well, that's what can happen if the publisher hasn't implemented semantic markup for the content. It turns out that with just a little effort, publishers can affect what appears when people share their content. This chapter explains the markup that makes it possible to take control of what's shown when people share your content.

Semantic markup is just as much about search engine optimization (SEO) as it is about social media optimization (SMO). Although some purists may prefer to think of this topic as purely one for the SEO team, the simple fact of the matter is that implementing these markup standards not only positively affects SEO, but also delivers significant benefits on key social media channels, including Facebook, Twitter, Google+, LinkedIn, and Pinterest.

Introducing Semantic Markup

Simply put, *semantic markup* is a standardized way of writing code that makes a web page easily understandable by dumb machines, such as search engines. It's a way to annotate the content of a web page so that it can be understood properly by search engines (or by Facebook, Twitter, and other automated systems). You need to know about it for two reasons:

- ✔ Semantic markup can improve the presentation of your content on search engines, Facebook, Twitter, and other social sharing channels.
- ✔ Research shows that properly marked-up content ranks higher in the search engines than content without semantic markup.

Put another way, semantic markup makes your content look better and perform better.

This is where the confusing stuff begins. Four standards for semantic markup are in place right now:

- ✔ Schema.org
- ✔ RDFa
- ✔ Open Graph
- ✔ oEmbed

We're going to take a stance here and say that, as an SMO practitioner, you need to care only about Schema.org and Open Graph. To be frank (and to run risk of being criticized by the purists out there), many people need to care only about Open Graph.

Some commentators refer to these standards collectively as *social meta tags*.

Making Sense of Schema.org

Schema.org is a structured data markup system promulgated by Google, Microsoft, and Yahoo!. The system was designed to help a search engine understand the information on the web pages it scans and to allow it to provide richer search-result output.

This concept is best understood with an example. Take a look at Figure 9-1, which shows a typical product listing on an e-commerce site — in this case, a product listing for a vintage mechanical watch by Hamilton.

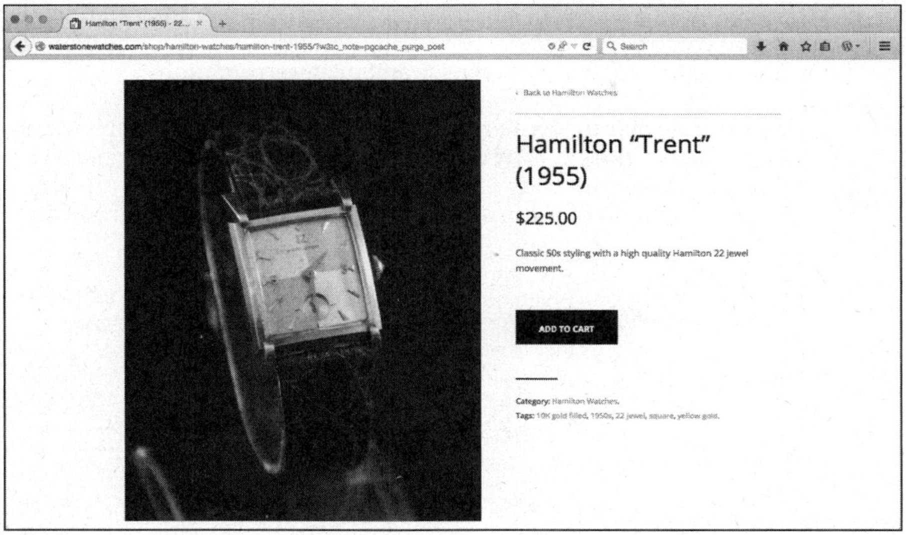

Figure 9-1:
An
e-commerce
product
listing.

The listing shows you all the things you'd expect to see:

- ✔ A photo
- ✔ The brand
- ✔ The model
- ✔ The price
- ✔ A description

To all us human beings, this listing makes perfect sense. We're able to process the context and view the information holistically. A listing of this sort, particularly in the context of an e-commerce website, presents no confusion or ambiguity. The viewer has no doubt this Hamilton Trent model watch is for sale at the price of $225.

To a dumb machine, however, this listing is just a bunch of data with no context. Here's a simplified view of what the machine sees:

```
<img src=" http://waterstonewatches.com/hamilton-trent.jpg"/>
<h1>Hamilton "Trent"</h1>
<p>$225</p>
<p>Classic 50s styling with a high quality Hamilton 22 jewel movement.</p>
```

The search engine that spiders the web page containing the product and receives the preceding information has very little idea what the information represents. The best search engines look at other information on the page and try to draw some conclusions about the content, but there's still a large amount of room for ambiguity and misinterpretation.

Semantic markup was created to help those dumb machines make sense of the data. It does this by adding tags (or markup) to the code. The markup is added inside the body of the web page, right by the items it affects. Here's the information for the same product, with semantic markup added:

```
<div itemscope itemtype=http://schema.org/Product>
<img itemprop="image" src="http://waterstonewatches.com/hamilton-trent.jpg" />
<h1 itemprop="name"><span itemprop="brand">Hamilton</span> <span
        itemprop="model"> "Trent"</span></h1>
<p itemprop="price">$225</p>
<p itemprop="description">Classic 50s styling with a high quality Hamilton
        22 jewel movement.</p>
</div>
```

All that `"itemprop="` stuff is the Schema.org markup. As you can see, the added markup gives meaning to specific pieces of information — in this case, the image, brand, model, price, and description. A search engine encountering this richer markup can better process the information it contains and is more likely to present it properly in response to a search query.

Google provides a tool for checking your markup: the Structured Data Testing Tool. You can find it at `www.google.com/webmasters/tools/richsnippets`.

Schema.org was designed to help search engines, but it's also useful in other contexts. Some social sharing sites look to see whether a page has Schema.org tags in place, and if so, they use that information when someone shares the page containing the markup, thereby affecting the appearance of the shared item. Although Schema.org can be used by Facebook and some other social sites, there's actually a better system that's tailored specifically to Facebook and social sharing: the Open Graph protocol (see the next section).

Because these tags affect the content and appearance of shared materials, they can affect greatly conversions and click-through rates.

Applying Facebook's Open Graph Protocol

The Open Graph protocol is a semantic markup standard introduced by Facebook in 2010 and now widely accepted. Some people view Open Graph as being in competition with Schema.org, but in reality, the two standards are complementary.

It's possible to implement both the Schema.org microdata and the Open Graph markup. The standards don't conflict.

Both these standards have the same goal: to better describe the information on a web page. The key differences can be summarized this way:

✔ Open Graph metadata describes the page as a whole.

✔ Schema.org microformats describe specific elements on the page.

Open Graph markup contains less information than the Schema.org microdata does but is easier to implement. To make your web page Open Graph–compliant, you need to add basic metadata to your page. Like traditional metadata, the Open Graph metadata goes into the `<head>` tag of the web page.

In Open Graph–speak, a web page is an *Open Graph object*.

Open Graph has four required properties:

✔ `og:title:` The title of the page as you want it to appear in any system that reads the Open Graph data.

It's best to keep the title tag shorter than 88 characters. Although you can add more characters, Facebook displays only the first 88.

✔ `og:type:` The type of your object. Types are specified by the protocol and are fairly numerous.

`type` is an interesting property, as it controls where the share appears in the user's interests on Facebook. If, for example, you set type of the object to "movie" and the user shares the object, the share shows up as one of the user's interests below the heading Movies in the person's Facebook profile.

To find out about all the various object types, visit `http://ogp.me`.

✔ `og:image:` The URL of the image you want to represent the page.

`image` is an important tag, because a good image can help your content spread. Use this tag to control what appears when your content is shared and make sure that it's optimized to fit nicely in Facebook. (A ratio of 1.9:1 works best. Keep it larger than 400 × 209 pixels.)

Don't leave this tag blank. If you do, Facebook will simply pull some other image from the page — possibly leading to inappropriate results.

✔ `og:url:` The URL of the page. The content of the `url` tag determines where the user goes when he clicks the Share button.

Some of the required elements have additional optional attributes, and you can provide multiple values for some of them if you so desire.

The options include

- ✔ **og:audio:** If you want an audio file to accompany the object, use this tag and specify the URL of the file.

- ✔ **og:description:** Use this tag to provide a one- or two-sentence description of the object.

  Facebook displays only the first 300 characters of your description.

- ✔ **og:determiner:** This tag allows you to specify the word that precedes the object's title in a sentence — typically, *a, an,* or *the.*

- ✔ **og:locale:** This tag specifies the locale for the page — in other words, the language on the page. If your content is in American English, for example, the value for this tag would be en_us.

- ✔ **og:locale:alternate:** If the page is offered in multiple languages, you can list all of them by using this tag.

- ✔ **og:site_name:** If the web page is part of a larger site that has a different name, use this tag to specify the site's name.

- ✔ **og:video:** If you have a video file to include, use this tag to specify the file's URL.

Using the tags is easier to grasp with an example. In the following example, we show how you can implement the Open Graph markup for a web page about a book titled *HowTo: WordPress 4:*

```
<meta property="og:title" content="HowTo: WordPress 4">
<meta property="og:type" content="book">
<meta property="og:url" content="http://wordpresshowtobook.com">
<meta property="og:image" content="http://wordpresshowtobook.com/ photo-
             200x300.png">
<meta property="og:locale" content="en_us">
<meta property="og:description" content="Learn to how to use WordPress with
             this practical how to book filled with WordPress tutorials
             and solutions to the most common WordPress CMS issues.
             Written by Ric Shreves and published by water&stone digital.
             Available now on Amazon.com, Google Play Store and on this
             website. Published in ePub, Mobi and PDF versions.">
<meta property="og:site_name" content="WordPress How To Book">
```

Your Open Graph tags go in the <head> tag of the page. Note that if you're using a popular content management system (such as WordPress, Joomla!, or Drupal), plug-ins will handle this task for you so that you don't have to write any code.

The result of implementing the Open Graph metadata is controlling what's displayed when someone shares the content on the web page. If someone shares the page with the markup shown in the preceding code, it looks like Figure 9-2.

Figure 9-2:
Sample
Facebook
share
output.

If you're not sure that you did one your Open Graph markup correctly, test it with Facebook's handy Open Graph Debugger at `https://developers.facebook.com/tools/debug`.

Although the Open Graph metadata is key to your content's success on Facebook, it's also used by several other important social sites, including Twitter, Pinterest, LinkedIn, and Google+.

Does Open Graph markup work? It certainly does! E-book site Kobo claims to have achieved a 50 percent increase in traffic from Facebook after implementing Open Graph tags.

Dealing with Twitter and Pinterest Microformats

Although Schema.org and the Open Graph protocol take care of the vast majority of social sharing situations, two of the big players — Twitter and Pinterest — have systems of their own. Twitter and Pinterest use Open Graph if you haven't used the network-specific tags, but if you master their specific standards, you can achieve better results when your content is shared on their sites.

Implementing Twitter markup

Twitter provides an option called Twitter Cards, which are simply templates for displaying tweet content. There are seven types of Twitter Cards:

- ✔ **Summary Card:** This card is the default type. It includes a title, a description, a thumbnail, and Twitter account information.
- ✔ **Summary Card with Large Image:** This card has the same content as the Summary Card, but instead of a thumbnail image, it shows a large image.
- ✔ **Photo Card:** This card shows a photo only.
- ✔ **Gallery Card:** This card shows up to four photos inside the tweet.
- ✔ **App Card:** This card provides a link to download an app.
- ✔ **Player Card:** This card has a media player.
- ✔ **Product Card:** This card is optimized to show product information.

Twitter Cards provide enhanced display of content inside of a tweet, allowing you to essentially move beyond the 140-character limitations. As a publisher, you want to implement the appropriate Twitter Card for your page so that when someone tweets a link to your page, the content displayed is rich and compelling.

If a user publishes a tweet with a link to your Twitter Card–enabled page, the tweet looks like Figure 9-3. Note that the card contents don't show up automatically; instead, the viewer sees a clickable link labeled View Summary.

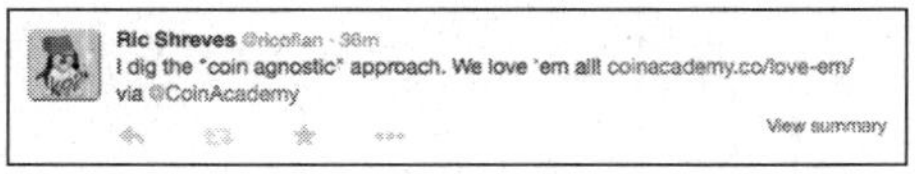

Figure 9-3:
A tweet containing a link to a Twitter Card.

> **Ric Shreves** @ricoflan · 36m
> I dig the "coin agnostic" approach. We love 'em all! coinacademy.co/love-em/ via @CoinAcademy
>
> View summary

When a person clicks the View Summary link, she sees the Twitter Card. In Figure 9-4, you see a Twitter Card display — in this case, a Summary with Large Image Card.

Figure 9-4:
Twitter Card
content.

To achieve the results shown in Figure 9-4, we had to implement Twitter Markup Tags. There are five basic tags:

✔ **twitter:card:** This tag holds the card type.

✔ **twitter:title:** Use this tag to contain a title for the page content.

   Keep the title shorter than 70 characters.

✔ **twitter:url:** This tag holds the URL the visitor will be taken to if he clicks the tweet.

✔ **twitter:description:** This tag holds a brief description of the page.

   Keep the description shorter than 200 characters.

✔ **twitter:image:src:** This tag holds the URL of the image you want to associate with the page.

   The image should be at least 280 × 150 pixels.

You can also use some optional tags. For the Twitter Card shown in Figure 9-4, I created these tags:

```
<meta name="twitter:card" content="summary_large_image"/>
<meta name="twitter:description" content="We're often asked;What's your favorite
            currency? It's such a loaded question we usually try to sidestep
            it as gracefully as we can. Of course it never works. Everyone
            seems to have a "pet" coinage and the only right answer is when
            we validate their choice. The official position of Coin Academy
            is, however, we're [&hellip;]"/>
<meta name="twitter:title" content="We love 'em all!"/>
```

```
<meta name="twitter:site" content="@CoinAcademy"/>
<meta name="twitter:domain" content="Coin Academy"/>
<meta name="twitter:image:src" content="http://
            coinacademy.co/revolutionary-choices.jpg"/>
```

The Twitter tags go in the `<head>` tag of the web page.

Creating tags isn't the only step. When you get the tags on your web page, you have to request approval from Twitter. Requesting approval is easy, and you need to do it only one time. When you're logged in to Twitter, visit the Card Validator at `https://dev.twitter.com/docs/cards/validation/validator`, test your page, and then click the button in the Card Validator to submit your page for approval.

Don't want to code Twitter Cards by hand? If you're using a common content management system, plug-ins handle the dirty work for you.

Implementing Rich Pins

Pinterest provides an enhanced display functionality called Rich Pins. Rich Pins provide an improved presentation that goes beyond the basic display limitations of the system. Five types of Rich Pins are available:

- Product Pins
- Recipe Pins
- Movie Pins
- Article Pins
- Place Pins

Implementing Rich Pins is slightly more complicated than the approaches discussed elsewhere in this chapter. If you have only one item per page, you can use Open Graph meta tags. Each pin has a different set of tags associated with it. Though each pin has a set of basic tags you can implement quickly, if you want to add a range of details and tap into the full power of the pins, you must use additional Open Graph meta tags.

Product Pins are the simplest to implement. Here's the code you'd use for a listing about a simple clock:

```
<meta property="og:title" content="8" Landmark Studio Wall Clock"/>
<meta property="og:type" content="product"/>
<meta property="og:availability" content="in stock"/>
<meta property="og:price:amount" content="30.45"/>
<meta property="og:price:currency" content="USD"/>
```

Open Graph metadata goes into the `<head>` tag of the web page.

Figure 9-5 shows what the Product Rich Pin looks like when someone pins this product to a board on Pinterest.

Figure 9-5:
A Product
Rich Pin.

This example looks really simple, right? It is, but this process applies only when you have one item per page. If you have multiple items on a page, you can't use Open Graph meta tags; instead, you need to implement Schema.org or explore a system known as oEmbed. oEmbed is another microformat that works a lot like Schema.org. The markup goes inside the `<body>` tag of the web page and describes specific items on the page.

If you want to find out more about oEmbed, visit `http://oembed.com`.

Both Schema.org and oEmbed require a significant work to implement. The results can be quite effective, but if you don't need to use these systems, stick with Open Graph and make your life easier.

After you decide on a method for implementing Rich Pins on your site and complete the work, you need to go to Pinterest to validate the work and submit your request for approval. You can find the Rich Pin Validator and approval link at `https://developers.pinterest.com/rich_pins/validator`.

If you're using a common content management system, plug-ins will handle this task for you.

Part IV
Mastering Practical SMO

In this part . . .

- ✔ Promoting your content with social media
- ✔ Using SMO to improve marketing of a product or service
- ✔ Publicizing events with your social media profiles
- ✔ Building brand and establishing expertise
- ✔ Improving reputation management with SMO
- ✔ Dealing with crisis management and negative public relations

Chapter 10

Promoting Your Content

- -

- -

C reating the right mix of channels is more art than science, and the formula for success tends to vary by the type of content, the nature of the target markets, and the amount and nature of your resources. Some basic principles remain, but the ratio of the ingredients in the recipe can change.

In broadest terms, there are three categories of channels:

✔ Channels where you control the exposure

✔ Channels where you earn exposure

✔ Channels where you buy exposure

The first category of channels really shouldn't require any explanation. We will say, however, that your content should "live" on your channels; in other words, you should always try to publish all original content on the channels you control and then push the content out to other channels from there. Don't make the mistake of putting your content exclusively on channels outside your control. You want to own it. Always.

The second category — that is, channels where you earn exposure — is the primary focus for the social media optimization (SMO) practitioner and the focus of this chapter. The third channel shouldn't be ignored, however. If you have the budget for it, paid promotion on social media channels — a topic touched on in the chapter — is a proven winner.

Getting the Big Three to Work for You

When it comes to marketing your website content, three channels dominate the field: Facebook, Twitter, and LinkedIn. If you can be successful on the Big Three, you've largely won the battle. Although other channels are deserving of your attention, if you have limited resources, focus on the Big Three. Indeed, even if you have unlimited resources, focus first on the Big Three; then look elsewhere as time and money permit.

Farming Facebook

Perhaps no channel today is as influential as Facebook. In addition to having a huge potential audience, it's an unmatched social news channel. More people than ever get their news from Facebook (which is kind of scary when you think about it, isn't it?).

If business-to-business (B2B) is your thing, you may find LinkedIn a better channel for your content than Facebook, and you may want to skip to the "Loving LinkedIn" section.

There are three keys to turning Facebook into an effective channel for your content:

- ✔ Great images
- ✔ Great headlines
- ✔ Frequent posting

Making the most of images

One of the easiest ways to make your content more compelling on Facebook is to optimize your images for Facebook.

Your image needs to be close as possible to the ratio of 1.9:1 to show up in a Facebook post as a large image.

Figure 10-1 shows you what happens when an image isn't properly optimized. Note the small size.

Compare Figure 10-2, which started life as a 1.9:1 ratio image. Much nicer, eh?

Sizing your images properly can make a world of difference in the clicks you'll get on Facebook.

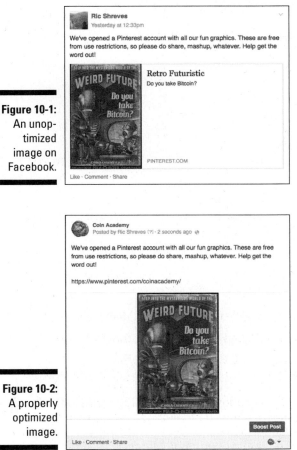

Figure 10-1:
An unop-
timized
image on
Facebook.

Figure 10-2:
A properly
optimized
image.

You can use any image you want in a Facebook post; you don't have to use an image from the article. Always use something attention grabbing, although you always want to make sure it is related in some way to the post itself.

Another neat trick is to create a custom image for Facebook and embed text in the image. Take a look at Figure 10-3. This figure has the same image as Figure 10-1 and Figure 10-2, but this one has a message inside to help inspire users to action.

Center-align the text to keep it away from the edges. Facebook trims the edges of images when it displays them on mobile devices. Keeping your text near the middle of the image prevents having it chopped off on mobile display.

Figure 10-3:
An image
with text.

The method you use to post an image is another consideration. You have three options for getting your post on Facebook:

- ✔ Share it directly from your web page, using a social sharing tool.
- ✔ Add it by creating a new post on Facebook, using the Add a Link option.
- ✔ Add it by creating a new post on Facebook, using the Add an Image option; writing the text you want; and pasting the link in the text.

The first two options result in Facebook's automatically pulling in the image and text sample from the page, leaving you to edit and optimize it. The last option has the advantage of allowing you to create whatever you want from scratch. The last option has a couple of other advantages:

- ✔ When people share the image, the text travels with the image as the caption.
- ✔ You can use a larger image.

Writing great headlines

The second key factor — writing great headlines — is one of those more-art-than-science topics. Great headline writers, like great copywriters, are worth their weight in gold. Although it's hard to teach people to how to write great headlines, you should always keep some basic principles in mind:

- ✔ Know what you're writing about.
- ✔ Remember who your audience is; your language should reflect their preferences.

✔ Speak directly.

✔ Use triggers to get people to act.

Some of the most effective trigger words are *free, secrets, easy, instant, discover, amazing, bonus, guarantee,* and *powerful.*

✔ Sell the benefits your content offers.

✔ Keep the headline short and clear.

Here are some simple tips that you can use to start creating great headlines:

✔ Use some emotion.

✔ Use actionable words.

✔ Ask a question.

✔ Build in some intrigue.

✔ State that you're presenting a list (if that's the content you're sharing).

✔ Create a sense of urgency.

✔ Use numbers to command attention.

✔ Create a problem/solution structure.

✔ Play to common needs.

See how the following headlines use the techniques mentioned in the preceding list:

✔ 10 Creative Ways to Turn Your Hobby into Income

✔ 5 Amazing Content Marketing Tips You Can Implement Right Now

✔ How to Write Blog Titles That Drive Traffic

✔ Little-Known Ways to Save on Your Utility Bills

✔ The 5 Questions You Should Ask Before Hiring an SEO Specialist

✔ What No One Tells You About SMO

✔ The Secrets to Social Media Success

✔ The Raw Food Revolution: Will It Change Your Life?

✔ Jet Lag: How to Beat It in a Day

✔ A Complete Guide to Facebook Pages

The simple fact is that your skill as a headline writer will develop over time. Practice, and practice again. No matter how experienced you are, one of the most effective ways to generate optimal headlines is to brainstorm your way through a list of six to eight variations. After you've listed all your ideas, look at them again, compare, and revise. If you're in doubt, test your ideas on a co-worker.

Timing your posts

The final key to Facebook content promotion is frequency. You need to feed Facebook regularly to develop a following and create an active community around your content. Many of the top brands post at least once a day; most publish multiple times a week. Posting less than once a week is pretty much wasted effort.

It's acceptable to post the same content multiple times on Facebook, but do this conservatively. We recommend that you do your first publication the day you publish on your website; do a second publication one month later and a third (and final) publication the month after that. Publishing the same item more than three times can wear on your followers. To avoid burning them out, change the title or the graphic on the subsequent publication dates.

Pay to play the Facebook way

After you create your post, you may want to think about looking at paid promotion of the post. On Facebook, paid promotion comes in two flavors: boosted posts and promoted posts. Both options mean paying to have your post displayed to people who meet the criteria you select.

Boosting a post is the quickest and easiest way to promote your content. When you click the Boost Post button, Facebook gives you the option to display it to your friends and the people who like your page, or to choose whom to target. The latter choice is better for most people, as it helps you extend your reach. After you make that choice, you're prompted to set a budget. As you enter your budget, Facebook projects how many people the post will reach. You can also elect how the budget is spent: as quickly as possible or spread out over a few days. During the period you specify, the post is boosted to appear higher in people's News Feeds, making it more visible. Boosted posts show up in the feed, along with the label "Sponsored." When people interact with your boosted post, their friends see that interaction.

Promoted posts work differently; they're essentially pay-per-click advertising. Promoted posts are created in the Facebook Ads Manager. It takes a bit more effort to get things going with the Ads Manager, but it offers you more control of the promotion of your post and slightly better audience targeting. Your budget can be set on a daily basis, and you typically bid for clicks, though you can choose among some other options.

Aside from the differences in ease of use and feature set, the big difference is what you're paying for. With a boosted post, you're paying for exposure; with a promoted post, you can pay for engagement. How you spend your budget should reflect your goals.

You can post on your Facebook profile and your Page and in Facebook Groups. If your goal is to drive traffic to your site, always post the site contents directly. If you also want to raise awareness of your Page, post it first to your Page; then share it to your profile and in Groups. That way, both your content and your Page get exposure.

Telling the Twitterverse

Twitter has a huge user base and is not to be ignored. It's a proven traffic spinner and is largely viewed as being one of the most effective channels for content marketing in the social media world. That said, you must deal with two significant limitations: a 140-character limit and the short life span of tweets.

The distinct characteristics of the Twitter format dictate how you approach content marketing on the channel. The 140-character limit really tests your skills as a headline writer. You have to capture your followers' imaginations and motivate them to click in a very short space. In 140 characters, you must do the following:

- ✔ Present a great headline.
- ✔ Add your URL.
- ✔ Include any tags.

Your best bet for moving beyond the 140-character limit is to implement Twitter Cards. With Twitter Cards, you can include a predetermined image, description, and other details, depending on the content being shared. Twitter Cards are discussed in depth in Chapter 9.

The short life span of tweets requires a different strategy. When a tweet appears in a user's timeline, it appears at the top of the list. As each new tweet arrives, it pushes down the old ones. That means that at some point, the tweet that was at the top of the page has been pushed down and no longer appears unless the user scrolls down the page to view his older tweets.

 Research done by one expert concluded that the median life span of a tweet is 18 minutes.

If a user follows a large number of accounts, the tweets roll by faster. As in any other medium, the content above the fold — that is, the content visible when the page loads — is the content that receives the most attention. Your tweets are largely effective only when they're above the fold of the user's Twitter timeline.

You can't control where your tweet will appear, but you can improve your chances of staying above the fold. Here's how to do it:

- ✔ **Include a link in your tweet.** Tweets with links are 86 percent more likely to be shared. Each time a tweet is shared, it pops up to the top of someone's Twitter timeline (and also extends your reach).

- ✔ **Add hashtags to your tweets.** Tweets with hashtags are twice as likely to be retweeted and are more likely to be found in a Twitter search.

    How many hashtags are optimal? No more than two. Research by Buddy Media (now part of Salesforce.com) found that tweets with more than two hashtags actually get a 17 percent lower level of engagement than tweets with fewer hashtags.

- ✔ **Get more followers.** More followers means more opportunities for someone to retweet your content.

- ✔ **Repost your own tweet.** There's nothing wrong with posting the same tweet multiple times. Just make sure you spread it out a bit. Don't post multiple times in a short period.

    Here's a suggested publishing schedule for repeating your tweets: Publish and then publish again two hours later. Post again once the next day, once the next week, and once the next month. This task is very easy to accomplish with scheduling software. Set it and forget it.

Another method for increasing the effective life span of your tweets is paying Twitter to keep your tweet in front of people. The service, known as promoted tweets, allows you to pay for priority exposure for a specific tweet. The tweet is marked clearly as promoted and is visible at the top of relevant search results on the timelines of targeted users and in the interface of official Twitter clients such as TweetDeck, Twitter for iOS, and Twitter for Android. Figure 10-4 shows you how a promoted tweet appears in a user's Twitter timeline.

A promoted tweet appears only shows once on the user's timeline. After its first appearance, it scrolls down the timeline list, just like any other tweet. Users also have the option to remove the tweet from their timeline by clicking the Dismiss link.

Promoted tweets are affordable, easy to use, and quite effective. You set up a campaign by specifying your goal, website clicks, followers, engagements, and so on. Then you bid for the results you desire. Twitter charges you based on its success in achieving those goals. If you set up a campaign with the goal of attaining engagement, for example, you're charged only when people interact with your tweet; you're not charged for tweets that get no engagement.

Figure 10-4:
A promoted
tweet.

Tweet is marked as a Promoted Tweet

Here are some tips for getting the most from the service:

- Keep the tweet short (less than 100 characters).
- Run three to six tweets as part of a coherent campaign.
- Use Twitter Cards to make the greatest effect.
- Use rich media. A good photo or video can make a difference.
- Don't just tweet; also interact with users.

Loving LinkedIn

Over the past several years, LinkedIn has come into its own as a vital publishing channel, particularly in the B2B space. Participants are motivated to learn and are looking for information that can help them get ahead in their professional lives. LinkedIn users are the perfect consumers for practical business and skills-oriented content.

You can post your content to LinkedIn in two ways:

- On your personal profile
- In a LinkedIn group of which you're a member

Of the two approaches, the latter seems to work better. Groups have a subject-matter focus that makes them good places to promote related content. Relevance is key. You don't want to be perceived as spamming the group. That practice can get you banned, and you'll miss a valuable opportunity to build expertise within your target audience.

Here are some tips for making the most of content promotion on LinkedIn:

- ✔ Post once to relevant groups.

- ✔ Always make an attempt to engage with the group members. One of the best ways is to post a question to the group members. Figure 10-5 shows an effective LinkedIn group post that uses this technique.

- ✔ If you're part of a team, encourage team members to engage in a discussion about the post. By creating activity about the post, you keep it at the top of the group, and your ranking as an influencer improves.

- ✔ Make sure that you respond to any feedback.

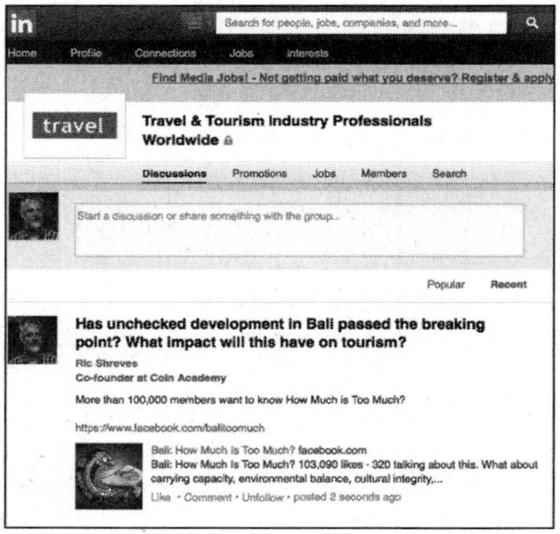

Figure 10-5:
An effective
LinkedIn
group post.

If you spot people who consistently respond and interact with your posts, reach out to them and connect with them on LinkedIn.

Like Facebook and Twitter, LinkedIn offers a paid promotion alternative. LinkedIn ads works similarly to other pay-per-click advertising systems. Indeed, LinkedIn ads look very similar to Google AdWords ads except that they include photos. Figure 10-6 shows a typical LinkedIn ad.

Runner-up to the Big Three: Google+

Although the Big Three — Facebook, Twitter, and LinkedIn — will probably generate the majority of your traffic and engagement, one other name bears mention: Google+. It's true Google+ ranks behind the Big Three in importance, but it's worth considering if you have the resources. The keys to publishing on Google+ are the same as the keys to publishing on Facebook. Although there are some formatting differences between Google+ and Facebook, as a general rule, the work you put into getting a post optimized for Facebook translates into usable material for Google+. If you have the time, definitely post to Google+. It may not deliver the same quick results as Facebook, but it's worth the effort.

Figure 10-6:
A LinkedIn ad.

MBA in Media in 1 Year
Online MBA in Media Leadership
Top UK Online MBA University of
Cumbria

Eventxtra, event solution
A smart IT event solution. Helping
you to shorten event checkin to 3s

Each ad includes a photo, a 25-character headline, a 75-character description, and a destination URL.

Ads can be targeted by a variety of criteria, and you can choose to pay for each click you receive, or you can pay for impressions, which are the number of times the ad is viewed. Minimum budget is $10 per day.

This chapter covers Facebook, Twitter, and LinkedIn for content marketing. You may be wondering what the right mix is. Our experience indicates that these three channels do different things well. Facebook is good for building community. Twitter is good for generating new followers and extending reach. LinkedIn is good for generating leads and recruiting.

Getting Visual

Working with great visual content on social media can be a joy. Powerful visuals have the best viral potential of any content, and even if your über-cool pic doesn't get thousands of shares, you often get more positive engagement from visuals than from anything else you post. People love fun photos, inspirational photos, and beautiful scenes. When you need an easy win, it's time to go to the graphics!

Several very popular sites focus on visual media. This section focuses on those sites.

Visuals work great on Facebook and on Google+, so don't forget about those channels.

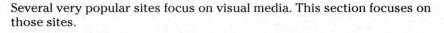

When it comes to creating visuals for maximum sharing impact, keep a few things in mind:

- ✔ If the goal is to generate awareness of your site, make sure that you include your URL in the image, in the description, or preferably in both.

- ✔ Tailor your content to your target markets.

- ✔ Video works well but can be expensive to produce. If you're on a limited budget, look at short-form video (10 seconds or less), as that content plays very nicely on multiple channels.

- ✔ Keep graphic quality high and your file dimensions to the appropriate sizes for your target channels.

- ✔ Be sensitive to copyright issues. If you don't have the rights to content, don't post it.

Using Pinterest and Instagram for images

Pinterest and Instagram dominate the image-sharing world. Pinterest, with its pin-boards approach to displaying photos, remains a strong player, but with the Facebook acquisition of Instagram, the popularity of that platform has soared.

Instagram recently passed Twitter in total number of users. It's now one of the most popular social sharing sites in the world.

Although brands are finding some success on Instagram, Pinterest remains the more effective tool for displaying your images. Pinterest provides better brand control, the ability to group your images into boards, and better analytics. Figure 10-7 shows how a Pinterest board can be used to group images topically.

Pinterest also provides a Rich Pins service that enables you to use social metadata to control what's displayed when someone pins something on your site. Rich Pins and social metadata are covered in detail in Chapter 9.

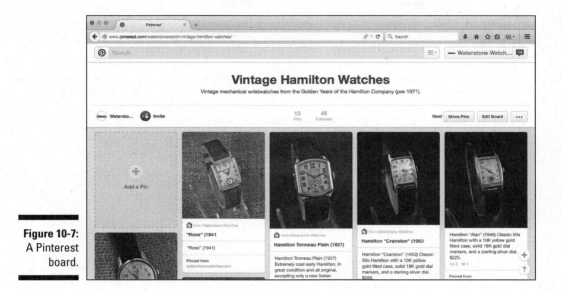

Figure 10-7:
A Pinterest board.

Instagram is the darling of the younger generation and is married to the mobile experience. The Instagram site itself offers little to brands in terms of creating a brand experience. What Instagram brings to the table are a huge user base, a massively popular mobile app, and a rich community of people who share images.

According to L2's 2014 Instagram Intelligence Report (www.l2inc.com/research/instagram-2014), images posted to Instagram see 15 times the engagement of posts on Facebook, Twitter, or Google+.

Using Latergramme and Gramblr with Instagram

Although the lure of Instagram is strong, the practicalities of using it can be frustrating. The major frustration is the fact that Instagram allows uploads only from its mobile applications. You can't go to http://instagram.com and add images. We've found two work-arounds that work reasonably well, however: Latergramme and Gramblr.

Latergramme (www.latergram.me) is web-based. Setup is a tiny bit convoluted and may keep some people from using this solution. To make it work, you need a desktop computer with a web browser and an iOS device with the Instagram app installed. To begin, point your browser to the Latergramme site and sign in, using your Instagram credentials. After you complete registration, download the free Latergramme app for your iOS device from the App Store. After you download the app, log in to Instagram, and you're ready to begin.

In the App Store, the Latergramme app is available for the iPhone but not for the iPad. Although you can install iPhone apps on your iPad with no problem, if you search for a Latergramme iPad app, you'll be disappointed.

Latergramme enables you to add images directly from your desktop computer or your iOS device. The website allows you to add multiple images at a time, along with descriptions and tags, and then drag them to a calendar to schedule their publication. Figure 10-8 shows the Latergramme dashboard with the scheduling calendar.

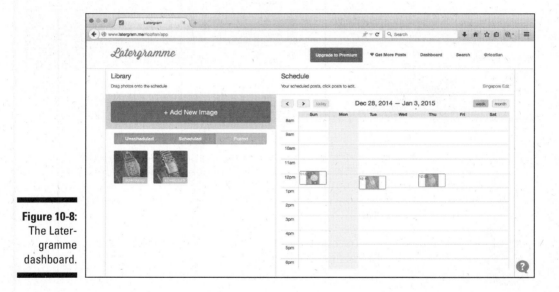

Figure 10-8:
The Later-gramme dashboard.

Aside from the setup hassle with Latergramme, there are two other down-sides: You're limited to 30 uploads a month in the free account, and after you schedule a post, you have to finalize the posting on your iOS device.

Gramblr (`http://gramblr.com`) works differently. Gramblr is a desk-top app that you download and install on your computer. Gramblr works on Windows (XP, Vista, 7,8) and on Mac OS X; it is not available for Linux. Gramblr is an emulator; it interacts with Instagram as though it were a mobile app. It has fewer features than Latergramme but doesn't limit the number of files you can upload.

Tagging photos on Instagram

Whereas Rich Pins are the keys to Pinterest, tags are the keys to Instagram. Instagram users are perhaps the most active taggers in the social media world. It's not uncommon to see a photo with a very number of tags, and a large number of tags doesn't seem have a negative effect on sharing the photo, perhaps because Instagram is mobile and tags make for easy discovery of related content. As a consequence, use tags liberally on Instagram.

To make the most of tagging, you can use the tag discovery service offered on these sites:

- ✔ Iconosquare (`http://iconosquare.com`)
- ✔ Websta (`http://websta.me`)

Simply enter a tag on either of those sites to get a count of tag frequency and a list of related tags. These sites are great ways to check out the effectiveness of your proposed tags and find ideas for others you might otherwise have missed.

Of the two services, our favorite is Iconosquare for its ease of use, reporting, and tracking. After we tie our account to Iconosquare, it generates automatic reports on our account activity. The Iconosquare reports enable us to discover the optimal time to publish to reach the largest number of followers. Figure 10-9 shows the Iconosquare reporting interface.

Whether you post your images to Pinterest, Instagram, or another image sharing site, always cross-post to your other channels. Leverage your social media presences to help people find you on other channels and increase your reach.

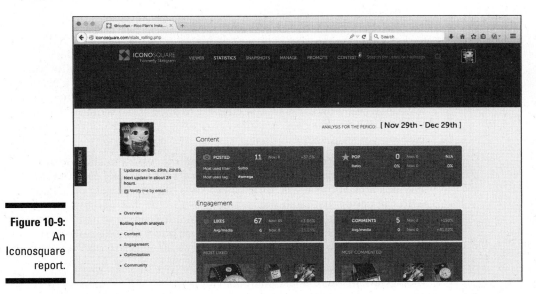

Figure 10-9:
An
Iconosquare
report.

Getting eyes on your videos

Are you creating video content? If so, that's great. If not, you really should consider adding video to your tool kit. Video can be powerful. As bandwidth has become ubiquitous in the developed world and the screen quality of mobile devices has improved, video has grown into a popular medium, and consumption has increased dramatically.

The trend is significant and totally understandable. Video is compelling, catchy, fun, and engaging. If a picture paints a thousand words, a video must paint a million words. Video is a strong contender to be the future of content marketing, and it should be an essential part of any SMO strategy. This trend is bound to continue, and the fact that it cuts across demographics makes it a no-brainer.

Cisco projects that video will account for 69 percent of all consumer Internet traffic by 2017.

The most popular video channel by far is YouTube, but other sites also deserve your patronage. Each of the following sites has strengths and weaknesses:

- **YouTube:** With a huge user base and close ties to Google+, YouTube remains the category killer. In 2014, an average of 400 hours of video was uploaded to YouTube every minute of every day! YouTube gives you a reasonable amount of control of your channel branding and also makes it possible to curate content.

  YouTube receives more than 1 billion unique visitors every month. Facebook is the only site that receives more.

- **Vimeo:** YouTube's better-looking cousin, Vimeo, doesn't have the reach of YouTube, but if you're brand-sensitive and want to project a bit more style, Vimeo is for you. The site offers a superior user experience, and for those who don't rely on the channel to supply large quantities of viewers, it's a great choice. Vimeo also gives you more control of who can see your videos.

- **Vine:** Vine is the new kid on the block and the leader in short-form video. A Vine video can be no more than 7 seconds long. Despite the obvious limitations of the format, Vine has become hugely popular with the younger set and the mobile crowd. Vine has also managed to achieve some impressive support from major brands, which find the format to be perfect for short commercials and promotional videos. Vine is tied to Twitter, which means that you can post your Vine videos directly to your Twitter profile as tweets.

- **Instagram:** Instagram also handles video. Instagram jumped on the short-form video bandwagon after Vine took off. The big differences are that you tap into the already-impressive Instagram audience and that your videos can be up to 10 seconds long. Because Facebook owns Instagram, you can expect closer integration of the two services in the future.

✔ **Facebook:** Facebook is on the rise as a video distribution platform. In November 2014, videos uploaded directly to Facebook exceeded YouTube videos shared on Facebook for the first time. If you're promoting video content, Facebook needs to be part of the mix. You can link a video from another source or upload to Facebook directly.

Facebook is now serving more than 1 billion video views a day, with 65 percent of those views being on mobile devices.

Although there's no doubt that getting the most out of video requires a bit of effort, the effort is worthwhile. If you don't think you can make decent video, think again. Production costs have dropped dramatically, and many easy-to-use tools are available, from Twitter's Vine app to stand-alone programs such as Camtasia (`www.techsmith.com/camtasia.html`). Creating content can be a challenge, but you have a few ways to avoid doing all the work yourself:

✔ Run a user-generated-video contest.

✔ Film product testimonials.

✔ Post product demos.

✔ Post interviews with key team members.

✔ Shoot video at trade shows and conferences.

Although these suggestions may not be equivalent to high-dollar video productions, you'll still see benefits — and the low production cost is very attractive.

Whether you use Vine, Instagram, YouTube, or Vimeo, cross-post to your other social media channels. Drive traffic to your videos, and raise awareness of your presence.

Reaching Out through the Social News Networks

Several years ago, social news was a significant trend in online content. That trend hasn't played out as many people thought it would. Instead of there being several high-profile news-oriented sites, there's. . . Facebook. Almost one third of U.S. adults get their news through Facebook.

The way that news is consumed on Facebook is also worth noting. The Pew Research Center refers to it as "drive-by news," meaning that most people who get news via Facebook get it as a byproduct of their other activities there.

For SMO practitioners, the popularity of Facebook as a news channel is good news; they have one fewer class of websites to worry about in promotional strategies. Social news sites aren't dead just yet, however. Several sites should still be part of your SMO strategy.

Reddit

Reddit (www.reddit.com) is a social news platform that lets people post and vote on content. Reddit calls itself "The Front Page of the Internet," and there's some truth in that motto. The service can pay handsome rewards in traffic for the right content.

There are three keys to Reddit success:

✔ Self-promotion is strictly against the rules — and the service polices it. That limitation greatly affects how you approach Reddit, but it shouldn't scare you away. Reddit can push huge amounts of traffic to your website.

✔ Reddit's audience is predominantly young and socially active. Make sure that the Reddit audience matches your demographic needs. If it does, don't skip it.

A typical Reddit user is male, between the ages of 35 and 44, with an average income between $25,000 and $50,000 a year.

✔ The site is organized into categories called subreddits. Each subreddit is essentially its own little community. Find the right subreddit(s) for your posts; otherwise, your efforts will be wasted.

Given the prohibition against self-promotion on Reddit, you have to post in a different fashion from the way you do with other social networks. You need to share news and engage the community, not broadcast to it. To get an idea of how strong the community aspect can be, take a look at the subreddit for the University of Texas Longhorns in Figure 10-10.

The moderators of the LonghornNation subreddit post game schedules, past scores, threads for each game, and links to related communities. The people who visit come for the community. Although this topic is admittedly noncommercial topic, the sense of community is typical of many subreddits, and you must harness that sense of community to prosper in this environment. Sharing news and articles is fine as long as doing so is useful to the community.

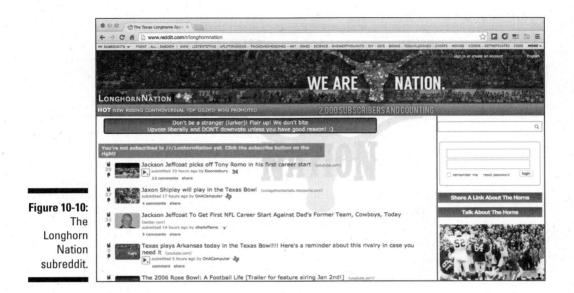

Figure 10-10:
The
Longhorn
Nation
subreddit.

Given the rather narrow demographics of Reddit, some types of content tend to do better than others. Among the winners are

- ✔ Technology-oriented posts (computers, Internet, gaming)
- ✔ Politics and society, particularly controversial topics
- ✔ Music
- ✔ Comics
- ✔ Food
- ✔ Adult content

You have to register and log in to post to Reddit. After you post, your content can be voted up or down, and as voting occurs, you gather karma points. Users with high positive karma points become trusted and valued by the community, and their contributions tend to attract more attention; those users becomes trusted sources. Therein lies the key to Reddit strategy: Invest in the community and become a trusted source.

Reddit offers paid advertising, sold on a CPM (cost per thousand impressions) basis. You can target by interest, by subreddit, and by location. The ads are affordable and can be quite effective. Find out more at www.reddit.com/wiki/selfserve.

Other social news sites

Several other social news sites are worth a look, though these channels should be a lower priority for you than Reddit because they have much smaller and less active user bases. Sites to investigate include the following:

- ✔ **Digg** (`http://digg.com`): Digg is a social bookmarking site with content voting. Digg can generate a fair amount of traffic if your link is voted up and makes the front page of the site.

- ✔ **StumbleUpon** (`www.stumbleupon.com`): Content on StumbleUpon is grouped by category, and users follow or browse categories to find articles of interest. Make sure that you join and find friends before you start adding lots of content; otherwise, your content will just sit there.

- ✔ **Delicious** (`https://delicious.com`): This site offers social bookmarking with tagging and keywords. You can create bookmarks that you can use for reference, and other users can follow or subscribe to a feed.

- ✔ **Pearltrees** (`www.pearltrees.com`): This social bookmarking site is easy to set up and use. It requires a bit of dedication, in that you really need to build a portfolio of links before Pearltrees starts to leverage your listings.

Of these services, Digg and StumbleUpon have the greatest potential to generate traffic. That said, this entire space has been fading away as Facebook and Twitter have grabbed social news traffic.

Tailoring Content to Specialty Channels

One of the best ways to get extra mileage out of your content is to repackage it and release it on different channels. If you have a blog post, in addition to promoting the post directly via social sharing, take that blog post and turn it into a downloadable PDF file. If the content is suitable, make a short slideshow that covers the key points.

Repackaging content can also help you get through dry spells or writer's block. Go back to what you published in the past and see whether you can find a way to it and update it. Maybe that blog post you put up a year ago is still relevant, but the underlying facts have changed, or perhaps something you wrote in the past would make a great presentation at your next event. If so, work up a slide deck to use at the event; then post the slide deck to one of your social media outlets. Even better, have someone record the presentation, and you'll have multiple pieces of new collateral stemming from one blog post.

Posting presentations to SlideShare

SlideShare (http://slideshare.com) is the most popular of the presentation sharing sites. Although the vast majority of the content is in presentation file-format, you can upload other types of media. SlideShare has an active community and is particularly suitable for business and skills-related content.

SlideShare is owned by LinkedIn, so it's easy to promote your SlideShare uploads on your LinkedIn profile and in LinkedIn groups.

Although creating presentations is beyond the scope of this book, here are some tips to make your SlideShare efforts more effective with regard to SMO:

- **Brand it.** Create a profile on SlideShare, and brand it appropriately. Link it back to your website.

- **Post regularly.** SlideShare is a community, and you'll find followers if you produce content regularly.

- **Keep presentations visual.** Text-heavy slides tend to be dull and less effective than strong visuals with limited text.

- **Keep it short.** The best-performing presentations tend to have fewer than 20 slides.

- **Link presentations.** Add a slide at the end that steers people to other presentations in your channel.

- **Put some effort into the description.** When you post the presentation, add a description. Make sure that you include all the appropriate keywords in your description.

SlideShare has a handy widget you can use to embed presentations in your website. Use the widget to embed the presentation in your company blog and help push traffic to your SlideShare channel.

Creating document downloads

Turning a blog post or other content into a PDF file is a simple way to leverage your content-creation resources. Several great sites are designed for sharing downloadable documents. Among the leaders are

- Scribd (https://www.scribd.com)
- Issuu (http://issuu.com)
- Docstoc (www.docstoc.com)

Of the three, our favorite is Scribd. Scribd is a mature site with a well-developed audience. It's perfect for content marketing, as it gives you an extra little bit of exposure by putting your content in front of people who are not visiting your site. Tips for effectiveness on this channel are similar to those for SlideShare.

- ✔ **Brand it.** Create a Scribd profile and brand it appropriately. Link it back to your site.

- ✔ **Post regularly.** You'll find followers if you produce content regularly.

- ✔ **Link documents together.** Add links at the end of the document steering people into other publications in your channel.

- ✔ **Put some effort into the description.** When you post the document you can add a description. Make sure you hit all the appropriate keywords in your description.

- ✔ **Embed where possible.** Like SlideShare, Scribd offers a widget that lets you embed documents on your web pages. Use the widget to promote your Scribd presence.

Scribd claims to receive more than 50,000 document uploads a day. The service seems to work best for professional and skills-oriented materials.

Cross-post your slide shares and document downloads to your other social media channels. Drive traffic to your profiles and raise awareness of your presence.

Reaching Mobile Users

With the prevalence of mobile devices and the shift in the approach of the search engines, the mobile audience can no longer be viewed as a separate channel. You need to be thinking about mobile users at the time you create content. You have to keep in mind how your content will display as well as how it may be consumed.

Many commentators are embracing a "think mobile first" philosophy. Mobile consumption is clearly on the rise. Mobile accessibility is both a technical issue and a content marketing issue. The first step is defining the conditions that will affect your efforts. You need to do some research into the ways your target audiences are using mobile to better understand how to approach them. Conduct a survey of your target markets, or at least take a random sampling to try to determine the following:

- How do your target markets use mobile?
- Is your mobile audience on smartphones or tablets?
- Is your audience primarily focused on visual content?
- What social media apps are your users using on their mobile devices?

After you have answers to these questions, you can begin to fold those conditions into your content creation, tailoring your content to the particular needs of your audience.

Following are some basic principles you should apply:

- **Focus on your headlines.** All mobile users tend to be skimmers; you need to grab them.
- **Write great first paragraphs.** You need a great first paragraph for the same reason you need great headlines: to grab attention.
- **Be visual.** We're not just talking about good images, but also about things like effective use of color. Mobile devices' screens tend to favor high contrast and strong saturated colors.
- **Make sure that your formatting is mobile-friendly.** Test your site's usability on mobile devices, and create a style guide for your team.

Modern digital marketing needs to emphasize integrating mobile-friendly content into your work flow. Set up secondary monitors and have devices handy so you can look at your work to see whether you'd enjoy reading it on various mobile devices. If your content is something you'd enjoy consuming on a mobile device, you're well on your way.

Chapter 11

Using SMO to Sell Products or Services

Generating social media buzz and finding new followers is all well and good, but for a lot of people, those activities are less important than feeding the sales funnel. For the sales-conscious, social media success is merely a means to an end, and social media is effective only to the extent that it generates leads.

Although we would argue that the brand-building aspects of social media are never to be overlooked, we can appreciate that the bottom line remains the key driver for a lot of firms. The good news is that social media is very effective in promoting sales and generating leads. If you're more focused on turning social media followers into customers, you can apply several proven techniques, and those techniques are the subject of this chapter.

Generating Prelaunch Publicity

Great product and service marketing begins before launch. If you, as a social media optimization (SMO) practitioner, have the luxury of getting involved before the formal launch of the product, don't miss the opportunity, as it can pay significant dividends and jump-start the marketing push. Whether you are dealing with a product or a service, prelaunch is the time to start framing expectations, building excitement, and creating demand.

Prelaunch is the optimal time to stake out your turf on social media channels. After the product is launched and the name is in the market, it may be difficult, if not impossible, to secure profiles and URLs that employ the product name. Whether or not you intend to use a particular channel at the beginning of the campaign, secure your product name on all the major services. Grab your product name at the following channels (at minimum):

✔ Facebook

✔ Twitter

✔ Google+

✔ YouTube

✔ Instagram

✔ Pinterest

Build up the profile on the sites you intend to use, and keep the others private or unpopulated. It's important that you prevent competitors, or trolls, from grabbing the names and exploiting them to your detriment.

If you're planning to go big with this product, you should look at securing your name on additional networks. The cost is low, and the benefits are significant!

After you've nailed down your territory, it's time to start plotting world domination.

Employing sneak peeks and video teasers

By far the most fun and the best prelaunch promotion takes the form of sneak peeks and teasers. This area is where you can let your creativity run rampant. That said, moderate your wild side with solid practice skills:

✔ Define who you'll be selling to.

✔ Figure out the audience's hot buttons. What is likely to tweak their interest?

✔ Decide which channels audience members use.

✔ Harmonize the target market's characteristics with your selling plan. Where will you sell? Where can you afford to maintain a market presence?

✔ Always be thinking about customer service . Where are you going to engage with people who have questions, problems, returns, or complaints? Be ready for all these scenarios; they're inevitable.

✔ Your prelaunch message creates expectations. Don't promise what you can't deliver.

Begin by mapping out whom you're selling to and exactly what and how you plan to sell, then start working on your sneak peek and teaser content.

The first thing you need to define is how much you want to give away and when you want to reveal it. In other words, how much do you want to say about the product in your teasers? For some companies, the less information given away, the better; for others, a more moderate approach is in order. There's no right or wrong approach; the choice depends on your strategy and the competitive nature of your industry segment.

If you're in maximum stealth mode, you won't want to use your product name profiles to begin your campaign. In that case, you'll use either the company profiles or your personal profiles, as in this example: "I was just assigned today to start work on our new product launch. Can't tell you much about it, except it's going to be awesome!"

Heck, if obscurity is a necessary part of your plans, embrace it. Give the product an intriguing code name and use it as follows: "I just got assigned to the Project Kasbah team!" Use the code name in all your posts. There's nothing like a bit of mystery to tweak interest. Post teasers to your primary channels or at least to Facebook, Twitter, and Google+.

As you move closer to launch, it's appropriate to be more forthcoming. Being able to reveal more makes your job easier, giving you ammunition for posts and discussions. As soon as the wraps are off the name, it's time to get the dedicated profiles out there and build a community around the name. If you're still restricted in terms of the content on those channels, at least get "coming soon" messages up to start raising awareness and generating interest.

Video teasers are fabulous ways to get people interested in a product before launch. Although budget and resources can be issues in producing videos, one of the easiest work-arounds is to shoot the videos yourself and use members of the product launch team as the subjects. Showing a product in development can be an incredibly effective way to build excitement. Periodic behind-the scenes videos work very well. As people see the effort involved in creating the product and appreciate the quality and the craftsmanship, they become believers.

Believers become not simply purchasers, but also evangelists.

Short video clips are effective teasers and super-easy to produce. Short videos are your chance to leverage Vine and Instagram's short video service (and don't skip Facebook!). These videos can be personal in nature and low-budget. You can even make them on a smartphone and upload them directly from your phone. Create several videos and schedule their releases in the lead-up to the launch. Make sure that you use tags to help your audience find the videos.

The role of paid promotion

If a lack of followers is a problem for you before launch, you can explore paid promotion. Promoted posts on Facebook and Twitter are ways to start drawing eyeballs to your teaser content. Our advice is to budget for some paid promotion regardless of your follower count.

The whole purpose of a prelaunch campaign is to generate the maximum amount of excitement before the product hits the market. That means you want to ramp up the size of the audience quickly, and paid promotion is your best bet for achieving quick results.

Going old-school: The press release

We've lost count of how many times we've heard the press release pronounced dead in the past five years. To paraphrase the old joke about jazz: The press release isn't dead; it just smells that way.

But seriously, it's accurate only to say that the press release is about half dead. Much its original purpose — to keep the news media informed of company happenings — has been co-opted by alternative channels, including social media. But there's one context in which the press release remains very useful: launching a new product, service, or website.

You see, reporters are (believe it or not) human beings just like the rest of us. They're sometimes lazy, and they're always looking for ways to fill column inches. This situation is where press releases come in. If you have a relationship with reporters and editors, your press release will be read, and you may be very surprised to see how often your exact words wind up in print.

The big key to success in press releases is the relationship between you and the media. You must cultivate your connections with journalists.

You can't expect to send out one press release a year and have it work for you. Instead, you need to be in touch with key media figures. You must send them news items and be available when they need research and quotes. In other words, you must become a trusted source.

Your press releases must be written in such a manner that they're useful to media without heavy editing, as follows:

- ✔ Write in journalistic style — not marketing style.
- ✔ Create an appropriate headline.
- ✔ In the first paragraph, state clearly why this news is important.
- ✔ Use facts and figures, and state the sources.

✔ Add quotations from known people in your firm. Attribute the quotations properly.

✔ Keep the release to one page (400 to 600 words).

✔ Attach suggested images. Your best choices for images are product shots and professional head shots of the people you quote in the press release.

✔ Add contact details for more information.

✔ Include links to more information online.

Send your press release to your media connections first, and give them a chance to be first to print. After that, use a press release distribution service. Though paid distribution services cost you money, they're surprisingly good at delivering traffic to your website and social media profiles, and they often give you a little boost to your SEO efforts by creating inbound links.

Spreading the Word with Snapchat

One of the social media darlings of 2014 was Snapchat, a mobile app that allows users to send photo or video messages that automatically disappear 1 to 10 seconds after being viewed. It's classic ephemeral media, updated with the computer age. What's cool about Snapchat — aside from the time factor — is that the application includes tools that let you mark up the image, so you can annotate, doodle, and even add a little story. Snapchat is meant to be fun, and it achieves that goal. Figure 11-1 shows just one of the many types of interesting images you can create and send with Snapchat.

Figure 11-1:
A Snapchat image.

Check your demographics. Snapchat has a younger audience. Statistics from ComScore and *The Wall Street Journal* indicate that one third of mobile users between 18 and 24 use Snapchat and that 70 percent of the audience is women.

To the surprise of many people, Snapchat has been embraced by marketers, who find that the unique nature of the channel suits creative uses. Here are some of the clever uses we've seen:

✔ A frozen-yogurt shop encouraged users to send Snapchats of themselves enjoying yogurt, and the shop would send back coupons via Snapchat. Because the coupon was a Snapchat image, it disappeared 10 seconds after it was opened, forcing users to use Snapchat at the register to display the coupon while they were checking out. To make the promotion more fun, the amounts of the coupons varied, from a little to a lot, and users wouldn't know the amount until they opened a coupon to use it.

✔ A cosmetics company used Snapchat to promote the release of a new line. Only people who friended and followed the company account could see the short-lived previews of the products, which nicely played to the exclusive nature of the line.

✔ A brand created a series of humorous Snapchat images and ran them throughout the course of the Super Bowl. The theme of the images dovetailed with the Super Bowl and were so well received that the company's Snapchat following jumped by more than 5,500 people during the game.

✔ A clothing brand used Snapchat to preview its new line and drive traffic to stores.

Snapchat isn't really about pretty pictures. It's about fun and authentic moments.

Reaching Out to Bloggers

When it comes time to launch a new product, you want to bring onboard the legion of citizen journalists who comprise the blogosphere. Outreach to bloggers should be part of every product or service launch plan. You want these people to cover the event and get the word out to their extended networks. Each positive article is another endorsement and independent validation of what you're offering.

The first step is identifying the right bloggers. Ask yourself these questions:

✔ Who covers what you're offering?

✔ Whose audience overlaps with your target markets?

✔ Who is an authority?

✔ Who is an influencer?

One of the best tools we've found for identifying bloggers to target for outreach is BuzzSumo (`http://buzzsumo.com`). This site is very simple to use. You simply type terms related to your product or service, select the type of people you want to see (bloggers, journalists, and so on), and then click Search. The system returns a list of people based on influence, number of followers on social media, and propensity to retweet and reply. Figure 11-2 shows the output of a search for influential bloggers and journalists who write about WordPress.

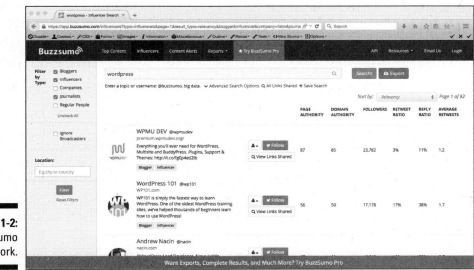

Figure 11-2:
BuzzSumo
at work.

From the results page, you can follow these people on Twitter, send a direct message to them via Twitter, or go to their websites to find out more.

We use BuzzSumo both to target bloggers for outreach and to find new influencers for our Twitter accounts.

When you've found the right people, the hard part begins. Blogger outreach is a process, and it can be a long process. The goal is to make these people aware that you exist and then foster a positive relationship with them. As in working with professional journalists, the idea is to establish yourself as a trusted source. When you have your foot in the door, so to speak, you can pass these people information and tips, and reasonably expect some coverage in return.

Bloggers are influencers and those with large audiences are especially valuable for influencing purchase decisions.

If you're launching a product or a service, one of the best ways to get a blogger's attention is to offer a free sample. Although there are mixed feelings about the ethics of asking for reviews in exchange for freebies, it never hurts to ask. Just approach the topic delicately, and don't push if the blogger says it's against his policy. We encourage you to send samples regardless. Even if you don't get a nice long-winded review, odds are that you'll get some mentions on social media, and the next time you want to approach that blogger, the door will be open.

Sending bloggers items in advance of the official release — giving them a first look — works very well. Another effective technique is to offer something the blogger can give her audience: a special discount or freebie she can extend to others.

Here are some tips for improving the effectiveness of your blogger outreach:

- Take time to read the blogger's About Me page. Find out what he likes and how he wants to be approached.
- Read the blogger's current and previous posts.
- Check out the content on the blogger's social channels.
- Make sure that what you want the blogger to do is a good fit for what she already does. Irrelevant pitches waste everyone's time.
- When you reach out to a blogger, make sure that you state clearly what's in it for him. Don't wait for him to ask; it simply won't happen.
- Gracefully take no for an answer. Thank the blogger for her time. Try again later. Eventually, stop attempting to work with this blogger if one rejection turns into a pattern.

Converting Followers to Customers

Up to this point, this chapter focuses on how to extend your reach and build a following. For many of you, however, the bigger issue is how to turn the relationships you create with social media into sales. Social media is quite effective in steering users toward the sales funnel, but as with anything else, success requires the right approach and dedicated effort.

In one important regard, lead development on social media is like lead development anywhere else: You have to create a relationship that encourages trust in you and whatever you're offering. Toward that end, you must work to build a consistent and trustworthy online presence, and you must s and cultivate relationships.

When it comes to lead generation, certain channels are more effective than others. For business-to-business lead generation, LinkedIn and Twitter are clear winners.

LinkedIn in particular deserves special mention. If your product or service is useful to businesses, LinkedIn will most likely be your go-to channel. This service is the proven B2B winner and your best chance of generating qualified leads with a reasonable effort.

You can generate leads anywhere, but the attributes of LinkedIn and Twitter and their user bases make them the most effective tools for generating sales leads.

When it comes to selling products to consumers, look to Facebook, Twitter, and Pinterest.

Facebook's incredible reach and wide demographics make it a solid place to present your products, particularly fashion and handcrafted items. As a general rule, anything people like to talk about and share with their friends has the potential to do well on Facebook. Great photos are key, as is willingness to provide information and be a resource for prospective buyers who want to know more and engage with you in comments.

Facebook keeps promising to launch selling tools that enable you to market products for sale directly on Facebook. If that ever happens, these tools could be game-changers, and Facebook would be a consumer channel not to be ignored.

Twitter can be an effective sales tool, but it requires a different approach from Facebook or Pinterest. With Twitter, you have to hunt down your prospects. Use Twitter's advanced search function to look for tweets that contain words relevant to your product, along with words that indicate buying interest. Look for the following words and phrases:

- *recommendation*
- *referral*
- *looking for*
- *want to buy*
- *anyone tried*

When you find a relevant tweet, reach out to the person who posted it. Respond to the tweet, offering advice or helpful information. When you've started a dialogue, you can move the discussion closer to conversion.

Another effective technique involves using a specialized Twitter Card known as a Lead Generation Card. Twitter created Lead Generation Cards to help companies promote their products, and these cards have proved to be quite effective. As with other Twitter Cards, you can create a richer tweet with an expanded message area and image. When the user clicks to expand the card, he sees not only your message, but also a call to action that enables him to express interest in your brand. If he clicks the call-to-action button (the Click Here button in Figure 11-3), the system captures and passes to you the user's contact details. Figure 11-3 shows a Twitter Lead Generation Card.

Lead Generation Cards are part of Twitter's paid advertising programs. They're not set up through the Twitter Cards interface; you must set these specialized cards up through the Twitter ads system. Read Chapter 9 for more information about other Twitter Cards, and find out more at https://business.twitter.com/solutions/lead-generation-card.

Pinterest is a different type of animal altogether. With Pinterest, the focus is on imagery and getting people excited about things through the use of compelling visuals. If you have really cool and unique products that lend themselves to photos, using Pinterest is pretty straightforward. If you're selling something that's less visually appealing or that's a service, it takes a bit of creativity to get Pinterest to work for you.

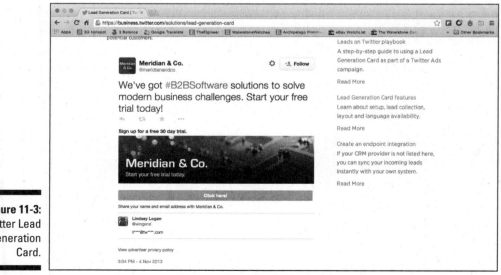

Figure 11-3:
Twitter Lead Generation Card.

The best approach is to create Pinterest boards that focus on specific are of interest. In that manner, after you attract someone to the board via a sp cific pin, you have a much greater chance of generating further engagement and getting the person to help you spread the word about your product. Figure out what your target market is interested in, and build your boards around those topics. If you're selling a service, look at it from the perspective of problems — that is, what problems your target markets are trying to solve. Build your board with a series of tips and information to help people solve those problems.

Putting coupons and discounts to work

Coupons and discounts create social media love. People love a deal, and when they feel they're on the inside of a special deal, they really love it! Social media is the perfect platform for offering special deals to your fans and followers, and it's a proven technique that you should seriously consider including in your repertoire of social selling tools.

Blanket giveaways are rarely the best approach. Instead, you should require some action on the part of the recipient:

✔ If you're running a campaign on Twitter, require a follow and a retweet to earn the coupon.

✔ If you're on Facebook, require a comment or a Like to earn a coupon.

✔ If you're on Snapchat, require a direct message for the coupon.

The whole trick with discounts is to offer something that your target audience desires without cannibalizing your business. That said, if your goal is to introduce a new product or simply to generate turnover, you may be less concerned with the short-term bottom line of a deep discount. The balancing act is worth the effort.

Although it's nice to make social sharing a part of the promotion, the most important thing is to require engagement of some sort. To that end, a simple direct message is sufficient. The point is to make a connection with the user. Make your coupons or special deals "social media only" to keep your user base motivated and to keep the offer exclusive.

Email isn't truly a social medium, but you can add social sharing tools to your email newsletters — a very effective way to promote coupons and special offers.

Rewarding the evangelists

An *evangelist* is someone who loves your brand enough to tell others about it. A diehard evangelist will follow your brand across multiple channels and frequently share and retweet your content, often with his own comments attached. Brand evangelists are always in the minority, but they're worth their weight in gold. They're social proof that your product or service is worth buying. They can help you in times of plenty and also when times are tough.

You should make an effort to reward your evangelists. The first step is identifying them. You need to be able to determine who is most active on your profiles and who generates the most activity. Keep track of who retweets your content on Twitter and who shares your posts on Facebook.

You have multiple ways to reward your evangelists, and not all of them have to cost you money:

- ✔ Share their posts and promote their content.
- ✔ Give them positive recognition; thank them by name.
- ✔ Send them a special discount. Make the discount even more special by allowing them to share it with others.
- ✔ Give them first peek at a new product or service.
- ✔ Invite their feedback on a new product or service.

Chapter 12

Enriching Events with Social Media

*S*ocial media and events go together extremely well. Any time you bring together a group of people for a common purpose, be it education, business, or just plain fun, you have a community, and a social media community is a great way to enrich and enliven an event.

Although you may associate social media with big festivals, it's also a great match for smaller events. You can implement social media optimization (SMO) in several ways, not only to make your event marketing more effective, but also to increase participant satisfaction. The best part? Handling social media for events is great fun! It brings together all the best parts of social media: easy user engagement, awesome content, and genuine buzz.

Generating Pre-Event Buzz

Pre-event marketing largely focuses on selling the event, and that's only natural. It should also be concerned with setting the tone for your event, however. So much of the success of an event, from sales to user satisfaction, comes from creating the appropriate tone. Are you promoting a sporting event? You need to build a sense of competition and excellence. Are you promoting a multiple-day festival? You need to build a sense of excitement and anticipation for the tribe. Are you building attendance for a business training seminar? The mood needs to reflect the professional and educational nature of the event.

Social media is a critical part of the marketing mix in any situation in which tone is a critical factor. Social media can provide significant help to your marketing and sales efforts, and lay the foundation for a successful event.

Leveraging the personalities involved

To a large extent, promoting an event is about promoting the personalities involved in the event. Although some festivals are big enough and have enough cachet to be treated as happenings in their own right, the vast majority of events, from seminars to concerts, are about the performers and the presenters involved. Given that the personalities are the draw, event promoters need to leverage the fan base and notoriety of the personalities to get the most traction in social media.

If, on the other hand, this is a recurring event that already has some reputation and buzz, your pre-event publicity should focus on the visual images of previous events. Photos and video of the things that made the event great in previous years are the key to generating buzz among new attendees and re-creating that awesome feeling among your previous participants.

Here are some examples of how you can ask your headliners to participate in pre-event promotional activities:

- ✔ An exclusive interview for your blog or for distribution to the media
- ✔ A short video interview
- ✔ A guest post (written by them) for your blog
- ✔ An expert tip for you to include in a blog post of your creation
- ✔ A sneak peek of what the headliners have planned for the event

No one buys a ticket to see the promoter. Your content plan needs to keep the headliners front and center. Sell the personalities, piggyback on their reputations, and leverage the personalities' popularity to promote your work with them.

Mention your headliners in tweets. Often, their social media teams will pick up those tweets and retweet them to their networks.

Working social magic with ticket giveaways

Ticket giveaways for events are among the most affordable tools in your tool kit. People love free tickets and are often willing to participate in promotions for a chance to win them. Ticket campaigns are easy to set up, have a strong viral component, and allow you to piggyback other promotional activities on them (such as interviewing the winners). Following are some great ways to execute this idea:

- ✔ **Retweet to win.** Put out the word on Twitter, inviting people to retweet a promotional message in exchange for an entry for a drawing to win a ticket or day pass.

- ✔ **Use hashtags to win.** Give people on Twitter and Facebook a chance to play with a hashtags campaign. All a person has to do is post a (positive!) comment and use the event hashtag for a chance to win a ticket or pass.

- ✔ **Share photos of past events to win.** If your event is a recurring one, offer users who post images of past events a chance to win. Get them to use the event's hashtag to gain more exposure (and make it easier to track the reach of your posts). Create galleries of the fan images submitted on Facebook or boards on Pinterest. Post images to Instagram with appropriate tags.

- ✔ **Add a blog comment to win.** Make commenting on a post in the events blog a requirement for entry in a drawing. This strategy works best when the blog post asks a question or requests specific feedback.

No matter which approach you use, keep it super-simple. If you make it hard to participate in a giveaway, numbers drop off quickly.

When your promotion is under way, engage with the participants. Use the contest as a way to identify active voices and motivated individuals. Follow people back, and consider giving shout-outs to participants. To gain some extra social media goodness, offer a discount to all the nonwinning participants. If you hold back the news that you're going to offer discounts that until after you reward the winners, you get more sales and a secondary social media bump as people share the news.

Check out Chapter 13 for some Facebook apps you can use to help you promote contests and giveaways.

Getting the event on key channels

It's possible to build event-specific pages on two key social media channels: Facebook and Google+. In addition, you may want to look at Eventbrite (`https://www.eventbrite.com`) as another location for hosting event information. When appropriate, get the event on all three channels.

Use Facebook and Google+ for any event type. The broad nature of the audience on those two channels makes the channels suitable for promoting anything from a concert to a business seminar. Eventbrite generally is more suitable for smaller events.

Facebook Events

A Facebook Event is a powerful tool. It gives you a place to promote the event and makes it very easy for Facebook users to share the event with their Facebook friends. Figure 12-1 shows a Facebook Event page.

Your Facebook Event should be active right through the event day. A Facebook Event is an excellent place for last-minute announcements, schedule updates, and day-of-event customer service activities.

Figure 12-1:
A Facebook
Event.

To create an event on Facebook, follow these steps:

1. **Log in to Facebook.**

2. **Click the Events label in the left column.**

3. **Click the +Create button (see Figure 12-2).**

The +Create button

4. **In the pop-up window that appears, enter your event details.**

   Make sure that you select the appropriate privacy settings. The options are:

   - *Public:* Makes the event open to anyone, even people not on Facebook.

   - *Open Invite:* Makes the event open to invited guests, their friends, and anyone else they invite.

   - *Guests and Friends:* Open only to people invited by the hosts and guests.

   - *Invite Only:* Open only to those people the hosts invite.

5. **Click the Create button.**

6. **When your event page appears, customize its appearance as follows:**

   - Add a photo by clicking the Add an Event Photo button.

   - Invite people by clicking the Invite button below the header image.

Google+ Events

The events feature in Google+ works in a fashion very similar to Facebook Events. Creating an event in Google+ lets you broadcast to either the people in your circles or to the public in general. Users who elect to attend the event can also add the event to their Google Calendars.

Figure 12-3 shows a Google+ Event page.

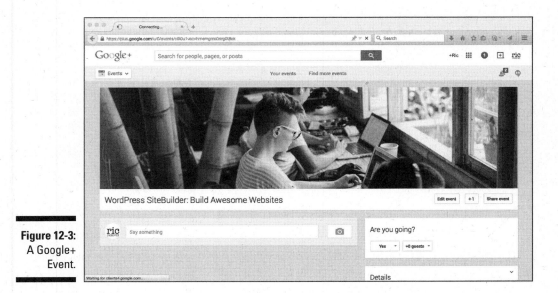

Figure 12-3:
A Google+
Event.

To create an event on Google+, follow these steps:

1. **Log in to Google+.**

2. **In Share What's New box, click the Event icon (see Figure 12-4).**

3. **In the pop-up window that appears, enter your event details.**

4. **Click the Change Theme button to add your own header image.**

5. **Choose invitees in the To field.**

6. **From the Event Options drop-down menu, choose Invite the Public to make the event open to the public.**

7. **Click the Invite button.**

Event icon

Figure 12-4:
The Event
icon.

Eventbrite

Eventbrite (`https://www.eventbrite.com`) is a dedicated events website. Although Eventbrite isn't as broad as Facebook or Google+, the site focuses on events and has a good following.

On Eventbrite, you can create events and handle ticket sales. The process of creating an event is simple and fast, and the whole system works quite well. It's particularly suitable for small conferences, seminars, and training programs. Figure 12-5 shows an Eventbrite event listing.

Create Event button

Figure 12-5:
An
Eventbrite
event page.

To create an event on Eventbrite, follow these steps:

1. **Log in to the site.**

2. **Click the Create Event button (refer to Figure 12-3).**

3. **Enter the event details.**

   Note that the required fields are marked with a red asterisk.

4. **If you don't want to sell your tickets on the site, choose the Free Ticket option.**

5. **Click Make Your Event Live to publish the event.**

   Note that you have to set up at least one payment method before the event can go live.

Unlike Facebook and Google+ Events, Eventbrite events have no built-in promotion mechanism. After you have created your event on Eventbrite you have to promote the event through your social media channels by publishing posts about the event and including the Eventbrite event URL.

Creating a Sense of Community for the Event

Events typically bring together very focused teams of people. As a marketing professional attached to an event, you need to make it clear from the beginning that marketing the event is everyone's job and that you'll be looking to everyone to contribute in some fashion, even if just by joining the event page on a social media channel and posting about the event to friends. The bigger the event, the bigger the team and the bigger the extended network you can tap to generate buzz.

Encouraging teamwork for event promotion

Early in your efforts, create a structured plan for event marketing. In addition to deciding on basics such as the timing and the channels for event promotion, agree on the tone you want to project for the event. Use that tone to inform the creation of your creative collateral, including the copywriting. Your tone helps frame expectations and is an important part of the message.

When your plan is in place, you need to communicate it to all the participants: your marketing team and event staff, the headliners, and the sponsors. If you're working with a major artist or presenter, they probably have at their disposal social media marketing resources that you should attempt to embrace. Get direct contacts for their team members, bring them into the conversation, and get everyone pulling in the same direction.

Don't forget your sponsors, who need to be included in your social media plan for the event. Get in touch with their social media personnel and bring them into the planning. Make sure that they're given the event collateral and kept in the loop about promotions and social media events.

Talk to your sales team about making social media support part of the requirements for sponsor involvement.

In addition to simply getting the marketing plan in front of everyone and building consensus for the approach, be proactive, and get people involved.

Often, key players in an event are busy with other obligations, so it may be up to you to reach out to them to get them involved. Approaching your headliners with a clear, considered request that helps them promote themselves is often well received. Refer to "Leveraging the personalities involved" earlier in the chapter for some ideas on ways to capitalize on the built-in fan base of your headliners.

Producing collateral for everyone to use

Event marketing collateral should be standardized to the largest extent possible. Work up nice graphics for the event, and share them with everyone on the extended marketing team. Following are some fun and useful ideas for collateral:

- ✔ Create specific, branded graphics for individual performers and presenters, and use those graphics in any mention of that person. Communicate with the performers' team to learn their branding requirements and share all materials with them.

- ✔ Ready-to-use tweets are a nice touch often welcomed by others. A ready-to-use tweet takes some of the work out of promoting the event.

  Don't forget the event hashtags!

- ✔ You should be running press releases before the events. Make sure that your press release is something that bloggers or journalists can copy and paste into their publications.

  Include photo collateral in your event press releases for better exposure.

- ✔ If your marketing plan includes reaching out to podcasters, write up a short script for them to use when mentioning the event.

- ✔ Event videos work very well. If you have material from previous events, edit it to different lengths for distribution on your various channels, including possibly Facebook, YouTube, Vimeo, Vine, and Instagram.

- ✔ If the event is a major festival with multiple performers, consider setting up an online press room where media members can access photos and bios of performers, as well as the collateral for the event itself.

- ✔ Interview performers and presenters. Both written and video interviews work well, and the interviews often attract the attention of bloggers and journalists.

Providing a Real-Time Channel

The work doesn't stop when the lights go down and the show begins. Indeed, the most fun and the richest engagement occurs during the event itself. Although the media you generate during the event may not do anything for your ticket sales this year, it can work wonders for programs in the future and can help you build a loyal following for your event (and the performers!).

Create a spirit of inclusion from the beginning of the event. Make sure that everyone who comes through the door is aware that your social media channels are part of the event and that they're invited to participate. The following techniques help you build a sense of community for your event:

✔ Provide selfie opportunities. Simple sets will do nicely.

✔ Provide a photographer or ask your staff to capture photos and video during the event.

If you can get a celebrity to show up for a selfie booth, you've struck social media gold.

Also let people know where they can find important information and schedule changes.

✔ Make sure that your event hashtags are displayed prominently at the event.

✔ If you're running a conference, invite people to introduce themselves on social media at the registration booth — for example, by posting a tweet. Provide an incentive.

✔ Run day-of-event promotions for people on the scene. Tie the promotions to something simple for attendees to do, such as using the event hashtag.

Whatever you do, make sure that your team is monitoring and engaging with people in real time. The social media team must be active during the event to retweet things, add tags, give shout-outs, and generally keep the momentum rolling.

Setting up a live social media event feed

Don't settle for simply publishing the content on the various social media channel. Go further by creating a social media aggregator to capture and display the content created by your team and your fans on the day of the event. A feed of your various social media mentions is a great tool for stimulating participation and creating a sense of fun for all involved.

An *aggregator* is a simple software tool that seeks out and displays all mentions of your hashtag or all the content on one or more channels. The aggregated content is laid out and shown on one screen. Aggregators typically are displayed in on event websites and live at the event.

Aggregators can be simple and affordable to create. With a little HTML skill, you can build your own by using the resources supplied to you by Twitter and Facebook. You can, for example, implement the Twitter feed widget and the Facebook Like box to create an aggregator like the one shown in Figure 12-6.

Figure 12-6:
A live
Twitter and
Facebook
stream on
an outdoor
screen.

At the other end of the cost spectrum, you can use a commercial product that aggregates social media content from a variety of channels. Following are some of the most popular products:

- ✔ **Crowd Reactive** (`http://crowdreactive.com`): Pulls in photos and video from Instagram, Twitter, Foursquare, and Facebook. Contact the company for pricing information.

- ✔ **Eventstagram** (`http://eventstagr.am`): Aggregates Instagram photos for your event. This free tool is produced by the same people who created Crowd Reactive.

- ✔ **Postano** (`www.postano.com`): Assimilates content from more than a dozen channels. This tool used by several large events, including South by Southwest and Coachella. Contact the company for pricing information.

✔ **Strea.ma** (`http://strea.ma`): Aggregates content from Facebook, Twitter, and Instagram. Basic plans start at $39 per month.

✔ **Tagboard** (`https://tagboard.com`): Uses tags to track posts across Facebook, Twitter, Instagram, Flickr, Vine, and Google+. The service can be used free of charge.

✔ **Tint** (`www.tintup.com`): Pulls social media content from more than ten channels. Contact the company for pricing information.

It's true that setting up a live social media feed to display at your event creates more work for you. In addition to finding or creating the aggregator, you have to plan for the hardware, and you must assign people to manage and deal with any contingencies that might arise with the software or hardware on the day of the event. Nonetheless, doing so is worth the effort because a live social media feed can enrich an event by making the event more fun and more memorable. Live social media also creates a sense of community. Additional benefits include

✔ Showing people who didn't attend what they missed

✔ Gathering quotes, photos, and other collateral for use after the event

✔ Providing a back channel for conversations (which is really useful for conference organizers looking for crowd feedback)

✔ Giving you an alternative channel for emergency management and customer service

✔ Providing a topic of discussion that further stimulates social commenting and interaction

Using video

On event day, make video a priority. Nothing is more effective at showing people what's happening — or what they're missing — than video. Don't be content to rely on fan-created video content. On the day of the show, have your own people on the ground shooting video of the event.

You can use day-of-event video in two ways:

✔ On your social media channels in near real time

✔ In post-event marketing

To use day-of-event video successfully, you need to have a plan in place for your crew. A planned shooting schedule helps make sure the team is in position for key moments and also ensures that you capture the video collateral you need for post-event marketing. Also leave your team some room to be creative by making spur-of-the-moment decisions about what to film. Short clips of audience participation and attendee interviews can be great fun.

Behind-the-scenes video can be very effective at generating engagement, but make sure that you clear it with everyone in advance and communicate to all when it will be filmed. Some performers dislike the distraction and won't approve unless they approve video recording in advance.

Live streaming of events is becoming more and more popular, with Google+ Hangouts being a popular channel for broadcasting. Although a live stream of your entire event may not be practical or consistent with your business goals, you may want to think about doing something more limited. It's much simpler, however, to live-stream a specific performance or a portion of the event — just the keynote speech or the daily press conference, for example.

Live streaming requires special resources. You need the right camera and the right microphone. Also, someone on your team should handle the intro and outro segments (short narration before and after the primary event). A narrator gives people context and frames the performance logically for the remote viewers.

After the event, edit your videos into a variety of lengths for use on different channels. Focus on creating video that people will want to share, and make it easy for them to do so.

When you've created your video content, get it out to your social media channels. At minimum, consider the following outlets:

- Host it on YouTube.
- Embed it in your website.
- Upload it to Facebook
- Get it up on Vine.
- Post it on Instagram.

Encouraging Fan-Created Content

Events bring people together, and you want to leverage people's social media connections. Have a plan to get attendees involved. Make it easy for them to post comments, tweets, photos, and videos about the event, and make sure that everything gets associated with the event by promoting the use of your official event hashtag. When you can get people working with you, magical things happen. Suddenly, you have more than a concert; you have a happening!

Tapping the power of hashtags

Hashtags are great tools for events. They're extremely popular on Twitter and on Instagram, and they're supported by services including Facebook. Users of social media channels that permit hashtags can follow hashtags to see all the posts that employ the tag. In other words, hashtags are easy ways for anyone who's interested in a topic to find out what's being said about it. Given the popularity of hashtags on key platforms, hashtags need to be part of your event marketing plan.

A hashtag is created with the # symbol before a keyword. The hashtag #sxsw, for example, is used for the SXSW festival in general, #swsi for the SXSW Interactive festival, and #sxswfilm for the SXSW Film Festival.

Choose a hashtag that can be used on multiple platforms, such as Twitter, Facebook, and Instagram. Follow these guidelines as you create a hashtag for your event:

✔ **Make it short.** By *short,* we mean eight to ten characters at the most.

✔ **Make it relevant.** Focus on your event positioning.

✔ **Make it memorable.** What good is a hashtag that no one can remember (or spell!)?

✔ **Make it unique.** Nothing is worse than discovering too late that someone else is using your hashtag for another purpose. If you're not sure whether your hashtag is in use, search for it at http://twitter.com/search-home.

✔ **Use only one.** Get everyone using the same hashtag for your event. Using more than one hashtag dilutes your efforts.

Before the event, make sure that your hashtag appears on all your marketing materials, including your email signature files. At the event, get creative by doing the following:

✔ Put the hashtag on your tickets.

✔ Display it at the front gate or the registration booth.

✔ Put it on attendee badges or on anything attendees will hold.

✔ Display it on the event's video walls.

✔ Write it on mirrors.

Creativity gets noticed. At one event, the hashtag was handwritten on the bathroom mirrors in lipstick — along with a big lip print.

✔ Display it anywhere that attendees may take pictures.

Hashtag etiquette

Hashtags are unregulated; anyone is free to create any hashtag they want. Nonetheless, some best practices for hashtag creation have emerged. Some pretty spectacular embarrassments have resulted from inappropriate hashtag use, so it's worthwhile to know the rules you should follow. In addition to avoiding potentially embarrassing hashtags (try doing an Internet search for *embarrassing hashtags* for examples of hashtag fails), you need to be aware of Twitter's official position on hashtag abuse. Make sure to review the Twitter terms of service at `http://twitter.com/tos` so that you're armed with the guidelines and don't find your account filtered from search or suspended because of an inadvertent violation.

Tracking fan-created content

So you have a great event; tons of fans, celebrities, and sponsors are tweeting about it, posting photos, and commenting on Facebook. How do you round up all that activity, monitor it, and amplify it?

The easiest way to track relevant posts is to track the use of your event hashtag. Several tools allow you to track the activity on your event hashtag. Two of the best free or low-cost tools are Hootsuite (`https://hootsuite.com`) and Social Mention (`www.socialmention.com`).

Hootsuite enables you to set up searches for your hashtags on Twitter, Facebook, Google+, LinkedIn, and Foursquare. The only real drawback is that Hootsuite lacks support for searching Instagram and YouTube. Figure 12-7 shows Hootsuite set up to search for the hashtag `#bitcoin` on Twitter and Facebook.

Social Mention works more like a traditional search engine. You can use it to search for hashtags, though the completeness of the results can be somewhat lacking. Twitter results are often poorly reported, but Social Mention does well with Facebook and with YouTube. The advanced search feature allows you to set a variety of filters (including language, location, and time frame), making it easy to zero in on relevant mentions of your hashtag. Figure 12-8 shows a Social Mention search result for the hashtag `#bitcoin`.

 Because Hootsuite doesn't search YouTube and Social Mention doesn't do well with Twitter, we tend to use both tools to get the widest tracking of hashtag activity. To pick up mentions on Instagram, we search for the hashtag on `http://iconosquare.com`.

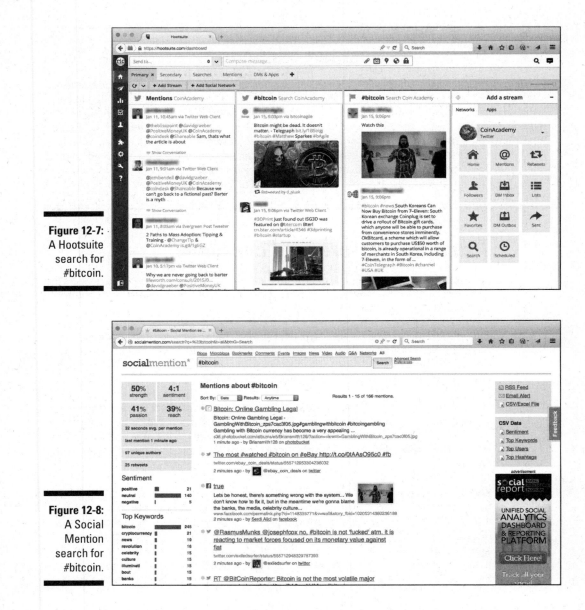

Figure 12-7:
A Hootsuite search for #bitcoin.

Figure 12-8:
A Social Mention search for #bitcoin.

If you have the budget to subscribe to commercial tracking tools, you have several options:

- ✔ **Keyhole** (`http://keyhole.co`): Keyhole provides near real-time tracking of social media mentions. The system offers a three-day free trial period; monthly plans start at $116 per month.

- ✔ **Tagboard** (`https://tagboard.com`): Tagboard hashtag search works across multiple channels and lets you set up a page where all mentions will appear. You can link to this page and share the contents. The basic version of the service is free of charge.

- ✔ **Talkwalker** (`www.talkwalker.com`): Talkwalker provides a dashboard for tracking social media mentions across multiple channels. You can search by keywords or hashtags. You can use the service free for seven days with registration; thereafter, you have to contact the company for pricing.

Chapter 13

Building Your Brand and Establishing Expertise

*Y*our brand is one of the most important things your business has. Without your brand, it's only a matter of time before you fade quietly into the night. You won't stand out in the crowd. Your potential customers won't be able to differentiate you from your competitors. Your business essentially doesn't have an identity if it doesn't have a brand. Just having any old brand isn't enough: Your brand has to be a strong one with positive *brand equity* (associations that come to mind when people hear or see something about your company).

This chapter shows you how to build your brand so that it fits seamlessly with your social media optimization (SMO) strategy. We explain how to use the capabilities of Facebook Pages and Twitter profiles to build positive brand sentiment. We take you through the process of establishing a company presence on LinkedIn and how to go about asking for recommendations. Finally, we give you tips on establishing your expertise so that you become a go-to resource for your customers.

Harnessing the Power of Social Media for Brand Building

The social media world is a big one, and the possibilities for using it to build your brand are virtually limitless. Having an SMO presence doesn't have to be expensive or complicate. The important things are that you have a presence and that you keep the content fresh and your conversations positive and engaging. See Chapter 16 for ideas on how to succeed in making SMO part of your long-term business goals.

These days, it's easier than ever to get your brand into the SMO game, but your effort can't stop at setting up your social media accounts. Those accounts aren't going to run themselves, you know! The following sections take you through how to polish your Pages and tweak your tweets to increase your *brand sentiment* (the public's thoughts and feelings about your brand) by becoming a go-to source for information.

Adding pizzazz to your Facebook Page

Chapter 3 takes you through the process of setting up a Facebook Page for your business. If you haven't already done that, check back there and get yourself set up. We'll wait.

Now that you have a brand-spanking-new Facebook Page for your business, you need to build it up with content that will keep your fans coming back for more! Content is king when it comes to all social media, of course, but the most successful brands go beyond posting links and uploading cute pictures of puppies and kittens. These brands go the extra mile to engage their followers, whether through running contests and promotions or building personalized apps and games to keep the atmosphere lighthearted. Figure 13-1 shows Charmin having a little fun with its Facebook followers by adding an app that lets them TP (throw toilet paper) all over their friends' Facebook profiles. Figure 13-2 shows the aftermath.

Your Facebook Page doesn't have to be all fun and games, either. You can add apps that let your followers sign up for your e-newsletter or even purchase items directly from a Facebook storefront. Some of these apps are free, and others are paid, but they all add some pizzazz to your Facebook Page. The best part is that after you sign up on the app's website, your spiffy new page is up and running with just a few clicks. In other words, the app creator does all the installation heavy lifting for you.

The following sections provide some examples to get you started.

Apps for selling

If you want to sell products from your Facebook Page, check out these apps:

- ✔ **StoreYa** (www.storeya.com): Plans run from free to $80 per month, depending on the add-ons you select for your store. With the free plan, you can import up to 20 products from 30 e-commerce platforms, including eBay, Etsy, Amazon, and Shopify.

✔ **Ecwid** (www.ecwid.com): Ecwid (see Figure 13-3) is the number-one e-commerce app on Facebook. Its robust set of features includes inventory tracking, discount coupons, and the ability to accept a variety of payment methods. The free plan includes 10 products, and prices go up to $99 per month.

✔ **Beetailer** (www.beetailer.com): Beetailer's plans start at free for 1 store with 30 products and go up to $80 per month for 5 stores and 2000 products. Beetailer integrates with your existing online store, so there's no complicated transition process. When someone is ready to make a purchase, he clicks the button in Facebook and is taken to your main e-commerce site.

✔ **Storefront Social** (http://storefrontsocial.com): Storefront Social is a great option for businesses that don't have an existing online store but want to give a Facebook storefront a try. After a free 14-day trial, plans range from $10 per month for 100 products and go up to $30 per month for 1,000 products.

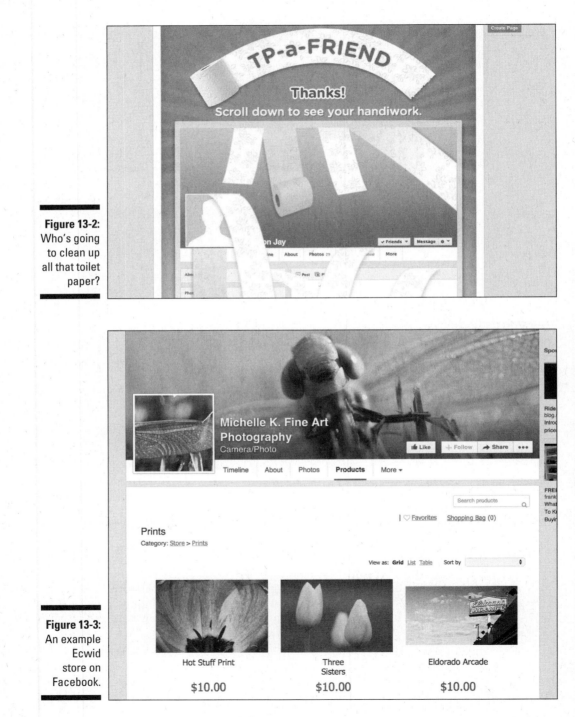

Figure 13-2:
Who's going
to clean up
all that toilet
paper?

Figure 13-3:
An example
Ecwid
store on
Facebook.

Apps for newsletters

There are apps that integrate with Facebook so you can gather email addresses and keep an eye on your open rates and clicks. Here are a few to check out:

- ✔ **AWeber** (www.aweber.com): Choose among more than 700 email templates, or have AWeber design one specifically for your business for an additional cost. AWeber also automatically converts your blog posts to e-newsletters, saving you time. It seamlessly integrates with Facebook, so you can use your fan base to grow your subscription list. Plans start at $19 per month for up to 500 subscribers.

- ✔ **MailChimp** (http://mailchimp.com): MailChimp is one of the best-known e-newsletter subscription services. Because MailChimp offers Facebook integration, it lets you keep an eye on the built-in analytics to see the engagement and website activity of each recipient. The service also gives you send-time recommendations to ensure that your emails are getting as much exposure as possible. MailChimp has a feature-rich free subscription service that allows for up to 2,000 subscribers, as well as paid and pay-as-you-go plans.

- ✔ **Campaign Monitor** (https://www.campaignmonitor.com): With monthly prices ranging from $9 to $700, Campaign Monitor has a subscription option for companies of all sizes. One of the most helpful features is real-time social reporting, which shows you the performance of your newsletter on social media sites such as Facebook and Twitter. In other words, you see how often your newsletter is being shared and tweeted.

- ✔ **GetResponse** (www.getresponse.com): GetResponse has more than 500 drag-and-drop templates that let you design a professional-looking e-newsletter in no time. It easily integrates with Facebook, so you can quickly collect new subscribers by using your existing fan base. Social sharing options are built in, so existing fans can share your newsletters with their Facebook friends. Plans start at $15 per month and go up to $450 per month.

Facebook Page design

It's important that your Facebook Page be nice looking and interactive to keep your fans coming back. These apps help you achieve that:

- ✔ **PageYourself** (https://www.pageyourself.com): Quickly change the look of your Facebook Page with one of PageYourself's highly customizable templates. Integrate a video channel, run a poll, and connect other social media accounts (such as Instagram) for real-time updates to keep your content fresh. PageYourself has a free plan that offers limited features for a small number of users. From there, plans start at $10 per month and go up to $60 per month.

- ✔ **Pagemodo** (www.pagemodo.com): One of the most popular Facebook Page design apps, Pagemodo offers custom tab builders to enhance your page capabilities, a Facebook cover photo designer, the ability to schedule posts, and more. The app has a free subscription plan that gives you access to a limited feature set, and the other plans range from $6 per month up to $33 per month.

- ✔ **TabSite** (https://www.tabsite.com): TabSite lets users pick close to 50 apps that can be implemented into Facebook Pages with a click of the mouse. Install video and podcast tabs, run deals for your customers, and hide special fans-only content behind a fan gate. Fully functional account subscriptions start at $30 per month, and each level has a free 14-day trial. TabSite offers a free plan that includes a few basic capabilities.

- ✔ **ShortStack** (www.shortstackapp.com): ShortStack offers an unlimited number of promotional campaigns with its free account. Any subscriptions with Facebook page personalization, such as custom subdomains and social sharing options, start at $30 per month.

Apps for contests

Contests and sweepstakes help bring in fans, and there's no better way to build up your email database! Here are some contest apps to consider:

- ✔ **Woobox** (http://woobox.com): Run sweepstakes, photo contests, deals, and polls, all from your Facebook Page. Woobox even has a feature that randomly selects a winner for you, ensuring that your promotions stay fair. Woobox has a feature-rich free plan, and all the more advanced features cost $49 per month.

- ✔ **Easypromos** (www.easypromosapp.com): Easypromos is great for sweepstakes, coupons, photos, and writing-based contests. It features registration forms to add a lead-generation feature to your Facebook Pages. You can pay per promotion or sign up for a subscription, which starts at $29 per month and goes up to $299 per month for large brands and agencies.

- ✔ **ContestCapture** (http://contestcapture.com): A simple yet extremely effective app, ContestCapture lets you keep track of Facebook contest entries such as likes and comments. The best part is that it's completely free!

- ✔ **Tabfoundry** (https://www.tabfoundry.com): Combine your contests with email signups by using Tabfoundry. A unique games feature lets you keep your fans entertained. Tabfoundry offers a free account, and its other paid level is Premium, which costs $14 per month.

Creating a Twitter business profile

Using Twitter for business purposes is much more than using 140 characters to announce your latest sale or providing the link to your latest blog post. Always keep in mind that using social media isn't all about you!

Using Twitter successfully for your business starts as soon as you sign up for an account. (See Chapter 3 to find out how to sign up for a Twitter account.) Sure, your business Twitter account may look exactly the same as your personal account, but you can do a few things to brand your account.

The rest of this section explains what you can do to properly brand your Twitter page, setting you on the path to commercial Twitter success. Here are a few tips:

✔ **Choose a profile image that represents your brand.** This image is not only shown on your Twitter profile page, but also placed next to every tweet you send out, so make it count! A logo is always a safe bet, but keep your business in mind. If you're a personal coach, for example, using a photo of yourself makes more sense. The ideal dimensions for a profile image are 400 × 400 pixels.

✔ **Get creative with your header image.** Your header image is the large photo that sits at the top of your page. It's visible only if someone visits your profile, but that doesn't mean it's not important! Unlike Facebook, Twitter allows you to add text to your header image, so take advantage of that feature. Add your company's tagline, website, or information about your latest promotion. The sky's the limit. The ideal size for the picture you use for your header image is 1500 × 1500 pixels. The image is resized automatically to fit, so make sure that it's as close to the recommended size as possible; otherwise, it could look squished or stretched.

If you prefer to use some beautiful stock photography for your header image, sites such as TwitrCovers (www.twitrcovers.com) have some great options. The best part? They're all free to use.

✔ **Pull readers in with your bio.** Your Twitter bio should be clear and concise (160 characters) explaining exactly what your business is, how you can help your customers, and what followers should expect when they follow you. Be sure to use keywords that describe your business to ensure that it shows up in search results. If you have space, you could also include your phone number or store hours. Don't waste space by putting your website address in your bio, because Twitter provides a separate section for that purpose.

> ✔ **Use the Tweet Pinning option.** If you tweet something that got a lot of retweets, for example, pin it to the top of your profile page so that it doesn't get lost in the shuffle. To pin a tweet, simply visit your Twitter profile page and click the three-dots icon below the tweet you want to pin. From the drop-down menu that appears, choose the Pin to Your Profile Page option. That's it!

Establishing a company presence on LinkedIn

Did you know that in addition to having a personal profile on LinkedIn, you can have a dedicated company page? Chapter 10 explains how to share content and engage with followers by using your personal profile. Although it's important to "humanize" your SMO strategy, it's also important for your company to have its own presence on LinkedIn.

What LinkedIn has that Facebook and Twitter don't have are dedicated Products & Services pages where you're encouraged to sell. Now, *that's* something you don't see much of in social media! The reason why it's more acceptable to sell on LinkedIn is that LinkedIn is a social network for professionals to connect with other professionals. Although overt, high-pressure selling is discouraged on LinkedIn (and in general), you have more leeway when it comes to elevator pitches (a succinct summary of your company and value proposition) and talking up your products and services.

Setting up a LinkedIn company page

Setting up a LinkedIn company page is easy. Just follow these steps:

1. **Point your browser to** `https://www.linkedin.com,` **and log in to your personal LinkedIn profile.**

   Every LinkedIn business page must be connected to a personal profile.

2. **On the top menu bar, right below the LinkedIn search box, click the Interests link, and choose Companies from the drop-down list.**

   You're now on your Companies home page, where you see the content updates of any companies that you follow on LinkedIn.

3. **On the right side of the page, below the Create a Company Page heading, click the yellow Create button.**

4. **On the resulting page, enter your company name and your email address at the company.**

   Only current employees with an @companydomain email address can create a company page. In other words, you have to use your company email address instead of your Gmail or Hotmail address.

5. **Check the box verifying that you're a representative of the company and then click the Continue button.**

   A confirmation email is sent to the email address you entered.

6. **Click the confirmation button in the email.**

7. **When you're prompted to do so, log in to your LinkedIn account again.**

Congratulations! You have your first LinkedIn company page! From now on, whenever you choose Interests⇨Companies, your company page shows up on the right sidebar.

Though doing so isn't required, you should upload your company's logo at this point. Doing so will "put a face to the brand" and help you stand out in LinkedIn searches.

Before your company page can be published, you have to fill out some required pieces of information (see Figure 13-4):

✔ Company Name

✔ Company Description

   Tell your company's story. Make sure to use keywords that help with search engine optimization (SEO).

✔ Company Type (Public, Self-Employed, Nonprofit, and so on)

✔ Company Size

✔ Company Website URL

✔ Main Company Industry

✔ Company Operating Status (Operating, Reorganizing, Out of Business, and so on)

✔ Main Company Industry

Seeking recommendations on LinkedIn

C'mon — now's not the time to be shy! You have satisfied customers out there who would love nothing more than to tell the world what a great experience they had with you and your company.

When your company has a solid LinkedIn presence, reach out to former customers, co-workers, and even employers, and ask whether they'd be willing to write you a recommendation. Recommendations are listed near the

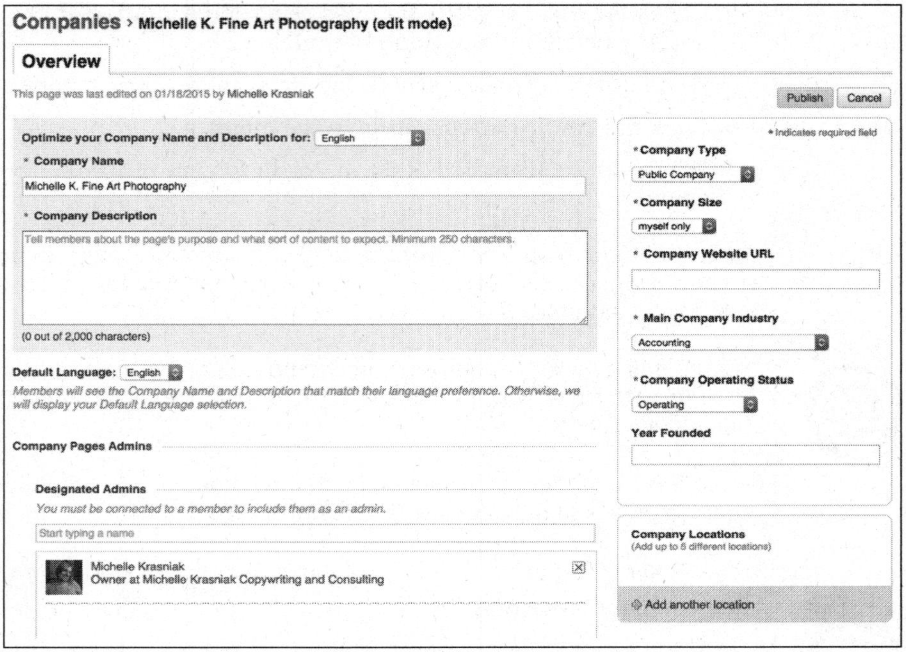

Figure 13-4:
Creating
your new
LinkedIn
company
page.

bottom of your LinkedIn profile and are great ways to highlight the great work you do and the varying skills you have.

Recommendations are different from endorsements. Endorsements, which are listed below the education section of your profile, show the thumbnails of those LinkedIn connections who acknowledge that you possess the skills listed in your profile. Social media marketing, technical writing, and editing are all skills that someone can be endorsed for. A person can't ask for endorsements through LinkedIn, though you can always contact a person directly and ask her to endorse you. Instead, LinkedIn occasionally presents your connections a prompt to endorse you for various skills — when he signs in to his LinkedIn account, for example, or (depending on his email settings) through an email from LinkedIn.

Although endorsements are great to have, it's super-easy to click skills mindlessly when you're prompted to do. You have the best intentions, but what you're endorsing your connection for may be far removed from what she *actually* wants to be endorsed for.

Recommendations (see Figure 13-5) are much more powerful than endorsements, because the person recommending you takes the time to sit down and write a personal account of his experience with you. There's nothing like hearing something from the horse's mouth!

Figure 13-5:
Let others say how great you are in their own words!

It's always a good idea to reach out to your connection ahead of time to ask her whether she'd be willing to write you a recommendation. If she doesn't feel comfortable, you can move on to someone else who may be more willing.

LinkedIn makes it easy for you to reach out to your connections to ask them for recommendations. Just do the following:

1. **Point your browser to https://www.linkedin.com, and log in to your personal LinkedIn profile.**

   You're now on your LinkedIn home page.

2. **Click the Profile link on the top menu bar.**

   The resulting page is where you can edit the sections of your profile. It also gives you a good idea of how your profile looks to other people.

3. **Scroll down to the Recommendations section (see Figure 13-6), and click the Ask to Be Recommended link at the bottom of that box.**

   Use the drop-down list to choose the position you want to be recommended for.

4. Start typing the name(s) of the connections from whom you're requesting recommendations.

You can add up to three names at a time. After you type the first name, more sections appear below that box (see Figure 13-6).

5. Use the drop-down menus to set your relationship to the connection, as well as the position of the connection from whom you're requesting the recommendation from.

The drop-down menu asking for your relationship lists both your professional and educational affiliations. If you're requesting a recommendation from a former professor, for example, choose that option from the first drop-down menu and then choose the school at which he taught from the second drop-down menu.

6. Personalize the message that will be sent with the request.

A default message is all ready for you, but it's a good idea to personalize it to show that you care enough about the person to take the time to write a special note. After all, you *are* asking him to write something about you!

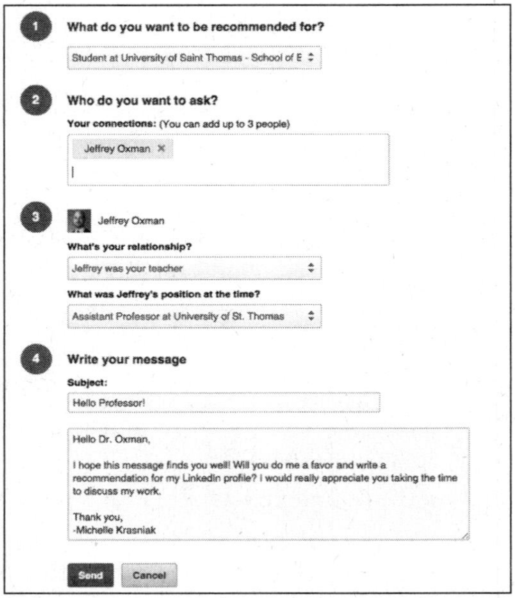

Figure 13-6:
Sending a message asking for a recommendation.

Figure used with permission of Jeff Oxman

7. **Click the blue Send button when you're finished, or click Cancel if you've changed your mind.**

Your message is sent to the email address that your connection has on file.

Creating the Perception of Expertise

If you've got it, flaunt it! You're in the business that you're in because you're good at what you do. People may even call you an *expert,* and if they don't . . . well, now's the time to change that situation.

Start by sitting down and making a list of all of your professional strengths. Are you incredibly organized? Are you a fantastic project manager? Are you able to recite the ABCs backward while standing on your head? If something relates to your business, by all means add it to the list.

Now take a look at that list and see how those strengths translate into reasons why your business is successful in its industry. For those who are organized, if you're a time-management coach or a professional organizer, it's safe to say that you're an expert at organizing pretty much everything. If you're a wonderful project manager, and you happen to run a construction consulting firm, we'd bet a paycheck on the fact that you know the ins and outs of that industry like the back of your hand. If you're a circus clown who performs at children's birthday parties, your head-standing, alphabet-reciting skills put you — ahem — heads above the rest.

The point is, there's no room for modesty in your SMO plan. You do have expertise, and as soon as you identify those areas, you're on your way to becoming a go-to source for useful information on social media.

The next section moves on to some ways in which you can showcase your knowledge.

Share knowledge freely

Your SMO strategy should be about having conversations, but sometimes, you have to be the one who gets the conversation started. Blog posts are great ways to start conversations, provided that you don't fill your blog with heavy-handed selling content.

Revisit your list about the areas that you would be considered an expert in (refer to "Creating the Perception of Expertise" earlier in this chapter). Those areas are perfect places to start when you're looking for ideas to blog about. You can even make them top-level subjects and then jot down a few ideas associated with those subjects. To return to the professional-organizer example in the preceding section, you're not only an expert in the actual organizing of things, but you probably also know a lot about filing systems and unique containers in which to store things. Take those secondary topics and write posts about them as well. The posts don't have to be long; they just have to be informative.

Chapter 5 talks about repurposing your content to use on other sites. Here's another great opportunity to do so. Reach out to the owners of blogs and websites related to your craft, and offer to write a guest post. This way, you produce more content that you can cross-promote on your other social media sites, and you're also getting your name and expertise in front of a new audience.

Engage in communities

Both Facebook and LinkedIn have Groups features that let like-minded individuals gather to share knowledge. Many people join to get questions answered, and many join to answer questions. Be one of the latter. Don't lurk and then all of a sudden jump into the middle of a conversation. Instead, join the group, introduce yourself, and pipe up when you see a topic that you can contribute to.

Under no circumstances should you take group discussions as opportunities to sell. Think of a group as a book-club meeting. If someone asked a question about the book, you wouldn't answer the question and then go into a discussion of your bookstore's sale on Italian cookbooks (and tell group members that they should hurry to buy some, because the sale is ending soon). Chances are that you won't be welcomed back to that club. The same goes for groups in Facebook and LinkedIn.

To find groups of interest in LinkedIn, log in to your account, click Interests on the top menu bar, and choose Groups from the drop-down menu. On the page that appears, simply type a search term in the search box at the top. The results will show any groups that meet your search criteria.

To find groups of interest on Facebook, simply log in to your Facebook account and then type your search term in the search box at the top of the screen. When the results appear, click the More link on the top sort bar to filter the search results to show only groups.

Be a resource

Another great way to show your expertise is to become a resource for people. Create content like FAQs (frequently asked questions) about your industry, and post the link on your Facebook page. One company even created a glossary of industry terms by using Facebook's Notes feature. That way, visitors to that company's Facebook Page can always refer to the note if they encounter terminology that they don't recognize.

A Facebook Group created a note containing links to all the retailers the Group leaders recommend for purchasing certain goods for craft projects. We've revisited that particular note several times to get links to these online resources.

In Figure 13-7, a professional time coach's website offers a free e-book download so that people can find out more about her industry, as well as get a feeling for the expertise she possesses. This strategy serves the dual purpose of making her a resource for information while collecting email addresses for her e-newsletter.

If you use this strategy, just make sure that your visitors know what they're signing up for!

Figure 13-7: Download some free resources.

Figure used with permission of Julie Gray

Protecting your brand in the social world

After you've put a lot of blood, sweat, and tears (but we hope not too much of the latter) into your SMO endeavors, it's important for you to ensure that sentiments about your brand (thoughts and feelings about it) are positive.

Sure, you can't keep everyone happy at all times, but you can do your best to keep *most* people happy *most* of the time. You do this by continuing to do what you're already doing: providing quality products and delivering impeccable customer service.

Chapter 14

Managing Reputation

*R*eputation management used to be considered a public relations discipline, but the rise of the Internet in general and social media in particular has changed all that. Today, reputation is largely a byproduct of what people see about you online. This means that search results and social media have become significant factors in reputation management.

You can use social media to project a personality for a company or a brand. You can also use it to set expectations and build an online reputation. At some point, you may even find it necessary to defend your reputation; when that happens, social media can be your best friend or your worst enemy.

Building and Preserving Reputation with Social Media

There's an old saying: You are your reputation. On the Internet, that saying is largely true. Unfortunately, a lot of firms don't think about reputation management until something bad happens. Waiting for bad things to happen isn't the way to protect your firm's reputation; rather, you should be actively striving to build a positive perception from day one. If something negative occurs at some point (and it almost certainly will!), you'll have built some credibility that will serve you well in dealing with the crisis.

The best way to protect yourself from negative publicity is to cultivate a positive reputation online. Build a reputation as being a person or firm that provides great products, treats people fairly, and is concerned about the effects of actions.

Social media is very effective in influencing perceptions of a person, product, or brand. Your social media goals should always take into account this aspect of the media, which should influence the formulation of your online tone and voice.

A good reputation can't be built by social media alone, of course. Some basic practices have a significant effect on your reputation:

- Producing a great product
- Practicing meaningful customer service
- Listening and responding to reviews, comments, and feedback from your customers and vendors
- Enforcing ethical business practices
- Being part of your community

These items reach far beyond social media, but these five principles should be reflected in your social media content. Your company values need to be communicated clearly in your social media channels. Let people know what you stand for, and back it up with appropriate action.

Nothing is wrong with telling the world that your company has solid values and that it acts in line with those values.

Building a great reputation

If you want to be known in a specific area and build a great reputation, you need to build two things:

- Credibility
- Visibility

Ask yourself the following questions to define what you want to be known for:

- Do I produce a specific product?
- Do I have expertise in a particular area?

✔ Do I have a strong social conscience?

✔ Do I provide great customer service?

Define your goal clearly and then begin to take steps to establish yourself as an expert or leader in your chosen field.

Creating credibility in social media typically is a long process. Perceptions of expertise largely depend on what you publish and contribute to discussions. If you want to be a world-class expert on WordPress, for example, you'd better be thinking about publishing, running seminars or webinars to teach techniques for using WordPress, being part of WordPress communities, and contributing to discussions about WordPress. You also need to establish your presence on key social media channels and align it with your goals. I also recommend that you create a branded web presence, which gives you control over your personal brand and the power to publish when and how you see fit. The website becomes the nexus from which you push the content to the world and a focus of efforts to bring people in.

Creating a reputation with regard to intangibles, such as being a socially conscious organization or having great customer service, can be even more difficult. So much of your reputation in those areas derives from actions over time. It's one thing to say that your firm has a strong commitment to the environment, for example, but in the absence of action to back up your claim, merely making a statement just talk and will do little to establish credibility. The same is true of customer service. Until you've delivered great customer service over time and dealt successfully with crises, claims of great service are as yet untried.

When you have a goal and strategy for establishing your credibility, you need to focus on getting the message in front of people — that is, you need to focus on visibility. Social media is a tremendous help, as are search engine optimization (SEO) and paid marketing. Visibility, in other words, is marketing.

Some of the most effective techniques for increasing your visibility include

✔ **Publish awesome content.** Great content is the keystone of social media success. Publish it on your site. Share it via social media. Seek out guest blogging opportunities. The more great content you can publish, the more visibility you'll have.

✔ **Monitor and respond to comments.** Be aware when people post comments and replies to your content and be responsive to them.

✔ **Curate content from other sources.** Piggyback on the work of others. Help people discover great content from other sources, and you'll win the gratitude of both the audience and the publisher.

> ✔ **Be transparent and honest.** People have a nose for frauds. Don't try to hide your activities, and don't claim to be something you're not.
>
> ✔ **Participate in a targeted community.** Be visible in the key communities for your specialty. Be helpful. Be positive, and be a resource for people. Your mere presence on the channel raises your brand visibility and creates associations.

You have three types of channels for building visibility: owned, earned, and paid. All three need to be part of the marketing mix. This concept is discussed in more detail in Chapter 10.

Optimizing social media to control search results

Although some factors that affect company reputation are outside your control, you can do some effective things with social media optimization (SMO) to manage reputation. Two of the most important things are to use social media to stake out and control your brand's online visibility and to affect what people see when they search for the brand. Search engines are key. Always use your best efforts to control your brand's presence on the search engine results page. Although it's nearly impossible to get your website to the point where results from your website alone dominate page one of Google, with strategic use of social media channels, you can control a large hunk of the territory on page one and beyond.

Social media profiles on key channels tend to rank highly in the search engines. Google considers social media sites such as Facebook, Twitter, LinkedIn, YouTube, SlideShare, and Pinterest to be high-authority sites by Google, so when your brand profile appears on those sites, it's likely to show up high in the search results. Therefore, staking out your turf on the key social media channels is strategically important. Claim any profiles related to your brand name and company name on the major channels. If, for example, you are working with company ABC, and they also have a brand named XYZ, then you should try to obtain the profiles for both ABC and XYZ on all the major channels. Build at least enough of a presence to make sure that the profile registers as a brand presence on the channel.

Creating solid brand profiles on key social channels can help ensure that the page-one Google search results reflect the legitimate presence of your brand. Control of that territory can act as partial insurance against negative reviews and other destructive public relations. If you hold the high ground on a search engine results page, you can marginalize the effect of posts, comments, and reviews by detractors.

Page one of Google is the most important territory for your brand's reputation. Rank well so that if a crisis strikes, you have plenty of visible channels that can help you get your message out.

Take a look at Figure 14-1, which shows Google search results for Costa Coffee. With the exception of a Wikipedia entry and the Google News items, page one of Google is dominated by brand-controlled properties.

If you look past page one, you see that Costa also controls most of page two. The firm has leveraged Facebook, Twitter, and YouTube to its advantage, using the strength of those high-ranking sites to strengthen its presence in Google. This strategy is highly effective (and legitimate) for staying in control of your brand presence and, therefore, for staying in control of what people see when they search for your brand.

Want to take this strategy further? Apply the same technique to control your company's product names in Google search results, or, if possible, for the primary keyword associated with your company or product.

Avoiding negative SMO practices

Though we want to focus on positive practices and hope that the ethical and appropriate techniques we discuss will guide your actions, we also need to point out that the SMO practitioner has the ability to damage a firm's reputation online. You need to avoid certain practices that are tempting for a quick win but can in the long run be hugely detrimental to your firm.

You shouldn't employ the following methods:

- ✔ Writing fake reviews or blog posts (aka astroturfing)
- ✔ Censoring negative or critical comments
- ✔ Lying or grossly exaggerating claims
- ✔ Trying to game search engine results with dodgy SEO techniques, such as creating gateway pages or using redirects

Engaging in any of these practices isn't in line with SMO best practices and shouldn't be part of your SMO tool kit. If you get caught using any of these techniques, the backlash can be extreme.

Figure 14-1:
Costa
Coffee on
Google.

TripAdvisor, for example, has a zero-tolerance policy for fake reviews. If TripAdvisor determines that any reviews are fake, it penalizes your firm in the rankings on the site, disqualifies you from all potential rewards and promotions, and adds a large red penalty notice to your page indicating that your reviews are suspicious.

Furthermore, make sure that you don't ignore customers who have reached out to you online, and don't promote your product or company to the exclusion of providing useful content; although neither of these points is an ethics issue, they tend to sour relations with people and have a negative effect on your audience's perception of your company.

Discovering the Pain and the Power of Review Sites

Review sites generate some of the most direct effects on the public perception of your firm. If you're in travel and tourism, in particular, the online review sites are critical for engaging with both past and potential customers. The list of review sites continues to grow. Some sites focus on specific industries, such as restaurants or hotels; others have broader appeal. Following are the leaders in this field:

- ✔ TripAdvisor (`www.tripadvisor.com`)
- ✔ Foursquare (`https://foursquare.com`)
- ✔ Yelp (`www.yelp.com`)
- ✔ Urbanspoon (`www.urbanspoon.com`)
- ✔ OpenTable (`www.opentable.com`)
- ✔ Angie's List (`www.angieslist.com`)
- ✔ Citysearch (`www.citysearch.com`)

A multitude of smaller, often highly localized sites focus on a specific industry or business, such as health care or legal services. The reviews trend is significant and unlikely to taper off. Even Google and Facebook provide review functions these days.

One of the worst aspects of negative publicity on popular review sites is the visibility of those reviews. The search engines tend to rank the content from major review sites highly in the search results — often higher than the company website itself. That kind of visibility means that reviews are influential, and you ignore them at your own risk.

One detractor costs you more than a promoter earns you, so it's important to do your utmost to earn goodwill. Dell Computer, for example, calculated that an average online promoter earns the company $32, whereas an average online detractor costs it $57.

TripAdvisor

TripAdvisor is the major player among the review sites, especially for hotels, restaurants, and related businesses. The site is large, highly influential, and active. The site also has a reputation as sometimes being a difficult place for business owners to defend themselves, due to TripAdvisor's policy of not getting involved in adjudicating disputes between customers and venues.

TripAdvisor claims to have more than 315 million unique monthly visitors and 200 million reviews. If you're in hospitality, you can't afford to ignore TripAdvisor. The site is very influential among travelers. Figure 14-2 shows a TripAdvisor review page.

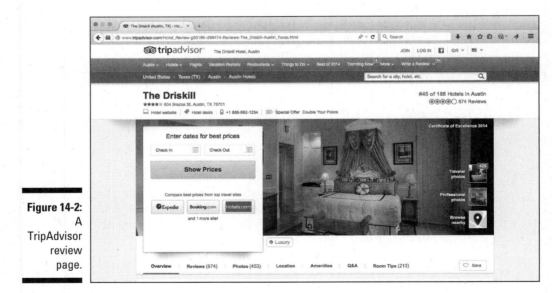

Figure 14-2:
A
TripAdvisor
review
page.

There are several keys to keeping a handle on things on TripAdvisor:

- ✔ **Take control of your company profile.** Claim the listing of your business. Be visible. Add a signature photo to your listing to set the tone, control expectations, and reinforce your branding. Make sure that your listing is accurate and up to date.

  To claim your listing, search for your business, visit the listing page for your business, and look for the Manage Your Listing link at the bottom of the review (see Figure 14-3).

Friday   7:00 am - 8:00 pm
Saturday   7:00 am - 8:00 pm
Cuisine: Indonesian

Owners: What's your side of the story?

Register now for free — and start getting automatic notification of new reviews, responding to traveler feedback, adding new photos to your listing and much more.

Manage your listing

Questions & Answers

- ✔ **Consider upgrading to a paid business listing.** Basic listings on TripAdvisor are free. For a small fee, you can upgrade to a business listing, which offers better visibility and typically generates more traffic.

- ✔ **Give your company a face and a voice.** Be present by keeping your listing current and by replying to reviewers. It's the single biggest thing you can do. You need to show you care.

- ✔ **Stay on top of things.** Failure to respond to anything for a long period means that damage has been done. No response to a review results in the perception that is the review is true and you don't care.

If you think that a review is a fake, TripAdvisor provides a mechanism for reporting suspect reviews. Simply click the Problem with the Review link.

Foursquare

Foursquare focuses on sharing locations and exploring the neighborhood around you. It provides reviews and ratings for businesses across a broad range of categories. The emphasis is on mobile users; the vast majority of users access Foursquare on the go. Figure 14-4 shows a Foursquare business review page.

Figure 14-4:
A
Foursquare
review
page.

Foursquare has more than 55 million users and almost 1.5 million active business pages.

To make the most of your business presence on Foursquare, try these tips:

✔ **Claim your listing.** After you claim your listing, you can customize your page. Add your company info, recent photos, tips, and so on. Make sure to keep the listing up to date.

To claim your listing, search for your business, visit the listing page for your business, and look for the Claim It Now link at the bottom of the right column (see Figure 14-5).

Figure 14-5:
Claim your
listing on
Foursquare.

✓ **Try the Foursquare For Business app.** The app lets you manage your listing on the go and improves your ability to react quickly to user feedback.

✓ **Try offering specials to Foursquare users.** Because Foursquare is used heavily on mobile devices and provides a check-in mechanism, you can tie promotions to check-ins. You could offer people a free coffee when they check in on Foursquare, for example.

Foursquare offers a variety of specials that can be triggered by different actions. Play around with the options and find what works best for you. To get started, click the Create a New Special button on your Business Manager Home Page.

✓ **Curate a list.** Foursquare lets members create lists of locations or tips. If you managed the Driskill Hotel in Austin, Texas, for example, you might want to create a list of public parks close to downtown Austin. Set up a curated list that shows your local knowledge, which make your business more visible and build goodwill.

Yelp

Yelp is one of the largest and most influential review sites, as well as one of the most controversial. There have been numerous complaints that Yelp gives preferential treatment to paid advertisers and that negative reviews are sometimes emphasized on nonadvertiser pages. Even if Yelp gives preferential treatment to paid listings, anyone can create a review page for a business. The page can't be deleted, so you have little choice but to jump in and engage.

The up side is that Yelp has a very large user base (more than 139 million unique visitors per month), so your Yelp listing page will likely rank quite highly on Google. Figure 14-6 shows a Yelp business listing.

To thrive on Yelp, consider the following:

✓ **Claim your listing.** Claim your listing by pointing your browser to `https://biz.yelp.com`. Use the search interface shown in Figure 14-7 to find your listing and claim it. Add as much information about your business as you can. Make sure to keep your listing up to date.

✓ **Post great photos.** Great photos encourage customer visits and shape perceptions of your business. Don't just show the premises; also show people and, where relevant, promotions or events.

Figure 14-6:
A Yelp
review
page.

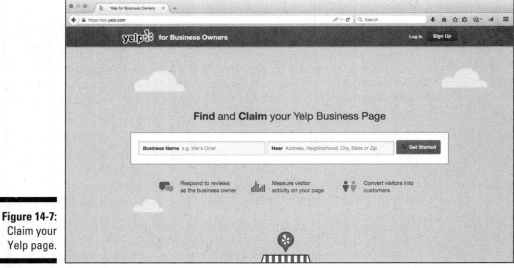

Figure 14-7:
Claim your
Yelp page.

✓ **Use the About This Business section creatively.** In addition to providing basic info, all listings have an optional section called About This Business. Use this section to tell your story. Communicate what makes you special and why people should visit.

About This Business is also a great place to use keywords that will help your business show up higher in search results.

✔ **Post a Yelp Deal.** You can create Deals that appear on your listing page. Yelp also offers gift certificates, a call-to-action button, and a paid advertising program. To get started, look for the Deals link on your Business Page.

Encouraging Positive Reviewers

Maintaining a positive reputation online isn't just about avoiding negative public relations; it's also about encouraging positive PR. Always make an effort to spread positives. Share the nice things people say, and make sure people see that you notice when they say positive things about your company or brand. Make it a point to respond to positive posts frequently. A simple comment like "Glad your enjoyed the flight. We hope we can welcome you aboard again soon," increases your visibility and shows appreciation to loyal customers.

On some sites, adding a new comment to a post moves the post back to the top of the list, thereby extending the life span and reach of a positive comment.

Publicizing your presence on review sites

The best way to overcome negative reviews is to have positive reviews. A preponderance of positive ratings and reviews tends to offset any negative comments. People understand that sometimes things go wrong, and they're tolerant of a few negative reviews here and there. Indeed, a business without some negative reviews looks suspicious to some people.

The best way to build up the critical mass of positive reviews is to encourage people to leave reviews. Although it's against the rules of almost all sites to offer incentives for positive reviews, you can encourage people to leave a review.

Try a mix of the following techniques to get the word out and encourage reviewers:

✔ **Use comment cards.** TripAdvisor, for example, offers free comment cards (a one-time order of 250) that you can give your customers to publicize your presence on TripAdvisor and encourage them to leave reviews.

✔ **Incorporate review-site badges and buttons into your website.** All the major review sites offer badges that you can use on your web pages to publicize your presence on the review site. Many sites include the option to feature the most recent reviews or your overall rating. Foursquare offers a Like button that's similar to a Facebook Like button.

✔ **Publicize your social media profiles.** Cross-promote your review-site presence on your other social channels.

✔ **Make social media information visible at your physical location.** All the major review sites offer ready-to-use graphics for publicizing your presence on those sites. Display Find Us on Yelp table tents, or put a sign by the register calling for a review. At your request, Foursquare will send you one of the window stickers shown in Figure 14-8. Yelp provides a code that people can scan to find your page, which makes it easy for smartphone users to check out your Yelp page and add a review.

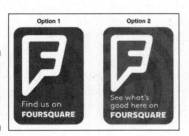

Figure 14-8:
Foursquare
promo
stickers.

Rewarding reviewers

Though it may seem counterproductive, it's actually against the rules of most review sites to offer incentives for users to leave reviews, regardless of whether the reviews are good, bad, or merely indifferent. Both TripAdvisor and Yelp have taken a hard line against rewards of any sort for reviews of any sort. The theory goes like this: Reviews generated by incentives tend not to be accurate reflections of the user's experience.

Be careful here, as the sites tend to define incentives broadly, including drawings or raffles, discounts, and any other type of special treatment. Similarly, putting a computer or a kiosk on-site to encourage reviews is discouraged, and some sites, such as Yelp, are believed to track IP addresses of reviews in order to detect the use of kiosks.

The best you can do is make people aware of your presence on the review sites and encourage them to visit your listing and to leave a review if they feel it is appropriate.

Managing Online Detractors

There's an old saying in the PR business: There's no such thing as bad press. That may have been true in the offline newspaper era, but it certainly isn't true in the world of social media. Bad social media buzz is nothing but bad — pure and simple. The sad truth is that bad news travels faster than good news.

No business is without its critics. It's impossible to make all the people happy all the time. Try as you might, there will always be people who feel that they didn't get what they wanted, deserved, paid for, or expected. Some people will be unhappy for legitimate reasons; others won't be. How you deal with detractors on social media has a huge effect on your company's reputation. Social media tends to amplify things. Negative social media buzz in particular can spin out of control very quickly.

Precisely how you handle negative comments and reviews is up to you. Some companies provide refunds or compensation; other firms offer additional assistance or resources but draw the line at refunds or compensation. The path you take should reflect your brand identity.

People are very good at detecting insincerity. When you address critics, make sure that you're not just spouting the company line without any intention of taking action to help the critics. It's very easy to have a set of stock responses and just stick to them; unfortunately, that approach is also likely to backfire on you. Stock responses that fail to recognize the issues specific to the user and their complaint run the risk of losing the trust of the customer. The customers who feel abandoned or betrayed by a brand are likely to become vocal about their feelings.

Responding appropriately

If someone calls your firm to lodge a complaint, would you feel comfortable ignoring him? Would you hang up on him or not take the call? Of course not. None of those behaviors are an acceptable customer service practice. You should apply the same rationale when engaging with customers online. If a customer feels strongly enough about something to lodge a complaint or post a negative comment or review, you need to respond to her. Although doing so may at times be difficult or awkward, you still need to do it. Responding to complaints is a matter of courtesy and of respect, and it's just good business.

Even if a complaint seems to be frivolous or lacking in sufficient proof, you should respond. Your brand will garner good will from showing concern, and you'll develop a positive reputation for transparency. No one wants to deal with a cold, indifferent corporation.

You can't hope to fix every problem to the satisfaction of every customer, but you can make a genuine effort to understand the problem and come up with a solution that's fair to the customer and to the company. If nothing else, you've acknowledged and validated the person, which often is sufficient to preserve the relationship, even if a complete solution for the problem isn't found.

If an issue is resolved quickly and efficiently, 95 percent of unhappy customers will return.

Use the following guidelines when dealing with negative reviews and comments:

- ✔ **Respond as soon as possible.** Delays can be fatal. The longer a negative criticism remains unanswered, the more people see it and assume it's true — and the more irritated the poster becomes.

  Failure to respond to negative comments leads people to believe the comments are true.

- ✔ **Always thank reviewers for writing about your business.** Don't be obsequious, but anyone who cares enough to write a review or comment deserves some acknowledgment.

- ✔ **Don't lash out at people.** It's never good to lose your cool, particularly online where lots of people are watching and where such incidents can live long and embarrassing lives.

- ✔ **Keep your tone professional.** Make sure that your responses have an even, respectful, professional tone. Don't use ALL CAPS. Don't use slang. Write a response that's helpful and concerned rather than defensive or insulting.

- ✔ **Highlight positives.** If you've made changes (or plan to make them) in response to the problem, tell the reviewer so.

- ✔ **Put yourself in the reviewer's shoes.** Try to see the problem from the reviewer's perspective, and respond to him the way you'd want someone to respond to you.

- ✔ **Don't make a mountain out of a molehill.** An individual criticism may be the result of an isolated bad experience or the reviewer's idiosyncrasies. Look at your entire set of reviews when assessing whether your firm has problems that need to be addressed. Look for trends and patterns.

Getting rid of unfair criticisms

For a criticism of your firm to be actionable on a reviews site, it typically must be objectively false or fake. A false review is one in which the customer misrepresents the situation. A fake reviewer was never a customer at all. In either event, you likely have grounds to get the site administrators to take action. Some sites, such as TripAdvisor, are pretty good about taking action when the business owner is able to provide even a small amount of objective evidence. You can do a few things:

- ✔ **Understand the rules of the site.** If a review violates the site's guidelines, you'll most likely prevail in any request to remove a review. This technique is powerful. Know the rules, and use them to your advantage.

- ✔ **Request that site administrators remove any review with foul language.** Profanity and abusive language are legitimate grounds for having a review removed.

- ✔ **Be prepared with evidence.** If a review is factually wrong, you need to have solid evidence to back up your complaint. Most review sites don't want to get into the middle of a "he said, she said" kind of argument. Be prepared to demonstrate that a review is false.

Don't feed the trolls

If you've spent any time managing social media profiles (or, heaven forbid, a forum site!), you've run into trolls — not the fairy-tale kind, but the mean, nasty individuals who do their best to derail rational discourse through needling, hectoring, or even mindless abuse. Trolls will post and post again in their attempts to humiliate and demean.

Techniques for dealing with trolls are based on removing either of the two things that feed trolls: a victim and an audience. To remove yourself from the role of victim, don't engage the troll directly. We're not saying that you should just sit there and take the abuse; instead, you should respond by addressing the presence of the troll in the group. Other people in the group can see that the troll is the person who has the problem. Restate the need for civility, and call for mutual respect. If you engage trolls directly, bad things tend to happen. When you feed a troll by engaging with him or her, things can spin out of control quickly, as there may well be other trolls waiting to jump in.

The second tool at your disposal is direct-messaging the troll in an attempt to take the discussion out of the public forum. This way, you can clear the negativity from your channel, and you may be able to turn the troll around. That said, if you're dealing with one of the hardcore trolls who lives just to make other people's lives hell, responding privately will never work. The troll will continue to engage you publicly, attempting to get you to respond in anger or to dominate the channel and derail your presence there.

If all else fails, it may be time to think about deploying your ultimate weapon: blocking or banning the user. Some sites give you the power to delete comments and to block users. Other channels give you a means to report abusive behavior. If appropriate, don't hesitate to block someone, but remember that a motivated troll will find another way to get back in action, usually by using a different account or working through another user.

If you're the object of an attack by one of the variety of professional trolls who reside on the Internet, you're in for a difficult time. The important point is to never hit back. You simply can't win against these people in direct confrontation. The only route to victory is to find a way to deny them what they need.

Tracking Online Reputation

If you don't know about an issue, you can't respond to it. It's absolutely essential that you take steps to track online mentions of your name, product, or brand. The first thing you need to do is define what you want to track. At a minimum, you should track the following things:

- Company name
- Specific brands inside the company
- Specific product names
- Names of key employees

Next, you need to find the right tools for tracking mentions. Several commercial systems serve as online "clipping services," providing a variety of alerts at a frequency you determine. Some of the leaders include

- **Chatmeter** (www.chatmeter.com): Chatmeter is the broadest of the solutions listed in this section. In addition to review monitoring, it performs a variety of other tasks, including reporting, competitor monitoring and workflow management. Chatmeter is fairly complex and is priced accordingly, but it does allow to compare your reputation and reviews with those of your competitors, which is a nice feature.
- **Reputation Ranger (**http://reputationranger.com): This service monitors more than 70 review and ratings sites, and provides specialty coverage for several industries, including travel and tourism.
- **ReviewPush** (www.reviewpush.com): ReviewPush monitors the major ratings and review sites for mentions of your brand or business. It offers a free trial period and tiered monthly subscriptions.
- **Review Trackers** (www.reviewtrackers.com): This service offers review monitoring for more than 50 sites. It offers a free trial period and a reasonable monthly fee for single-location businesses.

Although you can always subscribe to one of the commercial services, the easiest way to stay on top of what's being said about you online is to create a Google Alert. Here's how:

1. **Go to** https://www.google.com/alerts.

   In Figure 14-9, a new alert is being set up.

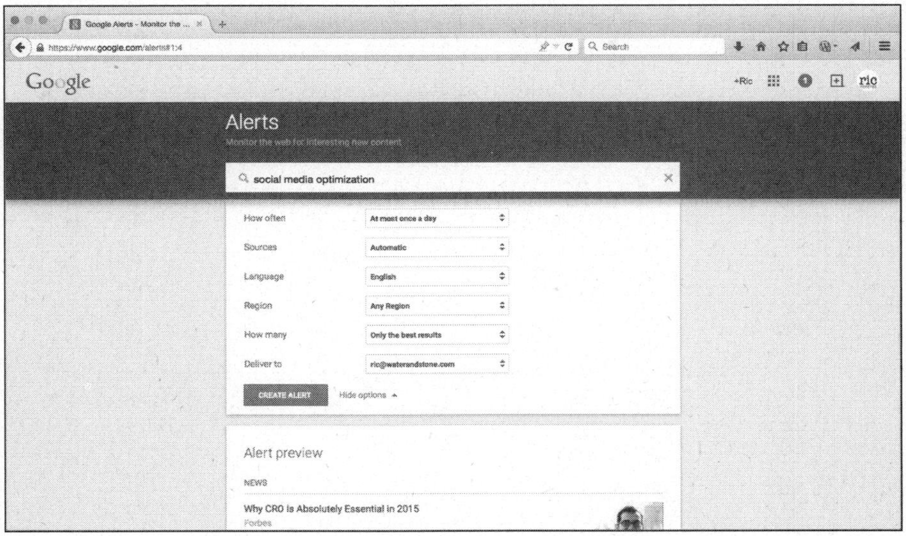

Figure 14-9:
Create a
Google
Alert.

2. **In the search field at the top of the page, enter your name, product name, or brand; then press Enter.**

3. **Review the results to make sure you're getting what you want.**

4. **If everything looks good, click the Show Options link.**

5. **Configure the options to suit your needs.**

   Select options that are appropriate for your business or production. Options include frequency of notifications, sources, languages and regions, and delivery address.

6. **Enter your email address in the field provided.**

7. **Click the Create Alert button.**

   If you're not signed in to Google, you need to do so to finalize setup.

A couple of other low-cost or free tools you may want to consider are

✔ **Hootsuite** (`https://hootsuite.com`): You can use Hootsuite to monitor Twitter, Facebook, and LinkedIn.

✔ **Social Mention** (`www.socialmention.com`): With Social Mention, you can monitor social media mentions on channels such as Facebook, YouTube, Reddit, and Photobucket.

Chapter 15

Creating a Crisis Management Resource

In This Chapter

▶ Dealing with the need for immediacy

▶ Building a resource for crises

▶ Maintaining control over the discussion

*A*t this point, the purists in the crowd are likely saying, "Crisis management is not really a social media optimization issue." Technically, the purists are right, but this chapter is here for one simple reason: If you get this part wrong, all your other efforts have just been wasted. Although crisis management may not technically be a part of everyday social media optimization (SMO), it's a crucial part of social media management and therefore has a place in this discussion.

A switched-on social media practitioner can make a difference for his company in crisis management. When a crisis or an emergency erupts, social media can deliver amazing benefits for your company. Admittedly, if everything is rosy and nothing serious ever goes wrong, company leaders probably will never fully appreciate your efforts to prepare for disaster. On the other hand, if something goes horribly wrong and crisis management becomes job one, prepare to be a social media hero.

Embracing the Tyranny of Immediacy

Murphy's Law is "Whatever can go wrong, will go wrong." One corollary to Murphy's Law is "When things go wrong, it will be at the worst possible time." That sentence pretty well sums up our experience. Things never seem to go horribly wrong during business hours, midweek. Things go horribly wrong while you're sleeping, when you've left the office, over a long holiday weekend, and so on.

The inherent perversity of the universe can't be overcome, but you can prepare for it. Good crisis management is about anticipating the day that things will go horribly wrong and having in place mechanisms to limit damage and aid recovery. Social media can play a crucial role in managing crises and mitigating the damage that results. That said, if you don't prepare for problems, you may miss your chance to make a big difference while you're rushing about trying to get everything in order.

Given the ubiquity of social media, get used to the idea that it's going to play a role in your next crisis, even if you haven't prepared a crisis management plan.

There are multiple advantages to making social media part of your crisis management planning:

- Providing real-time coverage
- Reaching a broad target audience easily
- Saving time and money
- Keeping people informed and helping reduce panic or overreaction
- Publishing a wide variety of media and post links
- Providing two-way communication

Warren Buffett is credited with this observation: "It takes 20 years to build a reputation and 5 minutes to ruin it." If you think about that, you'll do things differently.

It's often a hard sell to get a company to invest in preventive tools for crisis management, but you should still argue to have them. Yes, costs are involved, and yes, there's management overhead. Those things pale in comparison to the harm that can occur if you don't have a plan and tools in place. Preparing for crisis is largely about three things:

- Actively listening to detect any crisis as soon as possible
- Having an escalation process in place to handle the crisis quickly
- Managing your message and communicating with your team, your customers, and your stakeholders

Establishing a crisis detection plan

The first and most critical key to dealing with a crisis is discovering in timely fashion that the crisis is occurring. Crisis detection enables you to triage the situation and respond before things spiral out of control. When you have a handle on the incident, you can implement the right escalation process.

Crisis detection is one thing that social media does extremely well. As they say, bad news spreads like wildfire. Social media is the tinder that fuels that fire. If you have your monitoring in place, you can be one of the first to know that a problem has occurred.

Not listening reflects badly on your brand. Failure to detect things quickly and respond is the fastest way to generate criticism of your company's professionalism and level of concern. You never want to be accused of being clueless or indifferent. With the existence of good social media monitoring tools, there's no excuse for not knowing about a crisis in timely fashion.

Numerous social media monitoring tools can help you find mentions of your name, your brand, and your products. Some of the best tools are commercial and can be quite expensive, but some low-cost alternatives work pretty well. One of the easiest-to-implement free solutions is Google Alerts (`https://www.google.com/alerts`), which enables you to set up an automatic notification for each time a particular set of words or phrases appears in Google search results.

You want a social media monitor with the broadest coverage possible. Don't restrict yourself to a tool that can search only the big channels (Twitter, Facebook, and LinkedIn). The goal is to find out about a crisis as quickly as possible, which means monitoring multiple channels.

Following are a few commercial social media monitoring products:

- Radian6 (`www.exacttarget.com/products/social-media-marketing/radian6`)
- Sysomos (`www.sysomos.com`)
- Trackur (`www.trackur.com`)
- Viralheat (`https://www.viralheat.com`)

When you have the monitoring tools in place, you need to establish a listening protocol that covers the following:

- Who is primarily responsible for listening?
- When is that person responsible for listening?
- How will you cover listening on weekends, holidays, and off hours?

When employees go rogue

It's a company's worst nightmare: An employee with access to the corporate communications channels turns the channels against the company. How bad can it be? Just ask HMV. The UK retailer laid off a large number of employees as part of a downsizing. Unfortunately, one of the employees had access to the company's Twitter account and turned it against the firm. The figure shows how the Twitter account was used against the company. As if that act weren't bad enough, management couldn't stop him, because no one at executive level knew the account password.

The HMV situation highlights one of the basic principles of internal information security: All company account access data must be kept on the company servers and associated with email accounts and personas that the company controls. These controls are easy to implement and should be part of your firm's standard operating procedures. You must have the ability to regain control if something is diverted. If you have a big budget, some social media publishing platforms provide a master "kill switch" that lets a senior manager exercise control of subordinates' online activities.

Acting quickly

Domino's Pizza once faced a social media nightmare. Two of the company's employees posted to YouTube a disgusting video about tainting customer food at Domino's. The video was clearly intended to be humorous, but real damage was done. It took two days for senior management to become aware of the video and mobilize resources to deal with it. By that time, the video had already received more than 1 million views.

Timing is everything. Waste no time getting involved in the conversation — even if it's just to say "Thank you for bringing this to our attention. We're looking at it right now and will provide more information shortly." Silence isn't an option!

If you're not sure what to say when a crisis explodes, try to put yourself in your audience's shoes. People typically want three things during a crisis:

- ✔ To feel that they're being heard
- ✔ To feel that their opinions matter
- ✔ To feel that someone is doing something about the problem

Providing that sort of basic assurance is the bare minimum, and you should be able to do that much regardless of the situation.

When you detect a potential crisis, go into triage mode. You need to quickly assess the situation and determine whether there's a legitimate crisis. If so, you have to be ready to take the next steps quickly. One of the basic skills is knowing what constitutes a true crisis that requires an exceptional response.

When a problem situation develops, ask yourself the following questions:

- ✔ Is it serious? If it's serious, how serious is it?
- ✔ Is it truly a crisis or merely a problem such as we encounter in the normal course of business?
- ✔ What's the nature of the crisis?
- ✔ Can it be confirmed or validated?

Some situations aren't crises, such as negative reviews, mean tweets, or complaints about a product or a service. Those situations are just part of the normal course of business. Refer the problem to your customer service personnel and let them handle it.

Characteristics of a crisis

A crisis has three characteristics:

- **Information asymmetry:** Information asymmetry occurs when someone other than your company has more or superior information about a situation. The classic example is finding out about a problem from social media before internal processes bring the matter to the attention of the right people in the organization. Suppose that one of your company's planes just went down in the Hudson River. How do you know?? Oh. . . there are multiple videos of it on YouTube!

- **A meaningful deviation from the norm:** Look out for patterns that are different from the normal background noise generated by doing business. Some degree of criticism is par for the course. Be on the lookout for new issues that garner quick social media momentum.

- **Potential for negative effect on your business:** A person complaining that he didn't like the meal he was served at your restaurant isn't a crisis. Multiple persons complaining that they became ill after eating at your establishment is a crisis that can cause significant harm to your company.

Managing responsiveness in a 24/7 world

A key piece of preparing for a crisis is creating a flowchart that defines your internal process in the event of a crisis, including trigger points and key personnel who will manage the crisis. Anyone who reads the flowchart needs to understand where to turn for assistance in various scenarios. Following are some matters that the flowchart needs to address:

- Create tiers for various levels of severity.
- Define who is contacted for each tier.
- Define what steps should be taken automatically in each tier.
- Provide contact information for all the key parties.

  If a crisis erupts, can you get a video statement from your chief executive officer online within 24 hours at any time, regardless of where she is? If you can't, you're not prepared.

- Include contact details for emergency responders such as police, ambulance, and hospitals.

Get the flowchart approved by management, make sure that the document has an owner, and make sure that it winds up in the hands of all the right people. When a crisis strikes, go to the plan. Get the word out to all stakeholders, both on your internal team and outside the company. It's essential to bring your company personnel in on the plan and let them know what's happening; their friends and social media contacts are going to turn to them first for information.

In sensitive industries, any emergency response plan needs to be vetted by legal and corporate responsibility teams. In some industries, you need to go further by formulating preapproved preliminary messages. Crisis drills can also be helpful for identifying gaps in your planning and for helping to stave off criticism that your company didn't do enough to be prepared for a foreseeable incident.

If you own a small business or work as a one-man show, you can't possibly deliver 24/7 coverage. That's okay as long as you make it known that you are not responding 24/7. Manage expectations by telling people how long it will take you to get back to them. It's okay to put something like "We try to respond to all feedback within 72 hours" on the About Us page on your website, or on your contact form. Be aware that a promise to respond within a certain timeframe creates a time-based expectation and that you need to deliver on that expectation.

Becoming a Resource in a Time of Crisis

Some people talk about "owning a crisis." I've got news for them: You can't own a crisis. If you could, you wouldn't have a crisis. All you can ever hope to do is shape the tone of the discussion and the perceptions of your company's role in the crisis.

One of the best ways to earn the respect of those involved is to be a helpful and accurate resource in the time of crisis. In this capacity, you need to tap all your content resources. Your website, your social media presence, and your media releases need to be brought to bear on the crisis. By taking a multichannel approach, you extend your reach and make it easier to influence the conversation.

In the event of a major crisis, it may be best to set up a dedicated web page or a microsite that focuses on the crisis. You can use all your channels to drive people to the dedicated page, which is much easier than answering every question again and again on Twitter, Facebook, your blog comment thread, and beyond. A dedicated web page or microsite should include the following:

- ✔ An acknowledgement of the crisis
- ✔ Verifiable details on the incident

✔ An explanation of how you found out about the situation

✔ Coverage of who has been alerted and when

✔ Effects of the crisis, both present and future

✔ Specific actions taken in response to the crisis, including steps to prevent recurrence

✔ Photos and video

✔ Contact information

A resource of this nature positions you to be the key source for information about the crisis, and it will be referenced by media. It also gives you a single place where you can keep all the related materials organized and controlled.

A dedicated web page or microsite has the added advantage of keeping the crisis from dominating your company's website or blog.

If building a specific web page or microsite isn't practical or simply isn't necessary, designate one social media channel (or your blog) as the official source of information. Post all detailed information to that one channel and point everything else to that channel. You want to avoid posting the same information multiple times, which increases your workload and creates increased chances for mistakes and misunderstandings. You don't need to create more potential messes that you may have to clean up!

Establishing credibility as a resource

A crisis can be a slippery thing. Particularly in the early stages of a crisis, accurate information can be hard to come by. You need to position yourself from the beginning as an accurate and reliable source of information. Taking a transparent approach that emphasizes facts, even if those facts are detrimental to your firm, positions you as a trusted source and helps prevent misconceptions and incorrect interpretations.

The emphasis is on facts — not rumors or things you think may be true but can't verify. Few things are worse than having to retract previous statements, admit you were wrong, and try to rebuild trust. Mistakes happen, and sometimes you have to revise previous statements, but if you take a firm position from the start to endorse only verifiable information, you can minimize embarrassments.

Maintaining transparency aids you in your efforts to establish your credibility with people. People want the real story, and they don't expect perfection.

It's better to be up-front about things, which is easy to do. Statements like the following show transparency:

- ✔ We are aware of the situation. We're posting updates as we get more information. For the most recent information, go to [URL for primary site for crisis information].
- ✔ We anticipate that the following difficulties may affect you.
- ✔ Here's what we're doing to solve this problem.
- ✔ We are taking steps to prevent this from happening again. Here's what we plan to do.
- ✔ We welcome your feedback on this situation and our efforts to address it.

Asking questions of your audience

It's almost an anathema to suggest asking your audience questions about the situation, but in a world of almost a billion Facebook users and about half a billion Twitter users, it's silly not to think of your audience members as resources. If you need information now, or if you need to verify information, there's nothing wrong with asking whether anyone has knowledge that will help.

Typically, you ask your audience for information when you want physical observations on a scene. This sort of information, commonly referred to as situational intelligence, could include road conditions, what's happening at an event, the size and disposition of crowds, or whether emergency responders are on the scene — the sort of nonexpert information that you can readily verify by gathering reports from multiple sources.

Another situation in which it's good to ask questions relates to experiences with your products or personnel. By asking customers to share their experiences, you can find out whether a problem is common or what other problems people are experiencing.

The "wisdom of the crowd" is a bit of misnomer. As the intelligence community is fond of saying: Trust, but verify.

Owning the Discussion

Get involved in the discussion early, be consistently present, and be responsive. If you do only three things right, do those three, and you're likely to do fine. As stated earlier in the chapter, silence isn't an option, so you may as well try to own the discussion.

By taking the lead in the discussion, you'll be viewed positively by many people, including some of your detractors; even they have to admit that you didn't shy away from the controversy. Moreover, every firm has supporters among its stakeholders. When you provide a forum where people can interact with you, you'll find that some of your stakeholders come to your defense. If so, thank them, recognize them, and make them feel appreciated. By encouraging positive sources, you may even find that the good opinions outweigh the bad, and you help ensure that positive comments stay at the top of the discussion thread.

Always date and time-stamp your posts to prevent confusion, because some social media timelines aren't linear. Dating and time-stamping also make documenting your efforts much more complete — crucial should your legal team ever need to get involved.

By "owning the discussion," we mean that you exert a positive influence on the discussion and help maintain a productive tone. I'm not talking about draconian attempts to limit discussion, exclude critics, or delete criticisms. There's no doubt that sometimes dealing with a discussion during a crisis can be a challenge, but you have no viable alternative. If you're not taking an active role, you'll rapidly become a victim.

Leading the charge

One of your first statements on any crisis should be "We are aware [that this thing is happening]." Acknowledge the problem immediately, even if details have yet to emerge. If you don't, you're likely to be flooded with "Did you know. . .?" messages. Moreover, the sooner you can prove to people that you're on top of things and dedicated to addressing the issue, the more trust you establish.

Your channel for first response should be the channel where the news broke. After you make a statement there, move on to your other channels.

Your channels may be the first places where many people hear about the problem, which gives you a huge advantage. If you can be the one who tells people "There's a problem you need to know about, and here's what to do," you seize control before the momentum takes the situation out of your hands. You go from being on the defensive to being perceived as a concerned, proactive company. Put another way, you're no longer trying to cover your butt; you're trying to help people solve a problem.

After the first announcement, don't disappear for a long period. It's better to offer frequent updates, explaining when the audience can expect to know more. Keep up regular updates until the danger passes, and slow things down in the days that follow.

KitchenAid endured a social media crisis on Twitter by following these methods discussed. The crisis arose when the person who managed its Twitter account posted a personal message to the corporate account by accident. Figure 15-1 shows the message that went out on the company's Twitter account.

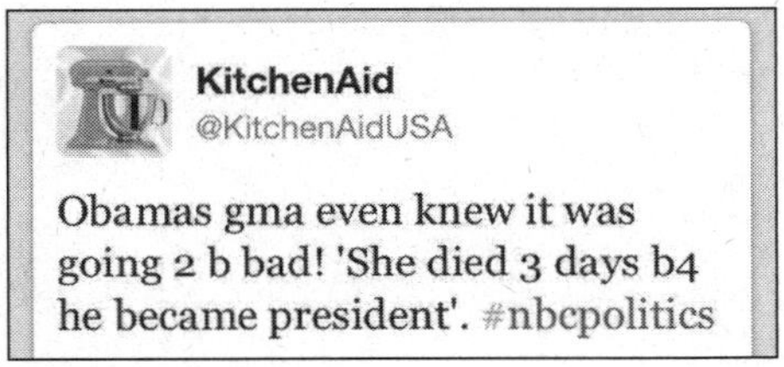

Figure 15-1:
The original KitchenAid tweet.

KitchenAid
@KitchenAidUSA

Obamas gma even knew it was going 2 b bad! 'She died 3 days b4 he became president'. #nbcpolitics

As you can imagine, the reaction to a message disrespectful of the president's dead grandmother wasn't good. A Twitter storm erupted.

KitchenAid wasted little time. It jumped on Twitter with tweets by the leader of the KitchenAid brand, Cynthia Soledad. Figure 15-2 shows the string of tweets she posted.

At the end of this crisis, KitchenAid came out fine. No serious harm was done to the brand, largely through timely intervention on the proper channel by a person who was clear and transparent, and owned up to the problem.

If you're dealing with an emergency or a major crisis, use the first posts to set a hashtag that people who track the event can follow. Declare this hashtag the official hashtag, and use it across channels. Although the hashtag may not be something you can set before the event, you can create a formula that will be applied, thereby removing any uncertainty from the process and speeding execution.

Preparing for tough questions

The very nature of a crisis means that people get upset. Some people may get very upset, and for them, social media is an amplifier. Be prepared for criticism and even anger. Expect it, anticipate it, and be ready to deal with it.

> **KitchenAid** @KitchenAidUSA   11h
> @Mashable My name is Cynthia Soledad, and I'm the head of
> KitchenAid. I'd like to talk on record about what happened. Please
> DM me. Thanks.
> Expand
>
> **KitchenAid** @KitchenAidUSA   11h
> That said, I take full responsibility for my team. Thank you for hearing
> me out.
> Expand
>
> **KitchenAid** @KitchenAidUSA   12h
> It was carelessly sent in error by a member of our Twitter team who,
> needless to say, won't be tweeting for us anymore.
> Expand
>
> **KitchenAid** @KitchenAidUSA   12h
> I would like to personally apologize to President @BarackObama, his
> family and everyone on Twitter for the offensive tweet sent earlier.
> Expand
>
> **KitchenAid** @KitchenAidUSA   12h
> Hello, everyone. My name is Cynthia Soledad, and I am the head of
> the KitchenAid brand.
> Expand
>
> **KitchenAid** @KitchenAidUSA   14h
> Deepest apologies for an irresponsible tweet that is in no way a
> representation of the brand's opinion. #nbcpolitics
> Expand

Figure 15-2:
The
KitchenAid
response.

Even when people aren't overtly angry and aggressive, they may ask tough questions. Don't shy away from engaging with these people. If they have questions, odds are that other people have the same questions and are watching to see how you reply. Be honest and up-front about any issues facing you or your company. If you made a mistake, admit it. If you don't know the answer to a question, say so. Your customers don't expect you to be perfect, but they do expect you to be honest and transparent, and that expectation isn't unreasonable.

When someone asks a tough question, take a moment to think before you respond. You need to formulate a thoughtful reply that responds to the question and doesn't create additional problems for you. Don't provide ambiguous responses, and don't lie.

After you provide an answer, it's critical to monitor the thread for reactions to your answer. You may have to engage with anyone who has further questions or who misunderstood what you said. In times of crisis, people tend to ask clarifying questions to confirm their understanding and to make sure that they're interpreting your comments correctly. You need to be there when those clarifying questions are asked. If you're able to respond quickly, you can often bring people peace of mind and close issues. The sooner you can close issues, the less likely they're to spin out of control.

Do we need to say this? Probably not, but we're going to say it anyway: Never lose your cool! You just can't take this stuff personally. You may disagree with people, but being rude or attacking is unacceptable.

The hidden gem during any crisis is the positive effect that solid responsiveness has on your brand reputation. Positive responses to negative questions can turn people around and change them from detractors to supporters. Your work in this area builds trust, which extremely valuable to your brand and generates strong positive word of mouth.

It's an ugly and inconvenient fact of life in the modern world, but people love to litigate. Protect your company by keeping detailed records of what happens during a crisis. Make copies of all tweets, status updates, comments, and blog posts. Keep copies of all emails. You may not need them, but if litigation results and you don't have these records, your legal team may be able to do little for you.

If things get really tough with a particular person on one of your social channels, try to take the discussion off the public channel. Encourage this person to contact you privately, or initiate the discussion yourself with a direct message. A fellow social media practitioner once said that she never responds to a detractor more than twice before offering to speak to them privately. That rule is a good rule of thumb. If the discussion takes more than two responses, see whether you can get the person to shift the discussion to direct messages, email, or even a phone call. In addition to getting the discussion off the public channel, direct interaction is more personal and gives the detractor a feeling that you're concerned and willing to engage with him individually to understand his specific concerns.

Apologizing when necessary

If people can forgive Exxon, Tiger Woods, Bill Clinton, Mike Tyson, and others, they can forgive you. The key is to say "I'm sorry." If your company has made a mistake, step up and ask for forgiveness — and mean it. The sooner you do, the better.

No matter how hard you try, you can't please everybody.

The reality is that people make mistakes, and when that happens, nothing beats the truth. It's best to have the guts to say, "We made an unfortunate mistake. We're terribly sorry, and it will never happen again." True, you may lose some fans, but what do you expect? You made a mistake. The majority of people, however, will forgive you, and you can move on. Some people may even respect you more for being human and for taking the high road.

If you need to issue an official apology, YouTube is a great place to issue it. A properly produced video by a known figure in your business can do wonders. Sincerity is key. An apology that's perceived as being halfhearted or false does more harm than good.

One of the most spectacular video apology failures occurred when TV personality Paula Deen released a poorly conceived 45-second apology video. (As one major news channel said, it bore "a striking resemblance to a hostage video.") That video was met with wide condemnation. Deen hastily pulled the video down and then almost immediately posted a second apology video. Unfortunately, the second video was only slightly better. Her career took a nosedive from which it has yet to fully recover.

When you post videos on YouTube, make sure that you select the option to moderate comments. Otherwise, things can go sideways quickly.

In contrast to the Paula Deen video apology fiasco, FedEx handled matters extremely well after a surveillance video surfaced showing a FedEx employee "delivering" a customer's fragile computer monitor by throwing it over the fence. This terrible situation had potential to do real harm to the brand. The video pulled in more than 4 million views the first week it was on YouTube.

Within days, FedEx posted a video apology from the senior vice president of U.S. operations, the leader of pickup and delivery operations across America. The apology was clear and unequivocal, and stated what responses had been taken by FedEx. The executive made no excuses and didn't try to sweep the problem under the rug, and in the end, his response served the company very well.

What to do when a crisis is over

After the crisis is resolved, you need to take some additional steps:

1. Mark the end of the crisis.

People need to know that the problem has been resolved, and they need to know what comes next. It's a good idea to publish an official statement by a senior person to wrap things up and explain the lessons learned. Where appropriate, also explain what the company is doing to prevent a recurrence of the problem. The message should also thank your supporters and members of your extended team.

2. Publish the wrap-up message on the channel you used to manage the crisis.

3. Monitor the wrap-up message closely over the next few days for any comments that require intervention.

If you have a microsite or a purpose-built page, leave it live for as long as it makes sense to do so. The only thing you can really do wrong is take it down too soon. When you decide to take the site or page down, make sure to archive it for internal purposes.

Part V
Building Your Social Media Presence

Followers

15,976 followers as of **1/12/2015** (days shown in Pacific time)

16.1K
12.1K
8,057
4,029
0

24 Sep   14 Jan   6 May   26 Aug   16 Dec   7 Apr   28 Jul   17 Nov

Interests
Most unique interests ⑦

69% Web design

67% Design

43% Graphics software

29% Marketing

26% Advertising

Top interests ⑦

73% Technology

69% Web design

67% Design

64% Tech news

43% Graphics software

39% Photography

35% Entrepreneurship

29% Marketing

28% Comedy (Movies and television)

26% Advertising

Location
Top countries and states

USA   UK
CA   TX   FL   NJ
NY   IND
   CAN
Other   ...
   IDN
   AUS

Top cities

5% New York City, US

3% Los Angeles, US

3% San Francisco, US

2% London, UK

2% Washington, D.C., US

Gender

72% M   28% F

Your followers also follow

45%   mashable · Profile

38%   ilovetypography · Profile

37%   TechCrunch · Profile

36%   abduzeedo · Profile

34%   DesignerDepot · Profile

32%   zeldman · Profile

30%   webdesignledger · Profile

30%   justcreative · Profile

30%   chrisspooner · Profile

For information on setting up a Hootsuite account, go to
www.dummies.com/go/socialmediaoptimization.

In this part . . .

- ✔ Making SMO part of your workflow
- ✔ Finding followers for your social media profiles
- ✔ Creating content with viral appeal
- ✔ Tracking your progress

Chapter 16

Integrating SMO into Your Workflow

*T*wo key ingredients of the social media recipe are consistency and perseverance. There's no point putting time and effort into establishing a social media presence if you allow your accounts to go radio-silent. Most people get into social media with the best intentions but find that over time, they make fewer and fewer posts. Soon, the cobwebs set in, and their social media presence is officially dead. All is not lost, though! The secret of avoiding common pitfalls is arming yourself with a plan.

This chapter explains how to start your social media endeavors with a solid plan to make sure that you're successfully set up to be in it for the long haul. We break down the most important factors in getting down to the nitty-gritty and staying on track. The chapter includes some great tools to help you manage your social media accounts. Finally, we provide pointers on how to ensure that social media doesn't overrun your life.

Planning for SMO

As the saying goes, if you fail to plan, you plan to fail. That's how the social media world is. It's not enough to set up your accounts, post a few times, and wait for the magic to happen. On the other hand, it's very easy to go overboard with your posts and end up burning yourself out. Neither option leads to a healthy social media presence.

If you put a little effort into mapping out how you want to approach and execute your social media plan from the beginning, you save yourself a lot of time and energy in the long run. It's easy to become discouraged if you're not seeing results quickly, but try to keep in mind that the turtle won the race, not the hare.

Target marketing on social media

You wouldn't walk into a room of urban gardeners and expect to sell fishing poles, would you? If you would, congratulate yourself on your amazing sales abilities! If you're like the rest of us, though, you know that you'd have an easier time getting leads if you walked in selling trowels or gardening gloves.

The same thing applies to social media. You have to know who your audience is and where they hang out online to gain access to them. How do you go about doing that, you ask? The first step is to have a clear objective. It's best to start with only one and follow it through to the point where you see measurable results. (We discuss measuring results later in the chapter.) Ask yourself what you want to accomplish by using social media. Some possible goals include

- ✔ Increasing brand awareness
- ✔ Driving traffic to your website
- ✔ Improving and/or increasing your customer service reach
- ✔ Growing sales

The social media channel where you should focus your attention (at least initially) depends on what your goal is. You may be thinking, "Of course I want to increase sales! Who doesn't?" But we urge you not to put the cart before the horse. People need to know you exist (brand awareness) before they can visit your website to buy something (growing sales). Building brand awareness is easier to do on some channels (such as Facebook and Twitter) than others (such as Pinterest); therefore, you know you should start with one of the former.

When you have your goal or objective, the next step is defining your target market. If you haven't completed this step yet, check out Chapter 4 for detailed information on identifying your target market.

Tailoring channel selection

When you decide what you want to accomplish with social media and who your target market is, the next step is figuring out where the people in that market hangs out on the Internet. To refer to the example earlier in this chapter, where would you put your social media efforts if your target audience comprises gardening enthusiasts? Ask yourself something like this: "If I were interested in gardening, what types of Internet sites would I frequent? What social media accounts, if any, would I follow?"

Leverage your existing customers; just ask them where they hang out online.

To answer those questions, you have to do some research. A good place to start is to check out what a few of your competitors are doing. The quickest way to find out what social media accounts your competitors have is to head on over to their websites and look for the social media tools discussed in Chapter 7 (see Figure 16-1). Do they have Facebook plug-ins or badges? Do they have Twitter and Google+ accounts? Click the available icons to be taken to the corresponding social media account pages.

Figure 16-1:
Check out
the social
media
accounts
of your
competitors.

When you're in a competitor's social media account, take note of a few things:

✔ Does this competitor post regularly? If so, what types of content are posted?

✔ How much interaction occurs? Do the posts get a lot of likes and shares, or frequent comments and @replies?

✔ Does the company do a good job of interacting with followers? Is the company consistently present in the conversations on its social media pages?

It's not necessarily the number of fans or followers a brand has that makes the brand successful in social media, but the quality and quantity of interactions with fans.

When you have answers to those questions, you can start narrowing down the social media channels that you want to spend your time and energy on. Your research may have turned up multiple social channels that your competitors use, but if you found that those accounts are full of cobwebs and crickets, it's a safe bet that those companies found those channels to be unworthy of their attention. The two biggies that most companies start with and find the most success with, regardless of their objectives, are Facebook and Twitter.

Have no fear, though. Social media is ever-evolving, and you'll be doing yourself a disservice if you don't give other applicable channels a chance at some point in the future. Just because you start with only one or two social media accounts doesn't mean that you can't expand after you acquire measurable success with your initial social media campaigns.

Pinterest, for example, works well when you have a more established online presence and have someplace to send Pinners (Pinterest users). If you have informative blog posts to link to, this service is worth a shot! (Chapter 10 explains how to make Pinterest work for your company.) Who knows — you may find success on a social media platform that your competitors didn't even bother trying!

Studying the performance of your posts

Social media is a 24/7 world, which stands to reason, because billions of people around the world are active on hundreds of social networking sites on a daily basis. In this always-on world, how do you know when to post?

First and foremost, take a look at your target market, and don't be afraid to make some general assumptions to give yourself a place to start. If your target market is stay-at-home moms with school-age children, chances are that they're not going to be on social media during the times when the kids are getting ready to go off to school or returning home. For these readers, dinnertime in general isn't a good time for social media posts.

Next, check out those research notes that you took when you were researching your competitors. (You took notes, right?) What times of day are those companies posting? Are there dates and times when their followers are more responsive and active on their accounts? If you have the answers to those questions, you should have a good idea of where to start with regard to the best times of day to post, so get posting! (See Chapter 3 for more information on tailoring your content to your audience and social media channels.)

When you have a week or so of posting different types of content under your belt, you have enough data to work with that you can really begin honing in on the best times to post, as well as the types of content that your target audience appreciates the most. Facebook and Twitter have built-in analytics, so you can try different approaches to test what works best for meeting your social media goals.

Facebook Insights

Facebook has a built-in analytics tool for all business Pages. This tool, called Insights (see Figure 16-2), is a robust analytics program, and the information that you mine from it's invaluable for planning and executing your social media content posting plan. Insights is visible only to Page administrators.

Facebook Insights specifically highlights three main areas: Page Likes, Post Reach, and Engagement. By picking up on any trends in Page visits and audience interaction (in the form of comments, likes, and shares), you can get an idea of when your target audience visits your page and what types of content they like (or don't like). Then you can adjust the types of content you post accordingly.

Analyzing Facebook Insights and making any necessary changes are very important tasks that you should do on a regular basis. If you don't analyze what you've done in the past, you're essentially flying blind when it comes to reaching your target audience.

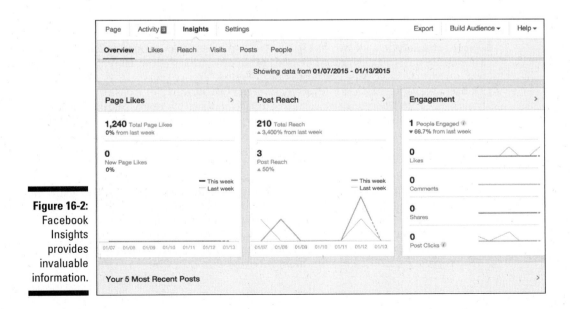

Figure 16-2:
Facebook Insights provides invaluable information.

To access Insights, follow these steps:

1. **Point your browser to www.facebook.com, and log in to your personal Facebook profile.**

   Every Facebook business Page must be connected to a personal profile.

2. **In the Pages section of the left sidebar, click the name of your Page.**

   You're immediately taken to your Page's timeline.

3. **At the top of the page, directly below the Facebook Search box, click the Insights tab.**

   You're taken to the Overview tab of your Insights dashboard (refer to Figure 16-2).

In the center of the page, you see three boxes: Page Likes, Post Reach, and Engagement. Clicking one of those headings takes you to a separate page with even more detailed information pertaining to that metric. You can also reach the detailed metric pages by clicking one of the six links below the menu bar that contains the Insights tab.

For more information on Facebook Insights, check out *Facebook Marketing For Dummies,* 5th Edition, by John Haydon, or *Facebook Marketing All-in-One For Dummies* by Andrea Vahl, John Haydon, and Jan Zimmerman (both from John Wiley & Sons, Inc.).

Twitter Analytics

Twitter Analytics, shown in Figure 16-3, isn't nearly as robust as Facebook Insights, but you can still mine a lot of helpful information from it to get a good idea of how your content is performing. You're given the typical, yet important, information offered by analytics programs: Impressions (how many people saw your tweet) and Engagements (how many people clicked your links, retweeted something of yours, favorited one of your tweets, and replied to you). Both statistics are important for deciding when and what to tweet about.

What Twitter offers users that Facebook Insights doesn't is below the Followers tab on the top menu bar. As you see in Figure 16-4, Twitter lists the top five unique interests of your followers, as well as their top ten general interests. The Most Unique Interests metric tells you the interests that are specific to your followers and what makes them different from the interests of the followers of other Twitter accounts. The Top Interests metric tells you the topics your followers are most interested in as a whole.

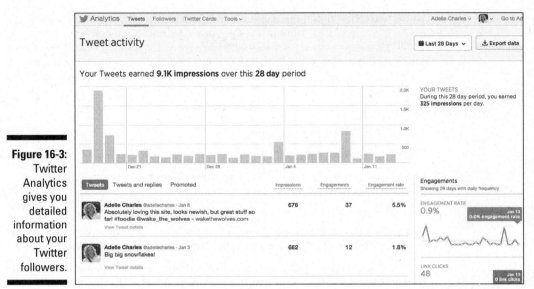

Figure 16-3:
Twitter Analytics gives you detailed information about your Twitter followers.

Interests column

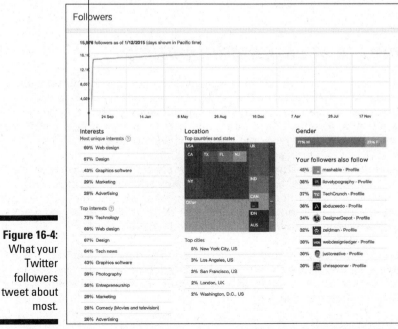

Figure 16-4:
What your Twitter followers tweet about most.

Combined with the Engagement data from the Tweets tab, this information is invaluable when it comes time to create your content. Now you have a good idea of the types of tweets your followers are most interested in and the times of day when they're most likely to see them. The idea is to give your followers what they want and are most interested in so they'll return for more.

Follow these steps to access Twitter Analytics:

1. **Log in to your Twitter account.**

   Your Twitter profile appears.

2. **Click your profile photo in the top-right corner of the page, and choose Analytics from the drop-down menu.**

   You go to your Tweet Activity home page.

3. **Click the tabs in the top-left corner of the page to toggle between your tweet analytics and detailed information about your followers.**

   Unless you have a Twitter advertising account, you don't have any need for the other two tabs — Twitter Cards and Tools — at this time.

For more information on Twitter Analytics, see *Social Media Marketing All-in-One For Dummies*, by Jan Zimmerman and Deborah Ng (John Wiley & Sons, Inc.) or the Twitter Analytics Help page at `https://support.twitter.com/articles/20171990-tweet-activity-dashboard`.

Defining a social media policy

If more than one person will be manning your social media accounts, it's important to draw up a social media policy that outlines your goals and expectations for conduct and for the types of information that gets posted. This policy should also include what company-related information employees can and can't post to their personal social media accounts.

Nothing is more cringeworthy than an employee's posting something that's offensive to your followers, leaving your company with quite a black eye. Granted, there's no way you can please every person all the time, but having some clear-cut guidelines on how to represent the company on social media goes a long way toward preventing a social media catastrophe.

Your social media policy should be in writing and should be signed by all employees — an important step to prevent "I didn't know that!" excuses in the future. Your policy should be specific to your company and industry, but here are some common examples:

✔ Any employee is free to associate himself with the company on social media provided that he brands his posts as personal and purely his own.

✔ Employees are forbidden to post any sensitive company information, such as trade secrets, legal, financial, or personnel information.

✔ Employees must uphold all intellectual-property rights.

✔ Employees should be careful when discussing sensitive subjects such as religion and politics, and should always conduct themselves in a respectful manner.

✔ Employees should be honest and transparent at all times. If they make mistakes, they should 'fess up and try to fix the problem.

As the landscape of social media evolves, you should adjust your social media policy to keep up with the changes. Revisit it frequently. Sticky situations such as off-color comments may arise, and you don't want anyone in your organization to tarnish your hard-won brand equity.

Mistakes will be made, and a few of your customers may become upset or offended by something that someone said or did. The most important thing you can do is own up to your "oops," apologize, and learn from your mistake.

Staying SMART

When you've defined your social media objectives, identified your target audience and found out where to find them on social media channels, used the data from analytics programs to determine the optimal time to be active on social media, and put a comprehensive social media behavior policy in place, you're ready to move forward to the next step in working search media optimization (SMO) into your workflow. You've put a lot of time, thought, and legwork into the research and planning you've done; now put your social media plan into action!

The next step in the process is something that marketing people everywhere call SMART marketing (specific, measurable, actionable, relevant, and time-related). Each of these points is described in the following sections.

Specific

The first step in defining your target audience (refer to "Target marketing on social media" earlier in this chapter) is setting the objective of your social media plan. You need to get more *specific* about that objective to clear away any fuzziness or ambiguity.

Grab a piece of paper and a pen, and then answer the five Ws:

- ✔ **What** do you want to accomplish with your social media accounts?
- ✔ **Why** is it important to accomplish this goal? What benefits will you realize if you do?
- ✔ **Where** on social media will you seek these goals?
- ✔ **Who** will be involved in accomplishing these goals?
- ✔ **When** will you know that you've met your goals?

Adding a "how" question and breaking your plan into steps helps you measure your progress as you go along (see the next section).

Measurable

Your goals should be measurable. How are you and your team supposed to know whether you've made any progress toward your goal if you have nothing to measure? Think of measuring goals as the before-and-after picture of your objective — how things looked before you began your social media journey and what they look like when you reach your first benchmark (at a time of your choosing). We recommend that you give your activities at least a month to take effect before checking to see how far you've come toward your goal.

Making your goals measurable goes along with the "When" question in the preceding section. Setting benchmarks shows you exactly how far you've come toward your goal and exactly how far you have to go. Measuring keeps your team on track, and you can make small adjustments as needed to make sure that your plan is moving forward smoothly.

These benchmarks depend on your overall objective, but they should be quantifiable. Here are some examples:

- ✔ How much have your website visits increased?
- ✔ How many more people have Liked your Facebook page since you started posting more often?
- ✔ How many more retweets have you had since you started tweeting more photos and videos?
- ✔ By how much have your sales increased since you've ramped up your social media efforts?

Using the analytics programs discussed in "Studying the performance of your posts" earlier in this chapter is a good place to start quantifying your progress.

Attainable

It's important to set realistic objectives. Getting 5,000 new Facebook followers in a month isn't very realistic, but getting 50 or 100 new followers in a month is. If you keep your goals reasonable (and therefore attainable), you and your employees will gain the confidence to keep pushing forward when you reach one benchmark and see that you're well on your way to meeting your ultimate goal — or, even better, that you've already reached it.

The flip side of that coin is that you have to be careful not to set the bar too low. A goal of gaining five new Facebook followers in a month is a pretty low goal, especially if you've been working hard to post appropriate content. Chances are that you could get that many new followers in a day or two, so your team really has no incentive to push themselves if they know that reaching the goal is going to be easy-peasy.

 It's okay to occasionally revise your idea of what's realistic for your team as you get more and more comfortable with social media. If you find that one benchmark is approaching a lot faster than you thought it would, feel free to extend the time to reach the benchmark a little to give your team more of a challenge. If you find yourself doing that frequently, however, it's time to revise your idea of what's realistic.

Relevancy

The *R* in *SMART* deals with the relevancy of your goals. If you sell fishing equipment, but your objective is to make sure that you clean out your email inbox by the end of the day, you're seriously lacking relevance. That example is an extreme one, of course, but the idea here is the irrelevance of that benchmark to your SMO goals.

Relevance covers a few aspects of your goal. It's important to answer questions like the following:

- ✔ Does this goal align with the long-term plans for the business?
- ✔ Is now a good time to pursue this objective?
- ✔ Do the ends justify the means? In other words, is all this time and effort going to pay off?
- ✔ Are the people who are involved the right people for the job?

If an objective isn't relevant to the current state of your company, it's going to lose steam quickly or — worse — turn out to be a waste of time and money.

Time-based

Having a timeline goes hand in hand with making your objective measurable, attainable, and realistic. You know how you're going to measure the progress and success of your social media efforts. You've made sure that you have attainable goals to keep progress moving forward, and you're confident that these goals are realistic for your company. But how long should you let your social media efforts continue before deciding that everything was a success or a failure?

In the earlier section titled *Measurable*, we recommended you keep your efforts going for at least a month. Social media is a slow burn. There are ups and downs. You have to stick with it, be patient, and not get discouraged if you get ten likes one day and don't get any more likes for the next five days. You have to be in social media for the long haul.

That said, it's important to set time-frame goals, which vary depending on your objectives. Here are some examples:

- ✔ How long do I give our effort to work before I designate it to be a success or a failure?
- ✔ If this effort doesn't pan out, is it worth revisiting six months from now or next year?
- ✔ Is it realistic to expect to see at least small changes on a weekly basis?
- ✔ What activities do we need to do every day?

Managing Multiple Social Profiles

When you're up and running with your social media accounts (if not, what are you waiting for?), you should get acquainted with some helpful online tools that keep your Facebook timeline and tweets straight and organized.

Some of these tools are more robust than others. Some are free; others charge a fee. All are invaluable for managing your social media profiles.

Hootsuite

Hootsuite (`https://hootsuite.com`) is an online social management dashboard. You connect your social media accounts to Hootsuite to control them from one central location. Hootsuite connects with more than 35 social networks, including Twitter, Facebook, Google+, Instagram, YouTube, LinkedIn, and Foursquare.

Hootsuite offers three subscription plans: a free one that manages up to 3 social profiles; a Pro plan that manages more than 50 social profiles and starts at $9.99 a month; and an Enterprise version made for large entities such as government agencies, corporations, and large organizations. The free option is perfect for companies that are just starting out in social media or that have few social profiles to manage.

One cool feature of Hootsuite gives you the ability to schedule posts ahead of time. That feature sounds like social media nirvana, right? Well, it is, and isn't. Scheduling posts is extremely convenient if you're going to be away from your social media accounts for a couple of days, but it's not wise to preload, say, a week's worth of social media posts and then walk away. Read more about post scheduling in "Use scheduling software. . . carefully" later in this chapter.

Hootsuite has built-in analytics (albeit fairly limited ones) with the free sub-scription. The service has ten report options, but only three are available in free accounts: Twitter Profile Overview, which shows things like follower growth and your most popular (unshortened) links; Facebook Page Overview, which shows your daily likes and daily post engagement; and the Ow.ly Click Summary report, which reports how many times your Ow.ly links were clicked. Users who have the free subscription are allowed to pull only two reports per month.

Figure 16-5 shows the free version of the Facebook Summary Report. Though it's better than nothing, if your main social media accounts are Facebook and Twitter, you'd get more out of sticking with those services' built-in analytics packages.

Ow.ly is Twitter's built-in URL shortener. If you prefer to use another URL shortening service, such as Bitly (`https://bitly.com`), Hootsuite doesn't keep track of analytics data such as link clicks and shares.

Figure 16-5:
Hootsuite gives you a basic snapshot of your Facebook Page statistics.

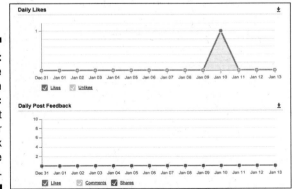

Signing up for a free Hootsuite account is easy. Just follow these steps:

1. **Point your browser to `https://hootsuite.com`, and click the green Sign Up button in the top-right corner.**

   You're taken to the page that explains the different options.

2. **Click the green Get Started Now button in the Free Subscription column.**

3. **On the resulting page, enter your email address, full name, and password, and choose your time zone from the drop-down menu.**

4. **Click Create Account.**

5. **Choose which three social media accounts you want to link to your Hootsuite account.**

   The choices are Twitter, Facebook, LinkedIn, your Google+ Page, and Foursquare. Each time you click one of the social network buttons, a box pops up, asking you to authorize Hootsuite to access that account. Go through this process for each account you want to add.

   As you add your social media accounts, keep an eye on the dial on the right side of the page. This counter estimates the amount of time you'll save each day, week, and year when you use Hootsuite to manage your accounts.

6. **After you add three accounts, click the Finish Adding Social Networks button.**

7. **When prompted, add another email address, or click the Skip This for Now link at the bottom of the window.**

8. **In the Welcome window that pops up, click the Get Started button.**

   Success! You have a Hootsuite account. The tutorial walks you through the intricacies of your dashboard (see Figure 16-6).

Other free tools for social profile management

Although Hootsuite is a popular social media management option, several other free platforms are available. The following sections cover some of the options.

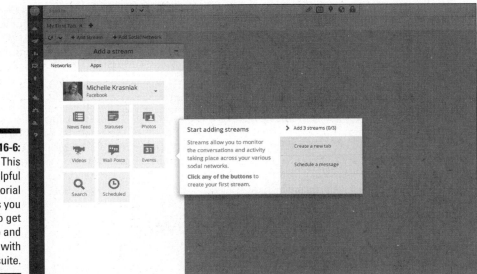

Figure 16-6:
This helpful tutorial shows you how to get up and running with Hootsuite.

TweetDeck

TweetDeck (`https://about.twitter.com/products/tweetdeck`) is a management platform for your Twitter account. You can get apps for Mac, Windows, iOS devices, Android devices, and the Google Chrome browser. With TweetDeck, you can do things such as manage multiple accounts, schedule tweets, filter, and search tweets and usernames.

SumAll

SumAll (`https://sumall.com`) is a robust account-management platform that enables you to connect 56 accounts to one dashboard. What's unique about SumAll is that in addition to letting you manage Twitter and Facebook accounts, it allows you to connect financial and e-commerce accounts. If you're a seller on eBay, for example, you can connect your eBay account and your PayPal account to manage all transactions from one convenient location. SumAll offers a free plan and a Premium plan that costs $9 per month.

Everypost

Everypost (`http://everypost.me`) claims to be one of the most robust mobile social account management apps. It's available for both Android and iOS devices and through its website. You can connect one account per social media network. Everypost supports Facebook, Twitter, Google+, LinkedIn, Pinterest, and Tumblr. A free version lets you schedule up to ten posts a month, and a paid version costs $10 per month or if you decided to pay yearly, you get a discount and the cost is $100 per year. With the paid version, you get an unlimited number of scheduled posts.

SocialOomph

With both free and paid ($40 per month) versions, SocialOomph (www.socialoomph.com) enables you to schedule posts to Facebook, Twitter, LinkedIn, and your blog. The free plan lets you connect up to five social media accounts per network; the paid version lets you connect an unlimited number of accounts.

Commercial tools for social profile management

The larger the company, the more complicated the SMO plan tends to be. That's why having a social profile management tool with more robust features comes in handy. Just keep in mind that extra features bring higher prices.

Sprout Social

Sprout Social (http://sproutsocial.com) offers three levels of subscriptions starting at $60 per month per user, with a 30-day free trial. All levels include what Sprout Social calls a "Smart Inbox," which aggregates all your messages from connected social media accounts into one manageable stream. You'll never miss another Mention.

Crowdbooster

With Crowdbooster (http://crowdbooster.com), you get recommendations about the most optimal time to post so that you can get the most engagement from your followers. You have access to real-time data so you can immediately see whether you need to change your content, for example. Crowdbooster offers a free 30-day trial; subscriptions start at $9 per month.

Postling

With Postling (`https://www.postling.com`), you schedule posts from an intuitive, all-in-one dashboard. Stay on top of conversations by having Postling bring in all comments from your social media accounts so you can see and respond to them from one convenient location. The price is $1 for the first 30 days; then paid plans start at $99 per month.

Sendible

Take advantage of the free 30-day trial that Sendible (`http://sendible.com`) offers to monitor, in real time, what's being said about your brand. It offers powerful analytics reporting across multiple social platforms so you'll always know how your content is doing and where improvements are needed. After the free trial, plans start at $60 per month.

The power of cross-posting

Few people have the time to create a brand-spanking-new piece of quality content for every social media network they use. Sure, it helps to share other people's content (with permission, of course) and to retweet links, but there's really nothing like content created from scratch.

These days, it's common, and maybe even expected, for content creators to share (relevant) posts across all their social networks. Every day, you may see the same content popping up in your Twitter stream; then it shows up in your Facebook News Feed; and finally, you see it in your LinkedIn feed.

Social media marketing professionals look for ways to maximize the effect of every post they create. That's why the social account management options discussed earlier in this chapter are so great. With little effort, you can post to all your connected accounts simultaneously. Figure 16-7 shows a business owner using cross-posting for her Twitter, Google+, and Facebook accounts. She knows that her target markets are spread over those three social networks, so she cross-posts her content to reach as many people as possible.

Figure 16-7: Cross-posting on Twitter (top), Google+ (center), and Facebook (bottom).

Figure used with permission of Julie Gray

Keeping Control of Your Social Media Life

It's easy to be swept up into the tide of instant gratification: getting your news as it's breaking, tweeting to or posting on the Facebook Page of a company and getting a response within minutes, posting fresh blog content to your Facebook Page and getting Likes or shares within minutes. Having positive responses virtually instantaneously is intoxicating, but this prompt feedback can also cause problems in your personal life in areas such as work/life balance. News outlets including CBS and The Huffington Post have run stories about how social media can ruin relationships. When we're out with a loved one and keep checking our Twitter feed or posting pictures to Instagram, for example, we're not present in the moment or paying attention to the person we're with. We're essentially ignoring them. How rude!

People who use social media for business purposes are sometimes given a little more leeway when it comes to letting social media infiltrate their lives outside work. After all, *social media is their job*. That doesn't make this infiltration into their personal lives acceptable, though. Fret not! You have ways to ensure that your social media life stays separate from your real life.

Set boundaries for SMO

As our mothers tried to teach us, there's a place and time for everything. SMO doesn't have to be everywhere at all times, and it shouldn't be! It may be tough to pull yourself away from your accounts at first, but you'll be better for doing so in the long run. Trust us.

Here are some ways to structure your social media life to make it more manageable:

- ✔ **Set aside a regular chunk of time for SMO, and stick to it**. Block out a chunk of time during the day to attend to your social media accounts. That chunk of time could be 30 minutes every 3 or 4 hours, or it could be 1 hour right when you come in every morning and right before you leave for the day. Test different times, and see what works best for you.

  We can't stress the "stick to it" part enough, but you must remain flexible. You'll have distractions at times, but stick with the length of time you decided on.

- ✔ **Delegate when you can.** If possible, hand the reins to your social media accounts over to a trusted colleague or employee. Doing so will allow you to turn your attention to other responsibilities, and it's good to get a fresh pair of eyes on what's going on in your company's social media world. Who knows — another person may have some great insight into ways to improve your SMO practices.

✔ **When other people are involved, put electronic devices away.** If you're in a meeting, at dinner with your spouse, or at your kid's soccer game, put your phone away. Put it in a desk drawer or a pocket, or leave it in the car. If you're in your office, turn your computer's sound and screen off. Show your visitors that you're present and care about what they have to say. Remove the temptation, and you won't feel the urge to look at your screen every time you hear the ding that signals a new tweet or blog comment.

✔ **If it's time to sign off, sign out.** Some of us have a hard time resisting the temptation to take a quick peek at what's going on out in the world of social media. If you're one of those people, we recommend that you sign out of your accounts and, if possible, shut your phone off, even if for only an hour or so. You may find that unplugging helps you relax more.

Let mobile apps help you

Taking your SMO endeavors on the road with you isn't *all* bad. At times when you're away from your computer, you realize that you're approaching your scheduled social media time, and — because you're so gosh-darn dedicated — you sign on to check out what's going on.

At other times, you may be at a marketing or tech conference where the organizers actually encourage attendees to stay connected. They may even provide with a specific hashtag to use on Twitter to make it easier to group updates from the different attendees.

The point is that sometimes you'll want to sign into your SMO accounts from your mobile device. Following are some helpful apps to help you do just that. You can find these apps in Apple's App Store or Google Play.

Buffer

Available for iOS and Android devices, Buffer is a comprehensive social account management dashboard. With both free and paid ($102 per year) accounts, Buffer lets you update multiple social media accounts from one convenient location (see Figure 16-8). You can also schedule updates to go out at a future time.

Facebook Pages Manager

Stay up to date on what's happening with your Facebook Page. You can do things like read messages, see how many new page likes you've received, and check out your post engagement stats. You can also compose messages and respond to comments. This app is available for free for both iOS and Android devices.

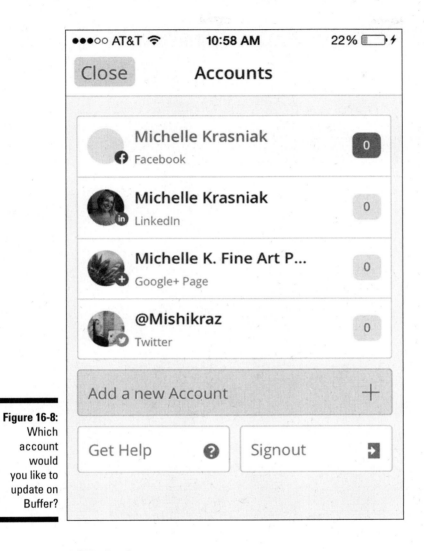

Figure 16-8:
Which account would you like to update on Buffer?

WiFi Finder

Heaven forbid that a team member sends out an inappropriate tweet or Facebook post while you're away from the office! If someone does however, WiFi Finder is a great way to get "plugged back into" your social media dashboards so you can mitigate any potential damage as soon as possible. This free app for iOS and Android devices shows you — in list or map view — the free and paid Wi-Fi hotspots in your vicinity. You can type in an address, or the app can find your approximate location by using the GPS feature of your phone. You can filter by service provider or select preferred locations such as coffee shops or libraries (see Figure 16-9).

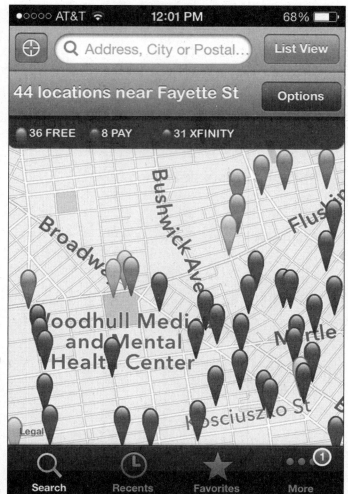

Figure 16-9:
Quickly find Wi-Fi hotspots near you with the WiFi Finder app.

Photo Editor by Avery

Photo Editor by Avery is a free app for iOS and Android devices. Use this app to apply fancy filters, add text, or give your photos frames. You can take a photo through the app, using your phone's built-in camera, or select an existing photo from your phone's camera roll. This app has one of the most comprehensive set of photo editing tools in any mobile app. When you finish editing your photo, you can share it on numerous social media channels, or you can send it via text or email. You can even send the print to a drugstore to get developed.

Republish to fill in the gaps

In the earlier section "The power of cross-posting," we talk about how helpful it is to cross-publish content to different social media channels to get the most bang for your buck. You can also republish content. Nothing is wrong with posting the same link to a recent blog post of yours, provided that you don't do it once an hour and that it's *all* you post. It's generally acceptable to repost the same content once a week for the first month and then maybe once every other month. That way, you get more mileage out of your content without annoying your followers and fans with the same content over and over.

You can also share other pages' content or retweet a link posted by another Twitter user. Luckily, Facebook and Twitter make it easy to give credit to the original sources. Be sure to always keep the content originator's username in your post so it doesn't look like you're trying to plagiarize someone else's content.

Use scheduling software. . . carefully

Being able to schedule social media posts ahead of time may seem like the bee's knees and the solution to all your time management issues. You should use this capability with caution, however.

All the social account management tools covered in the earlier section "Managing Multiple Social Profiles" offer post-scheduling capabilities because scheduling is a common practice these days. Scheduling helps keep social media accounts fresh and active even when a live person isn't manning them. These tools save time (except for some time on the front end scheduling the posts); they allow you to turn your attention elsewhere, focusing on more pressing issues; and they may even save you some money if you've been thinking about hiring a person whose sole job would be to manage your SMO.

What these tools won't do is automatically cancel posts if, for example, a natural disaster strikes somewhere else in the world. If a scandal arises in your corporation, for example, your scheduled posts don't pick up on that scandal and adjust content accordingly. You're essentially leaving the state of your brand in the hands of the universe, and you can look like you don't care about anything but what's happening in your business if you are still posting about your latest sale or blog article while something awful is happening somewhere in the world.

Here's an unfortunate example. On April 13, 2013, two bombs went off during the Boston Marathon, killing three people and injuring more than 260 others. Social media guru Guy Kawasaki illustrated the negative side of using Twitter automation when his account continued to post links to his blogs and other marketing messages, while the Twitterverse was lit up with news updates and tweets about the unthinkable tragedy. Failing to turn off his auto-posting feature resulted in him looking very insensitive, and people weren't afraid to let him know that.

Keeping Up with the Social World

Myspace was the largest social networking site from 2005 to 2008, surpassing even Google at one point. But just six years later, Myspace found themselves in 392nd place on the list of most visited websites in the United States.

The problem was that over time, users wanted bigger and better and faster and cooler-looking, and Myspace couldn't keep up with those demands. Other social networking sites like Facebook could, and we all know how that turned out.

Social media users are constantly on the hunt for the newest thing, whether that thing is the hottest website, tech gadget, or fashion trend. Brands rise and fall at breakneck speed. How do you keep up? The bad news is that you really don't. The good news is it's not hard to follow closely behind. How do you manage the complexity of this shifting landscape?

Luckily, several sites can do all the legwork for you. To know what's going on in the social world, all you have to do is log on to the Internet and head to one of these sites:

- **Mashable** (`http://mashable.com`): One of the most popular sites for social media users, Mashable reports on everything from technology and social media to business and world news.

- **CNET** (`www.cnet.com`): Head over to CNET for technology news for business-oriented readers. This site is a great place to go for computer-related news.

- **TechCrunch** (`http://techcrunch.com`): Another popular news source, TechCrunch offers Web 2.0-centric content. If something is happening on the Internet and trending on Twitter, it's most likely on the front page of TechCrunch.

- **Geek.com** (`www.geek.com`): If you love to be on the front lines of the latest hardware, software, and mobile device releases, be sure to bookmark Geek.com.

- **Social Media Examiner** (`www.socialmediaexaminer.com`): This site is all social media, all the time. Some big names in the social media marketing world write for this site, so you're sure to be kept up to date on the ins and outs of SMO.

- **MarketingProfs** (`www.marketingprofs.com`): Online marketing folks should have this site on speed-dial. It does a great job of keeping you up to date on the latest tips and trends in marketing in the social media age.

Chapter 17

Finding Your Followers

. . . .

. . . .

This chapter is for those people who are ready to dive into the task of finding their audience on social media. After all, social media isn't very social if no one is listening to what you're saying.

This chapter describes how to find a social media audience that you didn't even know you had. We show you how to leverage your existing network to get the word out about your company. We show you that Facebook is an important and invaluable tool for finding and engaging with your target audience by different methods, including Facebook ads. The chapter explains the importance of nurturing your Twitter relationships and the importance of finding the right followers to help make your search media optimization (SMO) plan a success.

Finding an Audience You Didn't Know You Had

One thing that those new to SMO may not realize is that *everyone* has an audience. That's right, everyone. If you think back to when you were knee-high, and you donned your superhero cape or lined up your stuffed animals for an impromptu performance of a scene from the latest Disney movie, you had an audience. Sure, your audience may have been filled with stuffing, but the point is that you were being watched, and you acted accordingly.

Now, we're not saying that finding an audience for your SMO accounts is going to be as easy as opening your closet and gathering your stuffed friends (if only). Finding followers is going to take some research, some effort, and some trial and error, but you'll get there. We promise. Locating your audience is just a matter of looking at things from a different point of view.

Turning everyone into a salesperson

Chapter 4 talks about some ways of finding new fans and mavens by engaging in online communities, and Chapter 13 talks about how you can establish expertise to gain the trust of people online with the ultimate goal of becoming the go-to resource whenever they had a question or need something having to do with your specialty. If you've been following our advice closely, you have a healthy following on your social media accounts. Now's the time to go back to those followers, use them to grow your community, and turn them into salespeople. You can do this in a few ways, none of which is a high-pressure tactic. Don't worry about angering or offending anyone.

Just ask

This first method of turning everyone into a salesperson is asking everyone to be one. No, we don't mean post job notices on Facebook or Twitter looking for a few good people. Chapter 13 describes how to ask for recommendations on LinkedIn. Take those methods and apply them to Facebook and Twitter. Ask your existing customers to write online reviews or testimonials to highlight the quality service they received from you. Reviews are generally left on sites like Yelp (see Chapter 14), and testimonials are typically longer, more detailed accounts of customer experiences that you put on your website. See Figure 17-1 for examples of testimonials on a website. Reviews and testimonials go a long way toward showing prospective customers that you have a history of providing exceptional customer service.

Be sure the customers from whom you're requesting testimonials and reviews are happy customers.

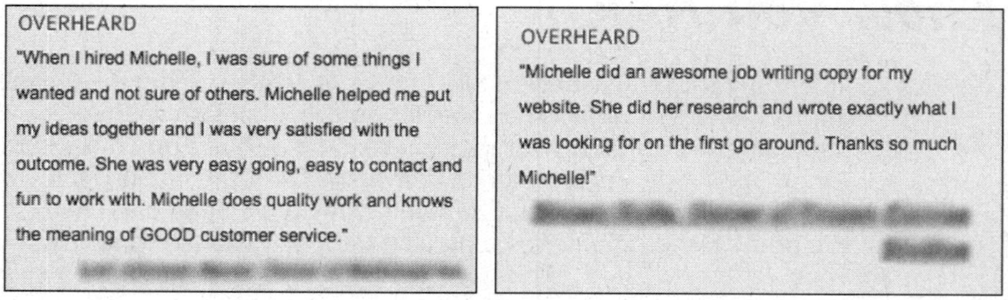

Figure 17-1:
Two customer testimonials on a website.

> OVERHEARD
>
> "When I hired Michelle, I was sure of some things I wanted and not sure of others. Michelle helped me put my ideas together and I was very satisfied with the outcome. She was very easy going, easy to contact and fun to work with. Michelle does quality work and knows the meaning of GOOD customer service."

> OVERHEARD
>
> "Michelle did an awesome job writing copy for my website. She did her research and wrote exactly what I was looking for on the first go around. Thanks so much Michelle!"

Give them a reason to help you

Referral rewards are great ways to entice your existing customers to spreading the word about your company and services. It's very common for businesses to offer coupons and discounts to people who send family and friends their way. We frequently purchase items and services based on referrals from people we know, so we trust their judgment on the quality of what we're purchasing. It's also a common practice to offer referral rewards to both the referrer and the person being referred. In Figure 17-2, Discover promotes its friend referral program in a Facebook post.

Use word-of-mouth marketing techniques

Word-of-mouth marketing has become so popular these days that the topic has its own trade association (www.womma.org). According to a study done by Nielsen, 92 percent of consumers trust recommendations and endorsements over traditional advertising.

The idea behind word-of-mouth marketing is that you provide your customers something, and in exchange, they shout from the rooftops how wonderful you're. The something can be anything from out-of-this-world customer service to free samples.

Figure 17-2:
Discover's
referral
program.

BzzAgent (www.bzzagent.com), a leading word-of-mouth marketing site, runs what are called BzzCampaigns, providing members (called BzzAgents) free products and services with the idea that the agents will review them and (ideally) spread the word via online reviews and social media points and by handing out the provided coupons. Each BzzCampaign is targeted to a specific audience identified through surveys BzzAgents routinely take. Figure 17-3 shows an example of a campaign invitation.

Figure 17-3: An example BzzAgent campaign invitation.

 You have even less control of who reviews your product than you do when you solicit support from people you know. Although you may reach a wider audience by using this method, you also run the risk of getting more negative reviews.

Encouraging your friends to invite others

Everyone is willing to help out a friend, right? When you take into consideration your network of friends, your friends' network of friends, and so on, the number of people you could be connected to grows exponentially.

Having this many people at your disposal is an invaluable resource in getting others to turn into salespeople for you. Facebook, Twitter, and LinkedIn make it easy for you to get your existing friends to introduce their contacts to your products or services.

Don't hound your friends. Ask them to help you once; then maybe send a reminder a week or so later. That's as far as you should go. If your friends are willing to reach out to their networks, they do it within a week.

Using Facebook

Facebook makes it easy for admins of business Pages to share their Pages with their existing connections. In fact, an admin can share his Pages *only* with people he's currently connected to on Facebook. Can you imagine what would happen if business Page admins were allowed to reach out to each and every Facebook user? Pandemonium would ensue, we're sure.

Sharing your Facebook Page with your friends is easy. Just follow these steps:

1. **Log in to Facebook.**

2. **In the Pages section in the left column, click the name of the Page you want to share.**

   You're on your Page's Timeline.

3. **Click the button with the three dots on the right side of the page and choose Share from the drop-down menu.**

   The button is located below your cover photo.

4. **In the dialog box that appears, click the drop-down menu to choose where you want to share the Page.**

   Your options are on your own Timeline, on a friend's Timeline, in a group you belong to, on a Page you manage, or in a private message to on of your Facebook friends.

   - *On your own Timeline:* Your Page is shared on your Personal Profile page.

   - *On a friend's Timeline:* Your Page is shared on a friend's profile. You can select only one friend at a time.

   - *In a Group:* Your Page is shared on the Timeline of a Facebook Group that you belong to.

   - *On a Page you manage:* If you're the admin of more than one Page, you have to first select whatever Page you want to share to. See Figure 17-4 for an example of posting on another Page.

5. **Type a message saying why your friends should Like this Facebook Page.**

   This step is optional, but it's a good idea to let your friends know why you think they'll enjoy the Page. Be sure to ask them to share it with their friends.

6. **Click the blue Share Page button.**

   That's it. You've shared your Facebook Page with your friends.

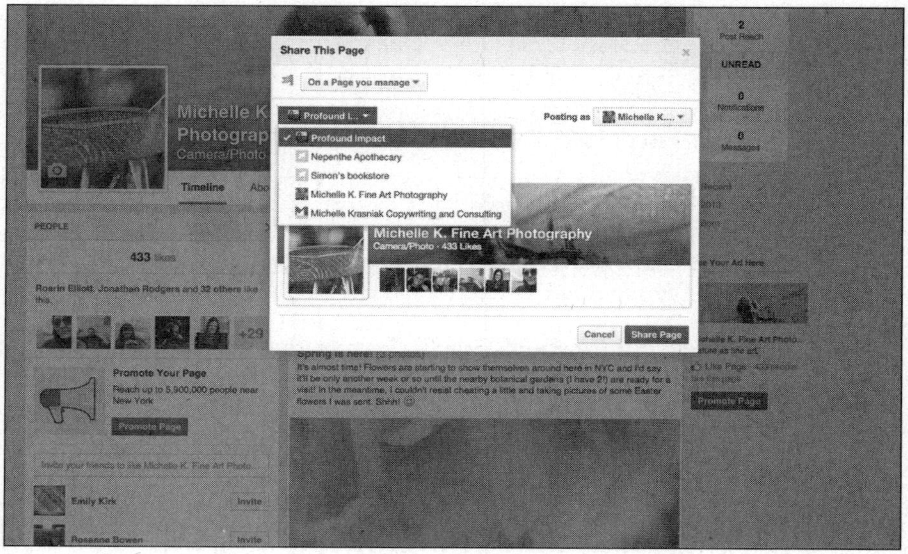

Figure 17-4:
Posting about your Page on a different Page you administrate.

Making connections through Twitter

If you follow someone on Twitter (and she follows you back), there's a good chance that you have a lot in common with that person. Maybe you're in the same profession, or you both love to read. Using a Twitter connection is a great way to get introductions to that person's followers. Just as that person has something in common with you, you probably have something in common with her Twitter followers. Introductions from your existing connections are quick and easy ways to grow your network.

It's a good idea to make a list of Twitter users that you would like an introduction to before asking your friend to make the connections. That way, you can ensure that any new Twitter contacts will be beneficial additions to your network.

Here are things to keep in mind when asking for Twitter introductions:

✔ Decide what angle you want your Twitter connection to use when making the introduction. Make sure that this angle aligns with your SMO goals.

✔ Do your research. Have a list of a few of your friend's Twitter followers to whom you'd like introductions.

✔ Offer to write the tweet for your friend to use to introduce you. It's often tricky to say everything you want to in only 140 characters. At the very least they will appreciate the offer.

✔ Be sure to acknowledge the introduction tweet immediately by thanking your friend and greeting the new contact.

✔ If you haven't done so already, by all means follow the new contact.

✔ Wait to get a reply from the other party before reaching out to him or her again. You don't want to seem to be badgering that person.

✔ After your new contact replies, try to keep the conversation going by asking open-ended questions. People love talking about themselves.

✔ Don't be afraid to ask the new contact for introductions after you've established a friendly rapport. Offer to do the same for him.

Harnessing the power of introductions on LinkedIn

Because LinkedIn is a social network that is geared to professionals, the service makes it easy for you to expand your network by giving users the capability to make new professional connections.

LinkedIn provides a link directly below the picture of the person you're requesting an introduction to. The caveat is that you have to have at least one second-degree connection with that person. In other words, at the very least, both of you have to be connected to the same person.

It's a good idea to send your connection a note ahead of time asking whether he'd be willing to make the introduction. He may be hesitant to do so for some reason. Maybe he doesn't have the best relationship with that particular connection, or maybe he doesn't know that person well. You never know about other people's connections, so it's wise to ask ahead of time.

After your LinkedIn connection agrees to make the introduction, you can act. Here's how to formally request an introduction on LinkedIn:

1. **Log in to LinkedIn.**

2. **Search for your existing connection by using the search box at the top of the page or click the Connections link directly below it.**

   If you use the search box, you get search results containing every LinkedIn member who has that name. Clicking the Connections link takes you to the page that lists all your connections. Find your contact either by using that page's search function or filtering the results.

3. **Click the name of your contact.**

   You're on her profile page.

4. **Click the blue number to the right of your contact's profile picture.**

   This number shows how many LinkedIn connections your friend has. You are automatically taken to the Connections section of your contact's profile.

5. **Click the magnifying glass icon on the top right of the Connections section, type a keyword related to your SMO, and then press Enter.**

   For example, if you run an automotive repair shop, then you'd type **car** into that box to single out her connections that use the word "car" in their profiles.

6. **Click a person's name to be taken to her profile.**

7. **Read the profile to make sure that the person is someone you'd like to network with.**

   Though there's a Connect button next to that person's name, we advise you not to click it. Instead, go for the introduction. You're much more likely to get a meaningful connection if you're introduced by a mutual friend.

8. **Click the Get Introduced link below the new connection's name on the right side of the page.**

   This box uses a flow chart to show how you're connected to this person. If you have any skills and expertise in common with this person, you see a big circle with a number below the flow chart (see Figure 17-5). Hovering your mouse over this circle shows you the specific skills you two have in common. This feature is a great conversation-starter.

Figure 17-5: Ask your LinkedIn connection for an introduction to one of hers.

9. **On the next screen, choose the person making the connection from the drop-down menu and then type a message in the provided box.**

   Be sure to mention why you want to be introduced to this person and how being connected could be mutually beneficial. See Figure 17-6 for an example.

Figure 17-6:
Make sure
that your
introduction
request is
clear and to
the point.

10. **When you finish composing your message, click the blue Ask for an Introduction button.**

    Congratulations! You're one step closer to making a new connection. Your mutual connection receives a message via LinkedIn, asking for the connection.

Structuring contests, promotions, and sweepstakes to raise visibility

Facebook gives marketers the opportunity to get contests, promotions, and sweepstakes in front of their fan base. The company recently loosened its promotional guidelines to allow businesses to run contests directly from their Pages, as opposed to having to use an outside application. Running promotions from your Facebook Page has never been easier.

TIP Be sure to read and understand all of Facebook's Page terms, specifically the Promotions section near the bottom, to ensure that you're complying with all the rules. You can find the terms at `https://www.facebook.com/page_guidelines.php`.

In case you prefer to use an application to run your contests, Chapter 13 has information about a few of the most popular ones that Page administrators use.

Many people don't know that there's a difference between contests and sweepstakes. Contests ask people to submit something for consideration to enter the promotion. That submission is then judged or voted on by other fans. Contests are wonderful opportunities to engage your fans, and they give entrants an opportunity to get creative with their submissions. Some examples are asking people to submit photos, essays, or recipes.

Sweepstakes, on the other hand, just require people to fill out a form to be eligible for a prize. Information typically requested is first and last name, email address, and maybe phone number. This method is a great way to build up your database of email addresses to use when you send out promotional emails or e-newsletters.

The more information you ask for, the less likely people will be to complete the entry form. Just ask for what you need. You can always contact the winner later to get more personal information.

Here are some things to keep in mind when running a contest or sweepstakes on Facebook:

- ✔ **Know what you want to accomplish with your promotion.** If you want to gain more fans, for example, a sweepstakes is the better option. If you want to increase fan engagement, a contest is the way to go.

- ✔ **Be realistic with your expectations.** The more effort a person has to put in to enter the promotion, the fewer entrants you're going to have. Also, the more hoops people have to jump through to enter, the more likely they are to not finish the form. Don't require a person to become a fan to enter and then have him click a link that takes him to a separate site, where you require him to create an account that asks for his name, address, phone number, and email address.

- ✔ **Match the prize to the effort.** Contests that require fans to submit homemade videos require a lot more effort than contents that require filling out a quick form, and the prize should reflect that fact. Don't expect fans to rush to make videos to win a $50 gift card. Make the prize worth their time.

Prizes worth $600 or more require the company to send the winner a Form 1099, and the winner is required to report the amount to the Internal Revenue Service. To keep everything simple, stay under that threshold.

- ✔ **Give fans the option to share the fact that they entered your contest.** Although you can't require participants to share something on their Timelines to enter the contest, you're allowed to encourage them to share their entries with their Facebook friends.

✔ **Get the fans involved.** In addition to asking fans for contest submissions, allow your other fans to vote for the winner. This method gives everyone the opportunity to participate, even if they aren't competing for a prize.

✔ **Use an app to choose a random winner.** When you're running a sweepstakes, you want it to be as fair and transparent as possible. Apps such as Woobox (`http://woobox.com`) randomly select a winner for you.

✔ **Run the promotion for a certain length of time.** There's no perfect number for how long to run your promotion. A good rule of thumb is to run it for at least a month to get a good number of entries, but a month isn't so long that your fans forget that the promotion is running.

✔ **Post your rules and guidelines.** Another way to ensure that everything is fair and transparent is to post your promotion's rules on Facebook ahead of time. Put them in a place where your fans are sure to see them. Pin them to your Page's Timeline, for example, to ensure that they're always available to read. Posting rules and guidelines will save you a lot of headaches in the future in case some fans try to play fast and loose with the rules.

Building an Audience on Facebook

It's imperative that you have a good handle on what you want to accomplish with your SMO efforts in order to succeed at building your Facebook audience. You should know who your target audience is, have a good idea about where they hang out online, and always work hard to post interesting content that makes people want to engage with you and your Facebook Page. If you have already gathered that information and have been posting great content, you're well on your way to establishing a strong Facebook presence! In the following sections we give you a couple more tools to add to your Facebook SMO toolbox.

Using Facebook ads

Facebook advertising is an affordable option for growing your Facebook presence. Whether you're looking to increase the numbers of fans you have or to entice people to head to your website, Facebook guides you through the process so that you're up and running in no time. Just follow these instructions to get started creating ads:

1. **Log in to your Facebook account, and click the Create Ad link in the left column.**

   This link is located below the names of the Page(s) you administrate.

2. **Select the objective of your ad.**

   You can choose from ten options, such as Promote Your Page, Send People to Your Website, Get More People to Attend Your Event, and Increase Views of Your Videos. The example in Figure 17-7 shows the Promote Your Page option.

3. **Choose the Page you want to promote, or enter its URL.**

   If you're the admin for more than one Page, chose the one you want to create the ad for from the drop-down menu.

4. **On the following page, name your ad campaign.**

   Facebook gives you a default name, and unless you're running numerous campaigns, the one offered should work fine.

5. **Choose who you want to target with your ad.**

   In the Who Do You Want Your Ads to Reach? box, select the location, age, gender, and languages spoken. Clicking the More Demographics button opens a drop-down menu of more targeting options, as shown in Figure 17-8.

6. **(Optional) Type some specific interests and behaviors in the next two boxes.**

   Facebook uses the data people provide in their profiles to identify the best people to view your ad. *Interests* refers to things like fishing, movies, and sports. *Behaviors* refers to things like purchase behavior and intentions.

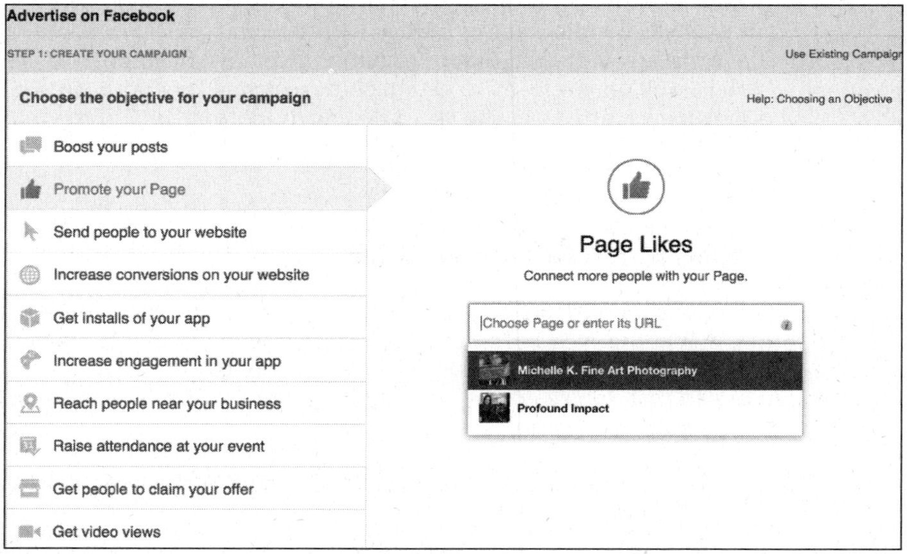

Figure 17-7: Select your ad objective and the Page you want to advertise.

Advertise on Facebook

STEP 1: CREATE YOUR CAMPAIGN   Use Existing Campaign

Choose the objective for your campaign   Help: Choosing an Objective

- Boost your posts
- Promote your Page
- Send people to your website
- Increase conversions on your website
- Get installs of your app
- Increase engagement in your app
- Reach people near your business
- Raise attendance at your event
- Get people to claim your offer
- Get video views

Page Likes

Connect more people with your Page.

|Choose Page or enter its URL

Michelle K. Fine Art Photography

Profound Impact

Who do you want your ads to reach?   Help: Choose Your Audience

Target Ads to People Who Know Your Business
You can create a Custom Audience to show ads to your contacts, website visitors or app
users. Create a Custom Audience

		Audience Definition
Locations ⓘ	United States	
	All United States	Your audience selection is fairly broad.
	Add a country, state/province, city or ZIP	Specific Broad
Age ⓘ	18 ▼ - 65+ ▼	**Audience Details:**
Gender ⓘ	All Men Women	▪ Location:
Languages ⓘ	Enter a language...	○ United States
	More Demographics ▼	▪ Not connected to:
	Relationship ❯	○ Michelle K. Fine Art Photography
	Education ❯	▪ Age:
Interests ⓘ	Work ❯	Suggestions | Browse	○ 18 - 65+
	Financial ❯		Potential Reach: 180,000,000 people
	Home ❯	
Behaviors ⓘ	Ethnic Affinity	Browse
	Generation	
	Parents (US) ❯	
Connections ⓘ	Politics (US)	....ected to Michelle K. Fine Art Photography
	Life Events	.... people not connected to Michelle K. Fine Art Photography

Figure 17-8:
Go through
this list to
narrow your
audience
even more.

7. Select the type of connections you want to target.

You can target all connections to your Page, only people who are currently fans of your Page, or only people who are not fans of your Page, or you can select more detailed criteria, such as targeting friends of specific friends.

Keep an eye on the Audience Definition meter on the right side of the page. Every time you add another targeting criterion, the number of people your ad will reach decreases. Keeping your criteria broad ensures that you reach as many people as possible.

8. Specify how much you want to spend on your advertising and when you want it to run.

You can choose to set a per-day budget or a lifetime budget; then you can decide whether you want your ad to run continuously or have set start and end dates.

9. (Optional) Click the Show Advanced Options link to specify greater control of how your money is spent.

Facebook uses a bidding system in deciding who to show your ads to, when, and how often. You can choose to be charged by CPC (cost per click) or CPM (cost per impression). Facebook optimizes the process to make it easier and to help you reach your objective. For that reason, we recommend that you leave these settings alone, at least until you have a better idea of how well your ads are working.

On the left side of the budgeting section is another meter showing your estimated daily reach. This meter takes the number from the Audience Definition section and manipulates it based on your budgeting and scheduling selections. The lower your budget, the fewer people will see your ad.

10. **Select an image to include with your ad.**

    Bright-colored images and those containing happy people often perform best. Your company logo would do, but unless it's really eye-catching, you may want go with something else.

11. **Write the ad copy.**

    Make sure that your ad message is clear and to the point. You have only a few seconds of the viewer's attention, so make every word count.

    After you create your ad message, the right side of the screen displays a preview of your ad.

12. **If you want to double-check all the details of your ad, such as targeting options and budget, click the Review Order button.**

    A box appears, giving you a rundown of all your selections.

13. **When everything looks perfect, click the green Place Order button at the bottom of the page.**

    Facebook has to approve all ads before they go live. Approval can take anywhere from 24 to 48 hours but often happens much faster.

Boosting Facebook posts

There will be times when you look at your Facebook Insights and see that one of your posts has racked up a lot of views, comments, and likes. Good for you. That piece of content is clearly what your target audience is looking for.

Unfortunately, Facebook made changes to the algorithm that decides the type of content that is shown on a user's Timeline. This has resulted in less organic reach for posts. In other words, fewer people are people being shown your content on their Timelines. The idea behind these changes was to make users' Facebook experience better and more applicable to their likes, interests, and use of the platform. The changes are great for average users and more than a little frustrating for Facebook Page administrators. The sad reality is that a Page's posts just aren't reaching fans the way they used to.

All is not lost, however. The good news is that Facebook offers a way to get your posts into more people's News Feeds. With the Boost option, you can pay to get posts in front of a larger audience.

You have two ways to boost a post. The first way is to create a Facebook ad (refer to the preceding section) and selecting Boost your posts as your ad objective (refer to Figure 17-7).

To get the most bang for your buck, boost only posts that take the user off the Facebook platform, such as to a blog post on your website.

If you have at least 50 fans, you can boost a post a second way. Follow these steps:

1. **Click the blue Boost Post button below the post that you want to promote.**

2. **In the dialog box that appears, select your desired audience and location (see Figure 17-9).**

   You can boost the post to people who already like your Page or to people who like your Page as well as their friends. A third option enables you to target your audience even further by selecting a country, a specific age range, or gender and by adding four to ten interests.

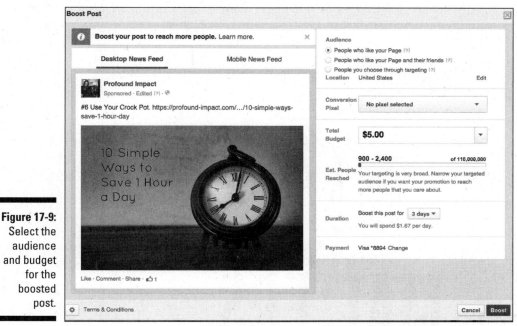

Figure 17-9: Select the audience and budget for the boosted post.

Figure used with permission of Julie Gray

3. **Specify whether you want to include a conversion pixel.**

   A *conversion pixel* is a small piece of code that you put on a specific page of your website; this code that reports back to Facebook when a viewer arrives on the website and clicks the Facebook link. In other words, if you choose to put a conversion pixel on the web page your post is sending the reader to, Facebook can tell you exactly how many people were sent your way. This tool is invaluable for measuring your return on investment.

4. **Select your budget amount and boost duration.**

   The lowest amount you can spend is $5. A meter below the budget selector estimates the number of people who will be reached with that amount of money budgeted. You can run the boosted post for one to seven days.

5. **Click the blue Boost button.**

   That's it. Your post is on its way to getting more views than ever.

When your post has been boosted in your Timeline, a little meter appears below the post (see Figure 17-10), showing the additional reach you achieved by boosting that post. The meter is split into two sections. The light orange section on the left is the number of organic views your post received, and the dark orange section on the right shows the number of paid views your post received.

Figure 17-10:
Boosted post on your Timeline.

Figure used with permission of Julie Gray

Clicking that meter brings up the post details box. As shown in Figure 17-11, you see the total reach of the post; how many likes, comments, shares, and clicks it has had; and any negative feedback you may have received, such as people hiding the post or unliking your Page.

Finding Followers on Twitter

Using Twitter in your SMO strategy is successful only if you engage in meaningful conversations with like-minded individuals as well as with people in your target market. Finding people to follow on Twitter is the first step. The second step is getting people to follow you back. After all, a conversation is a conversation only if people other than you are involved.

The good news is that others out there are looking to find interesting, like-minded individuals to follow. They're perusing the bios to find users who have similar interests, and maybe they'll come across your Twitter account at some point and follow you first. Who knows — they may be out there reading this book at the same time you are. Wouldn't that be nice?

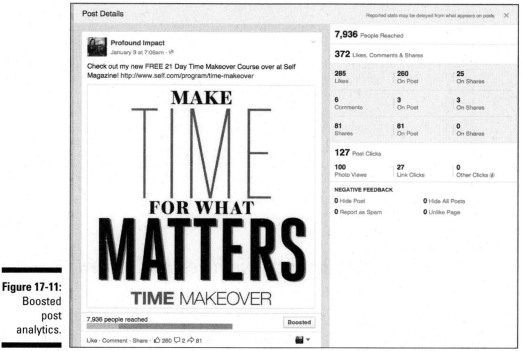

Figure 17-11: Boosted post analytics.

Figure used with permission of Julie Gray

Here are ten tips to keep in mind when building your Twitter audience:

- ✔ Always introduce yourself, and thank the other person for the follow. Reaching out shows you're invested in building some kind of relationship with them.

- ✔ Retweet interesting content. (See "Retweeting to build relationships" later in this chapter.)

- ✔ Don't use an automatic follow feature, as you have no control of the quality of person you follow. Spam accounts take advantage of this fact and sprinkle keywords throughout their bios and tweets to get picked up by these programs.

- ✔ Don't set up an automatic direct message to go out to a person who follows you. Automatic messages are incredibly impersonal, and people have been known to unfollow accounts who send them immediately. If you want to send a message to new followers, take the time to write each message separately.

- ✔ Post your Twitter username wherever appropriate. Some good locations are your Facebook and LinkedIn pages, your email signature, your website (of course), any guest posts you write for other websites, your business cards, and any bios you have. Be sure to include a call to action such as "Follow me on Twitter at @username."

- ✔ If you have a bricks-and-mortar store, include tent cards at the register or on tables, and put a cling-on sticker on your front window.

- ✔ Run a Followers advertising campaign on Twitter. Check out https://business.twitter.com/solutions/grow-followers for more information on this paid option.

- ✔ Don't fall for services that promise a certain number of followers a day. These followers are likely from spam accounts and useless for your SMO purposes.

- ✔ Tweet interesting stuff. As we mention earlier in this section, people just like you are searching Twitter for users who post interesting information.

- ✔ Use your ever-growing Twitter network to check out the followers of the people you follow. You clearly already have something in common.

Targeting the most influential users

Sometimes, you have to make the first move and search out influential users to follow. There's a good chance that when people see you've started following them, they'll check out your Twitter profile and tweets to see whether you're worthy of a follow in return. It's a good idea to thank people who follow you back, to introduce yourself, and to mention something that you have in common. Reaching out in this way opens the line of communication and may be the start of a lasting friendship.

Just because someone has a lot of followers doesn't mean that she's worth a follow from you. Look through her tweet stream to see the types of content she posts and how much she interacts with her followers. If she's active and engages frequently, she's definitely worth your time.

Here are some sites that can help you find some relevant influential Twitter users to follow:

✔ **TweetStork** (www.tweetstork.com): Type the Twitter username of someone who has an account similar to yours, and filter the results to find potential followers whose profiles and tweets contain the keywords of your choosing, as shown in Figure 17-12. TweetStork offers a free account and a premium account that costs $4 per month or $26 per year.

✔ **Wefollow** (http://wefollow.com): When a Twitter user joins Wefollow, he adds his interests. Wefollow is a free service that finds the most prominent users within interest groups. It has a prominence score that ranks these users according to influence.

✔ **Just Tweet It** (http://justtweetit.com): A free Twitter user directory, Just Tweet It breaks users into helpful categories based on the interests, tweets, and keywords used by Twitter users. Some of the most popular directories include bloggers, SEO and marketing folks, and social media mavens.

Figure 17-12:
Find highly
targeted
followers
with
TweetStork.

✔ **Twello** (www.twellow.com/splash): In addition to finding Twitter users who are in business categories relevant to you, Twello narrows these users to your geographical area to help you target those Twitter users even more. Twello users have their own profiles on their site, which gives you even more opportunities to find users who share specific interests. Twello is free to join.

Don't go on a massive follow campaign. Twitter imposes limits on the number of people you can follow in relation to the number of people who follow you. Also, following random people just to get your numbers up makes you look like a spammer. Remember that your follower list is about quality, not quantity.

Retweeting to build relationships

Retweets are integral parts of your Twitter SMO strategy. In addition to posting interesting, original content, you should always be retweeting relevant content of those you follow. The most influential Twitter users garnered as many followers as they have because they're always posting content that others consider to be helpful, interesting, and original, regardless of whether they created the content themselves. It's obvious that they have a lot to offer their followers.

By regularly retweeting the content of others, you accomplish a few things:

✔ You're providing your followers content that they may find interesting.

✔ You're keeping your tweet stream fresh by mixing tweeting original content and others' content.

✔ The number of times a particular tweet has been retweeted is displayed underneath that tweet. When a person clicks that tweet, and then the retweet number, they see the usernames of the people who retweeted. If you've retweeted that tweet, your profile will be listed and there's a Follow button right next to your username, so you can be followed directly from your retweet. (See Figure 17-13.)

✔ If you're a regular retweeter of one person's tweets, he'll take note, and there's a good chance that he'll follow you back.

✔ Retweeting shows you're not just on Twitter for your own selfish reasons. It shows other users that you're in it for the relationships and conversations, which will lead to the building of trust between you and your followers.

✔ People are more likely to repay you by retweeting your content if they see that you actively retweet other people's content. When this happens, your content will be in front of a much wider audience of users, which could lead to you gaining more followers.

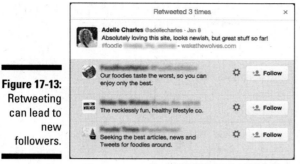

Figure 17-13:
Retweeting
can lead to
new
followers.

Always identify the tweet as a retweet, and credit it to the original source. You never want to seem as though you're trying to take credit for another user's content.

Chapter 18

Tapping Into the Vox Populi

In This Chapter
- ▶ Planning the creation of viral content
- ▶ Finding viral techniques that work

*V*iral marketing, *viral advertising*, and *buzz marketing* are terms that reflect successful attempts to tap the vox populi — that is, the people's voice. A piece of content goes viral when it's picked up, shared, and recirculated by large numbers of people who have no incentive other than sharing something that's cool, fun, or useful. A piece of viral content can have millions of views, and a piece of viral content is hugely influential as it leverages the power of the masses.

Getting a piece of content to go viral is often considered to be the holy grail of digital marketing, and there's a lot to be said that for that point of view. There's definitely value in getting your content viewed by a large number of people; the value is greatest if the viewers are the right audience for your business. Certainly, a lot of ad agencies spend a lot of money trying to create viral content. But big budgets and large creative teams aren't the keys to getting content to go viral. The key is something much, much simpler: great, compelling content that evokes a strong emotional response. Anyone can create it; just ask the guy with the grumpy cat.

The definition of viral content is content with a viral coefficient greater than 1. To put that definition in human terms, content has gone viral if the 100 people who see the content share it with at least 101 other people. Achieving those kind of numbers is rare.

Designing for Virality

Although it's easy to think that viral content has a magical serendipitous element, the fact is that you can create content that's highly likely to go viral. Though there's no guarantee that any particular item will go crazy online, garnering millions of views, you can take some steps to make it more likely that your content will see at least a degree of viral success.

Research and thoughtful, creative content planning are the core elements of a structured approach to courting virality. As in any marketing campaign, you should start by defining your goals. What are you trying to achieve with the content you're creating: social engagement, brand visibility, signups, inbound links, or something else? What you want from the campaign dictates how you structure the collateral and where you press for views.

The next step in the process is defining your target audience. Always keep in mind who you're trying to reach. When you have a profile in mind, do some research to figure out what will trigger audience action. Use the results of your research to frame your collateral.

See Chapter 4 for a more extensive discussion of how to frame your target markets.

Personas of online sharers

In a landmark study, *The New York Times* conducted an extensive survey of its users in an attempt to find out why people share content online. The study defined six personas of online sharers, based on emotional motivations, their desired presentation of themselves, the role of sharing in their lives, and the value of being the first person to share. Following are the six personas identified in the survey:

✔ **Altruists:** People who seek to be helpful to others with whom they're connected.

✔ **Careerists:** People in this group share content related to business, and they exchange ideas that can help their companies and their careers.

✔ **Hipsters:** This group is comprised of younger, cutting-edge, and creative people for whom social sharing is an integral part of their interactions with others and their definition of themselves.

✔ **Boomerangs:** People in this group tend to share and post provocative content. They want to be viewed as being engaged, and they seek reactions and validation.

✔ **Connectors:** Connectors use sharing as a way to interact with their friends and members of their extended networks. These people tend to be thoughtful and relaxed, and they enjoy using social content to make plans.

✔ **Selectives:** People in this group share only what they perceive to be specifically valuable. They're the hardest people to motivate and the least likely to share.

The *Times* analysis provides useful criteria for classifying your target audience and tailoring your content to match their motivations. Decide which persona you're targeting, and create content that matches that group's needs.

You also need think about the channel that you'll use, as it also affects the formatting of the creative collateral.

When you have a handle on your goals, your audience, and the channel for the content, your content creators should kick into gear. Your best bet for coming up with a winning concept is generating multiple ideas and testing them. For testing purposes, find a test audience that matches the persona you're targeting (see the nearby sidebar "Personas of online sharers"), and ask questions that will give you insight into whether a particular idea will meet your goals. Here are some examples:

✔ Do members of the test audience want to click the link?

✔ Would they share the link?

✔ Would they sign up for the mailing list?

✔ How does the content make them feel about the brand?

After testing your content options, pick the winner, and get ready to go with it.

When it comes time to launch, don't be shy about spending some money on views. You need to hit the ground running, as it were, and your odds of gaining viral traction are improved by obtaining a large audience for your content in a short period of time. The immediate postlaunch window is key. Fresh content has a much better chance of going viral than old content does.

Think about optimal times to post. Getting your content out at the right time can get things off to a good start. If you're in the United States, for example, think about noon Eastern Standard Time. At that time, people on the East Coast are breaking for lunch, and people on the West Coast are just coming into the office — two of the most popular times for people to surf for a bit for distraction.

Don't hesitate to spend big. By ensuring a large audience for your content, you're more likely to enjoy massive sharing. Some of the best ways to build audience with paid placements include

✔ Boosting a post on Facebook

✔ Promoting a tweet

✔ Buying paid placements in online publications

✔ Using Outbrain (www.outbrain.com) to display your content on premium media channels

✔ Trying paid promotion via Taboola (www.taboola.com)

If you structure your Facebook Ads properly, you can reach tens of thousands of people for a few hundred dollars.

Inspiring people to share

It's possible to find viral success with more than just cat videos. Many publishers tap the vox populi by providing content that people feel passionate about. People engage with and share content for a variety of reasons, including (but not limited to) entertainment. Here are five motivations for sharing content:

- ✔ To bring valuable and entertaining content to others
- ✔ To define oneself to others
- ✔ To grow and nourish relationships
- ✔ To achieve self-fulfillment
- ✔ To get the word out about causes or brands

Strive to make an emotional connection between your content and your audience. If your content arouses emotion, you're more likely to succeed. Emotion can be positive or negative. In a 2010 study, Jonah Berger and Katherine Milkman took a psychological approach to the sharing of online content. They examined the link between emotions and sharing behavior, and found some very interesting connections. The research suggested a strong relationship between emotion and virality. The conclusions included the following:

- ✔ The more likely a piece of content is to evoke emotion, the more likely it is to be shared.
- ✔ Positive content is more viral than negative content.
- ✔ Positive content that inspires awe and surprise is more likely to be shared.
- ✔ Sadness is less likely to be shared.
- ✔ Some negative content — specifically, content that induces anxiety or anger — does prompt sharing.
- ✔ There's no positive relationship between disgust and virality.

The report's findings shed some light on how to tap the passion of the crowd and how that passion should shape your creation of content.

In her book *Fascinate: Your 7 Triggers to Persuasion and Captivation* (HarperBusiness), Sally Hogshead describes seven personality triggers that influence people to take action. Check out this book to find out more about triggers that may inspire people to share your content.

The power of boredom

Although we talk about finding the power of passion, there's also a lot to be said for tapping the power of boredom. Targeting the portion of the population that's feeling bored at work or browsing with a mobile device while standing in line can be super-successful. The people in those situations are looking for distraction and amusement. The most-shared post on Facebook in 2014 was the entertaining promotional video Holiday Minions, shown in the figure. This video is a classic example of content designed to tap people who are looking for quick, light entertainment. If you can get entertaining content in front of these people and make sharing that content easy, you could be well on your way to viral success. The passionately bored will do a lot of the work for you!

92,469,900 Views

Hitting the right note

The tone and quality of your content are key execution factors. The content is more important than the production values, but you do want to make your best effort to create something that looks good. Visual appeal is a big part of any content, but if your goal is to make something with potential to go viral, you can enhance your chances of success by using great visuals.

Content needs to offer more than just appealing visuals. Great content also needs great titles. Indeed, a great title draws in traffic even when the content isn't spectacular. Conversely, a poorly created title may cause people to pass over an otherwise-fabulous item that deserves more attention.

Evoke emotion strategically to encourage your audience to make your content viral. When your content inspires one of the following emotions, you're positioning that content for possible virality:

- ✔ **Anger:** We're not talking about intentionally trying to make people mad; doing that is inappropriate. Creating righteous indignation about injustice or challenging cherished beliefs is a proper way to evoke anger in this context.

- ✔ **Anxiety:** The way to productively tap anxiety is to create a fear of missing something. You see this technique used often in calls to action that urge "Act now! This is a limited time offer!"

- **Awe:** Show people something amazing and awe-inspiring. Tap the "Wow!" factor.

- **Fear:** As with anger, you have to use a sense of fear responsibly. The right way to use fear is to drop a hint that the audience is doing something the wrong way — that they're making mistakes they may not be aware of. This technique shows up frequently in articles that promise to tell you about "mistakes you don't even know you are making."

- **Joy:** Make people happy. Evoking joy works like a charm!

  Don't forget about nostalgia. People often feel joyful when they're reminiscing about how things used to be and feeling nostalgic.

- **Lust:** In this case, we don't mean lust as in blatant sexual content (though a bit of titillation can be very effective). Instead, we're referring to lust for money, success, or recognition.

- **Surprise:** Surprise is anything that goes against people's expectations — a pretty broad definition, but it works. You don't need a big bang at the end to create surprise; you simply need things to turn out differently than expected.

Tapping emotion as a technique to increase the viral component of a campaign needs to be handled with some delicacy; you can overdo it and come off as insensitive or corny. This technique can also backfire on you, creating a strong negative reaction against you as the publisher — the old kill-the-messenger syndrome. Tread lightly in this area, and definitely, positively, always test your messages before you broadcast.

Discovering Techniques with Viral Appeal

If you consider the body of research on sharing behavior and the various examples of content that have gone viral, you start to get an idea of the type of subjects that have the most viral potential. A clear pattern has emerged:

- Target your content to particular personas (refer to the sidebar "Personas of online sharers" earlier in this chapter).

- Draft your content to meet known needs.

✔ Craft the message to evoke a strong emotional response.

✔ Push a bit. Don't play it too safe; if you do, you won't evoke sufficiently high emotional reactions.

If you look at examples of content that has achieved large numbers of views, certain subjects clearly trip the emotional triggers of the masses:

✔ **Things that are cute:** The masses seem to have an insatiable desire for cute animal videos and pictures.

✔ **Things that are shocking:** Outrageous content that makes people think "oh, my!" works well, particularly on video. Blendtec has done used this technique spectacularly with its Will It Blend? Series (www.willitblend.com), shown in Figure 18-1.

Figure 18-1:
Blendtec's
Will It
Blend?
video series.

✔ **Things that are humorous:** It's no surprise that humor always has an audience.

✔ **Things that are puzzling:** Content that's weird, unexpected, and unexplainable often goes viral. The more bizarre, the better.

✔ **Things that invoke a sense of relief:** Things that make people feel better about their lot in life work well, even though this technique may be distasteful to many people. Embarrassing images of important people fall into this category as well.

✔ **Failures:** Disasters of a personal nature — from accidents to idiots doing disastrously stupid things — get lots of shares. This category also includes failings of organizations. Content of this type tends to tap into people's frustrations with organizations and society.

✔ **Helpful information:** Content that's useful or helpful is always a winner.

✔ **Victories:** Positive content that shows accomplishment in a fashion that people can relate to is classic feel-good content. Good guys defeating bad guys and honest human moments are viral gold.

If you're struggling to come up with something, just remember: Originality is overrated. Often, it's much easier to curate existing content of your own or from other sources. Assemble a top-ten list from the Internet archives. Sure, some of your audience may have seen at least part of the content before, but you may also turn up some underappreciated gems.

Employing causes, controversy, and relatability

If creating emotionally provocative content is one of your goals, you should consider the role of causes and controversies. People like talking about causes and injecting their opinions into controversies; it's a type of social currency. Talking about things that are provocative shows that you're engaged and aware of the world. In short, people talk about things they care about. Moreover, as we all know from experience, people tend to talk about things in direct relation to how much they care about them, rather than how much they know about them.

Topics that relate to common causes tend to do disproportionately well in social media, including

✔ Animal rights and animal welfare

✔ Religious-themed content

✔ Political content

✔ Climate change

✔ Hot topics in the news headlines

These topics tend to push people's buttons and evoke emotional reactions, so this sort of content needs to be handled delicately and sensitively. You don't want to be perceived as using a popular cause for selfish or commercial purposes. If your goal is to position your brand as socially conscious or engaged and aware, however, common causes can work very well.

Though common causes can generate excitement and buzz, they can also generate a lot of controversy. If you decide to use common cause content, be prepared for the possibility that there may be people who have strong opinions. Watch your comment thread and be aware that you may need to step in and moderate the discussion if things start to get out of hand.

Another way to tap people's emotions is get them to relate to the content. This technique is used in the form of posts like these:

- ✔ 21 Problems All Sarcastic People Understand
- ✔ You Know You've Lived in Boston Too Long When . . .
- ✔ 10 Problems Tall People Understand

These types of posts immediately connect with at least a portion of the audience. Your job is to make sure that the group the content appeals to is large enough to achieve your content goals.

Looking at what works

What do people actually share more than anything else? Table 18-1 lists the top topics on Facebook and Twitter in 2014.

Table 18-1	Top Ten Topics on Facebook and Twitter	
	Facebook	*Twitter*
1	Music	Music
2	Television	Television
3	Holidays	Software
4	Software	Celebrities
5	Religion	Holidays
6	Celebrities	Film
7	Film	Internet
8	Books	Business
9	Business	Basketball
10	Food	Sports

The first thing that should jump out at you is how similar those lists are. There's a tremendous amount of overlap in terms of what people are talking about on these two key channels.

The Facebook and Twitter stats give you some idea of the topics that tend to get traction, but what types of posts were most popular in 2014? Table 18-2 lists the top ten shared posts on Facebook in 2014.

Table 18-2	Ten Most-Shared Posts on Facebook in 2014		
Title	*Topic*	*Media*	*Tone – Purpose*
1. Minions Holiday Greeting	Film	Video	Positive – Entertainment
2. Chucky Bus Stop Prank	Prank	Video	Positive – Entertainment
3. People Being Awesome	Animals / Human Interest	Video	Positive – Inspiration
4. Minion Halloween Costume	Human Interest	Video	Positive – Entertainment
5. Why We Need Best Friends	Relationships	Image (Text)	Positive – Inspiration
6. Crazy: Man Helps Dead Shark Give Birth to 3 Babies!	Animals / Human Interest	Video	Positive – Inspiration
7. If You Ever Fall In Love...	Relationships	Image (Text)	Positive – Inspiration
8. Weird Things Couples Fight About	Relationships	Video	Positive – Entertainment
9. Different Ways to Wear a Scarf	Fashion	Video	Neutral – Information
10. Remembering the Family Members and Friends We Have Lost	Relationships	Image (Text)	Positive – Nostalgia

What's interesting here, aside for the public's love for Minions, is the lack of overlap between the most-shared topics and the most-shared pieces of content. Several of the topics that show up in the Facebook and Twitter top ten (refer to Table 18-1) aren't represented in the most-shared content. Indeed, the ten most-shared items come from a very small set of topics:

- ✔ Film
- ✔ Pranks
- ✔ Animals
- ✔ Human interest
- ✔ Relationships

The difference seems to be emotion. People talk about a wide range of topics, but not all of those topics carry an equal emotional charge. The most-shared content was highly emotionally charged, almost exclusively positive, and almost exclusively entertaining in nature.

 Don't take Table 18-2 as a complete rethinking of what's come before in this chapter. These examples don't mean that positive, entertaining content about animals or relationships will go viral automatically. Content with these characteristics scored some big wins in the past, but other types of content also had viral success.

 It's not enough to create content that people share. If you want to get the most out of any social media campaign, you need to follow up, engage, and be present on the channels.

Chapter 19

Tracking Progress and Measuring Success

This chapter takes you through the key metrics to keep in mind when measuring your social media optimization (SMO) progress. You dig into the nitty-gritty of Facebook Insights, and find out how to harness that information and turn it into a successful Facebook Page. Finally, you delve into Twitter Analytics to see what these numbers are telling you and how to tweak your SMO approach in response to these numbers.

Identifying the Key Metrics

It is important to be able to measure the success of your SMO efforts because doing so will give you a clearer picture of your return on investment (ROI). After all, who wants to spend any more time and money than they have to on a failing SMO plan? The following sections discuss what we feel are the five most important metrics to keep a watchful eye on to know whether your social media efforts are successful.

Reach

In terms of your social media content, reach is the number of unique people who saw your post. By *unique,* we mean that when someone reads a portion of your post, clicks away from it, and returns at a later time, the view is counted as one visit rather than two separate views. That's why the reach of your posts often is a lower number than your page or site views.

Reach is affected by all the rest of the metrics in the following sections, and for that reason, all analytics programs include it. Without reach, there's no engagement, no influence, and no relationships. In other words, reach drives other important key metrics used to measure SMO success.

Reach has several categories: Page, Post, Paid, and Organic. Page reach refers to the number of people who have seen any of your page content within a particular time frame (day, week, or month), whereas Post reach refers to views of a specific post. In Facebook, Page reach is called total reach. Figure 19-1 shows a post reach chart in Facebook Insights.

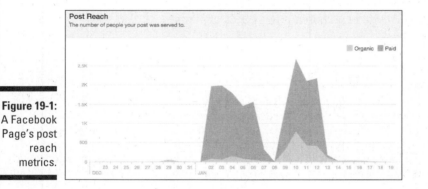

Figure 19-1:
A Facebook Page's post reach metrics.

Notice in Figure 19-1 that this reach chart is broken down into Paid and Organic categories. These two categories, used in both page reach and post reach, refer to the way viewers came upon your content.

Organic reach happens when people come across your content on their own, whether it's in their Facebook News Feed or through a Google search. Organic reach is free. Paid reach is exactly what it sounds like; it occurs when you pay for exposure, such as through promoted posts on Facebook or ads on Google.

Engagement

Engagement refers to how your viewers are consuming your content. Engagement comes in the forms of post clicks, Likes, shares, and comments on Facebook, and retweets and favorites on Twitter. Engagement can also refer to activities on your own website or blog, such as content downloads, new subscribers to your newsletter or new followers of your blog, and the time people spend with your content. Figure 19-2 shows the engagement metrics for a Facebook Page.

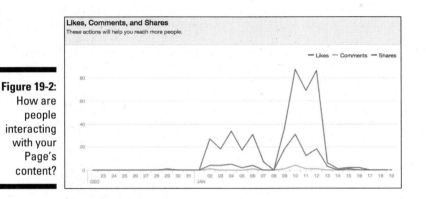

Figure 19-2: How are people interacting with your Page's content?

Engagement is a good way to gauge how your audience feels about the content you're posting. It's one thing to click a link and read something; it's an entirely different thing to take the time to leave a comment, click the Like button, retweet your content, or share your content with others. Use the engagement metric to judge what types of content people like and, more important, what kind they don't like. Use this information to drive your SMO content strategy.

Having a high level of engagement also shows you the health of your online community. If you find that most of your posts get comments and interesting conversations are taking place, you have a healthy online community. If no one ever comments on any of your posts, or if the comments are just fights between the people commenting, your online community could use a little tune-up. Step in and keep things positive by laying some ground rules for interaction. It doesn't matter if people are commenting if those who participate are mean-spirited and take things off-topic. You'll soon see your engagement rates drop as people stop coming back.

Influence

We all have both bad and good influences in our lives. Social media isn't any different. When a person sees that his Facebook friend has clicked the Like button on a company's Page, and he in turn visits that company's Page, he was influenced to do so by the actions of someone he's connected to on social media.

Influencers — people who have a lot of influence over their fans and followers — tend to have a lot of engagement in what they post on social media. People trust the opinions of and the information provided by influencers. Influencers encourage and inspire others to take action. They don't just talk about themselves; they know that social media is about having conversations, and being real and approachable. In other words, influencers are charismatic thought leaders.

Just because a person or company has a lot of followers on Twitter or fans on Facebook doesn't mean that that person or company has influence over those followers or fans.

Building up influence takes time and dedication. Just as Rome wasn't built in a day, you aren't going to immediately grow a dedicated following that hangs on every word you tweet. You have ways to grow your influence, however. One of the best ways is to research the biggest influencers in your field and follow what they do. Do they recommend a new social media tool? Check it out. Do they ask a question of their followers? Respond. After you get to know this person and how she works, don't be afraid to reach out to her directly to help promote your content. Influencers are inundated with many of these requests, but if you bring your A game and create informative, original content, you have a chance at catching their attention. Nothing is better for your engagement metric than being endorsed by an influencer.

Klout (`https://klout.com/home`) is a well-known website that tells you how big an influencer you are by means of your Klout score (see Figure 19-3). The Klout scale is from 1 to 100, and the higher your score, the more influence you have. How Klout calculates your score is a proprietary formula, but Klout scores are trusted tools for gauging influence.

Figure 19-3: This designer's Klout score is 60.

Figure used with permission of Adelle Charles

When you sign up for Klout, you're prompted to authorize the website to access your social networks, connect them to your Klout account, and calculate your score. At this writing, you can connect up to 14 social network accounts, including Facebook, Twitter, Foursquare, Instagram, and Google+. The more social network accounts you connect, the more accurate your Klout score will be.

Relationships

Social media isn't. . . well. . . social without relationships. After all, if you don't form relationships with people, who are you going to converse with? Technically, you could just put your messages out on Twitter and Facebook, but that would get your SMO plan exactly nowhere. That's why the relationships you create are an important metric to use in measuring the success of your SMO.

It's imperative that you keep an eye on this key metric, because it ties in closely with the influence metric discussed in the preceding section. Again, if you don't form relationships with anyone on social media, how do you expect to influence them to do anything, whether it's to visit your website, click links that you post on Twitter or Facebook, or even purchase things from you?

Social media success is not about the number of followers and fans you have; it's the quality of the relationships you form.

The following are some questions to ask yourself when you are measuring the strength of your social media relationships.

How friendly is the relationship?

Simple kindness goes a long way on social media. Treat your fans and followers like friends. How do you greet your friends in the morning? By saying good morning, of course. So say good morning to your social media following. How do you hold conversations with your real-life friends? Chances are that you ask questions about their lives and listen to what they say, which drives further conversation.

If a follower reaches out to ask you a question about a problem he's having, congratulations on establishing your expertise with this person. In addition to answering the question to the best of your ability, make a note to follow up with this person in a day or so to ask how things turned out. This simple act of remembering your previous conversation goes a long way to showing *all* your followers that you care about them.

How often do your followers reach out to you?

Do you find that your fans are saying good morning to you first or initiating conversations in general? That's a good sign that you've built a good relationship with people. Always respond when people reach out to you directly. Don't make someone feel as though he waved at you on the street and you ignored him.

As unpleasant as it may be, you should also respond if someone sends you a message complaining about your product or customer service. It's important that all your followers feel that they're being heard, whether what they have to say is positive or negative. If you find that a situation is escalating, however, ask the other person to take the conversation off social media. It does no one any good to witness public airing of dirty laundry. Keep the private conversation polite and professional, of course. You can communicated much more via email or over the phone than you can in a 140-character tweet or a post on Facebook.

Flamers and trolls are everywhere online, and pretty much every professional social media account encounters them at some point or another. Flamers and trolls are people whose main purpose is to start fights with you and other followers. Their comments aren't constructive; often, they're derogatory. Use your best judgment in deciding whether to respond to these people (to let them know that their behavior is inappropriate), but by no means should you continue to fuel the flames of their nastiness.

How much interest do your followers show in what you have going on?

Suppose that you're making a presentation at a conference, or your company is hosting an open house. How much interest do your followers show in these events? Are they asking questions, expressing excitement, or asking how they can attend? If so, you've cultivated some great online relationships through SMO.

When your followers show interest in what you having going on, don't be afraid of providing more details to sell more tickets or get more open-house attendees. Obviously, you've already shared that you have something going on, but expressions of interest are open invitations to talk about the topic more and in more detail. Your followers won't see you talking about your event as you selling to them. After all, they asked. As with everything in SMO, don't overdo these promotional posts. Making every single tweet or Facebook post about this topic gets very obnoxious very quickly. At that point, you're falling into the category of talking to people instead of talking with them — the exact opposite of what social media is about.

Traffic

The final key metric to keep an eye on to track your SMO progress is how much traffic is generated as a result of your efforts. You can tell how much traffic is generated the same way you know how much engagement you're having on your posts: through the use of analytics. We discuss both Facebook and Twitter analytics in more detail in the following section. Knowing how much traffic you're generating to your website drives your other SMO efforts.

Did you tweet a link to your latest blog post, for example, and see a major increase in the number of people visiting your website? When people were on your website, did they visit other pages and spend more time than usual on those pages? This traffic information tells you a few things:

- You have a decent following on Twitter, and people are paying attention to what you're saying.
- People like the content you posted.
- After people land on your blog, your website draws them in and makes them want to find out more about you, see what you do, and maybe read even more blog posts by you.

The take-away from this traffic is that you should keep doing what you're doing on Twitter.

On the other hand, if you aren't seeing any additional traffic being generated by your SMO efforts, it's time to rethink your strategy. Is your content boring and unhelpful? Are your posts not interesting enough to entice people to click the link? Are you even targeting the right audience? Take a look at all these things and maybe tweak them to see whether your traffic increases.

Change only one thing at a time so that you have a better idea of where the problem lies in your SMO program. If you change too many factors at once, you run the risk of changing something that works and possibly seeing a decrease in traffic.

Analyzing Your Facebook Page and Twitter Activity

Facebook has a built-in analytics platform for all business Pages, called Insights. Insights is a robust analytics program, and the information you mine from it is invaluable for planning and executing your SMO strategy. Insights is visible only to Page administrators.

Analyzing Facebook Insights and making any necessary changes are important tasks that you should do on a regular basis. If not, you're essentially flying blind in reaching your target audience.

Twitter Analytics, although helpful, isn't nearly as robust as Facebook Insights, but you can still mine a lot of helpful information from it to get a good idea of how your content is performing. You're given the typical, yet important, information offered by analytics programs: Impressions (how many people saw your tweet) and Engagements (how many people clicked your links, retweeted something of yours, favorited one of your tweets, and replied to you). Both numbers are important in deciding when to tweet and what to tweet about.

We discuss the helpful features of both in the following sections.

Facebook Insights

Facebook Insights highlights three main areas: Page Likes, Post Reach, and Post Engagement. By picking up on any trends in Page visits and audience interaction (in the form of comments, Likes, and shares), you can get an idea of when your target audience visits your page most and what types of content they like (or don't like). Then you can adjust your content posting initiatives accordingly.

Insights breaks down those three main areas even further to provide detailed information that's invaluable for tracking your progress and measuring your SMO success. Figure 19-4 shows the Insights Overview page, and Figure 19-5 shows more detailed information about Post Reach, as well as Post Engagement (Likes, comments, and shares). Facebook Insights puts all the statistics in helpful charts, giving you a clear picture of the health of your Facebook Page.

To access Insights, follow these steps:

1. **Point your browser to www.facebook.com, and log in to your personal Facebook profile.**

   Every Facebook business Page must be connected to a personal profile.

2. **Below the Pages heading on the left sidebar, click the name of your Page.**

   You're taken to your Page's timeline.

3. **At the top of the page, directly below the Facebook Search box, click the Insights tab.**

   You're on the Overview tab of your Insights dashboard (refer to Figure 19-4).

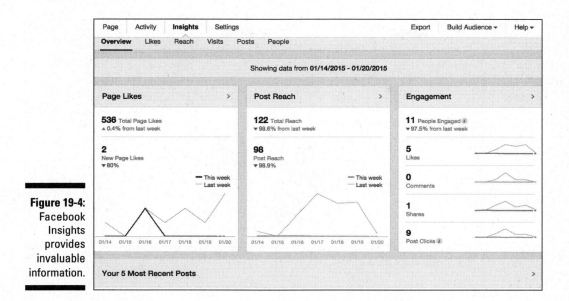

In the center of the page are three boxes: Page Likes, Post Reach, and Engagement. Clicking each of those headings takes you to a page with even more detailed information pertaining to that metric. You can also reach those detailed metric pages by clicking one of the six links below the menu bar that contains the Insights tab. The following sections describe the information you can glean from each of those links.

Overview

The Overview link is exactly what it sounds like: an overview of your Facebook Page for the week leading up to the current day. On this page, you see your Page Likes, Post Reach, and Engagement. Clicking any of those three box titles takes you to a page that provides a more detailed breakdown of the data.

Below those three boxes is a list of your five most recent Facebook posts. If you want to see more than five posts, click the See More link at the bottom of the Recent Posts box.

Additional information about each post is provided:

- **Type:** Photo, link, or text status update
- **Targeting:** The visibility of your post (public or a target group)
- **Reach:** Broken down by Organic and Paid
- **Engagement:** Broken down by link clicks and Likes, comments, and shares
- **Boost:** Whether you paid to boost or promote a post

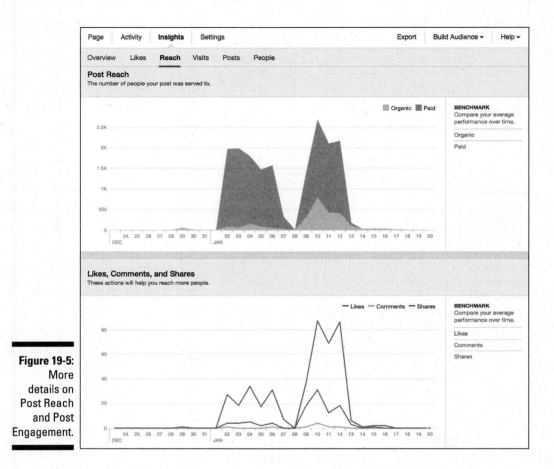

Figure 19-5:
More
details on
Post Reach
and Post
Engagement.

The final box on the Overview page is Pages to Watch. This page compares your Facebook Page with random Pages that Facebook deems to be similar. If you want to keep an eye on a particular Page, click the blue Watch Page button to the right of the Page's name to ensure that those particular Pages stay in your Pages to Watch section.

Likes

Next to the Overview link is Likes. Clicking this link gives you metrics about your Page Likes, such as total Page Likes and the total number of Net Likes, which is the number of new Likes minus the number of people who Unliked your Page. The Net Likes chart is broken down by color to show Unlikes (red), Organic Likes (light blue), and Paid Likes (dark blue). You can customize the time frame that these charts show by manipulating the dates at the top of the page. The default setting is one month.

The final box on that page is Where Your Page Likes happened, which is the number of times your Page was Liked, broken down by where it happened. If someone clicked the Facebook Like box on your website, for example, that Like would register as being from your website.

Reach

The next link shows the number of unique people who saw the content you posted on Facebook. The Post Reach chart is at the top of the page (refer to Figure 19-5 earlier in this chapter). This chart is broken into Organic and Paid reach types. Organic reach is when someone sees your content by clicking the link in their News Feed or happens upon it through a Google search. Paid reach refers to when a person clicks a post because you Boosted it (see the description of Boost in the "Overview" section) or because you paid for a Google ad, for example. You can also get to the Reach page by clicking the Post Reach box title on the Overview page.

Below the Post Reach chart is a chart showing Likes, comments, and shares. In other words, this chart shows the Engagement numbers for your Page. Use this chart to determine when your Page had the highest engagement levels, and look to see what content you posted at that time. This chart is a great indicator of what kind of content your audience wants you to post more (and less) of.

The third chart on the Reach page shows the number of times your fans hid a post, hid all your posts, reported your posts as spam, and Unliked your page. Sheesh! This chart isn't a very pleasant one; we hope that yours is empty. If you do see activity in this chart, however, take note. Just as with your Likes, shares, and comments, take note of the dates on which you had activity and then refer to the posts that went up that day. It's no big deal if just a couple of people Unliked or hid your posts. Things happen. If you saw a mass exodus on a particular day, however, or if quite a few people reported a particular post as spam, you definitely have to make some changes in your content strategy.

The final chart on the Reach page is Total Reach: the number of people who saw any activity on your Page, including posts by other people, Page mentions, and Page Like ads (if you purchased any). This information is broken into Organic and Paid.

Visits

If you have multiple tabs on your Page, such a contact form or a tab containing your podcasts, the top chart on the Visits page is where these tabs show up. If people are checking out different areas of your Page, it's a good sign that they're liking what they're seeing (and reading).

The External Referrers chart shows you whether someone linked to your Facebook Page, perhaps from one of their blog posts. Having someone share a link to your Facebook Page is a great thing. It means that your Page is getting attention, so be sure to keep the content fresh and interesting.

Posts

The bottom half of the Posts page shows the same chart as the bottom of the Overview page. In fact, if you click the Your 5 Most Recent Posts heading on the Overview page, this page is where you land.

The Posts page shows additional important information as well. The top chart is the total number of fans you have, and the second chart (When Your Fans Are Online) shows the times when your fans were engaging with your content. See? We told you that this information is important. This page helps you can decide at what times to post your content to reach the most people. As you can see in Figure 19-6, few fans are consuming the content of this page between midnight and 3 a.m. Then, from about 4 a.m. until 8 a.m., the number of views steadily increases and stays pretty consistent throughout the day, with a decline starting around 9 p.m. This person is lucky because she has a pretty large window in which to post.

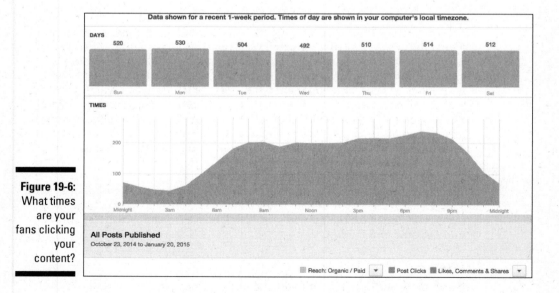

Figure 19-6:
What times
are your
fans clicking
your
content?

The Posts page is broken down even further. Directly below the six links at the top of the page (the ones we're discussing here) are three more links: When Your Fans Are Online, Post Types, and Top Posts from Pages. The default landing page when you click the Posts link at the top is the When Your Fans Are Online page. Clicking the Post Types link gives you a chart that shows the type of content you post, the average reach for that type of content, and the average engagement for that type of content, broken down by post clicks and Likes, comments, and shares. Figure 19-7 shows you how different types of content are performing for this page.

Using this information, you can determine the type of content seen by the largest number of people (Reach), as well as what types of content receives the most engagement from your fans.

The final link below Posts is Top Posts from Pages You Watch. This section is where you get to spy on your neighbors, so to speak. If you click the Watch Page button for a particular page (see the "Overview" section earlier in this chapter), the content posted on that page that has the highest reach and the highest engagement numbers is listed here. Hey, if fans of Pages similar to yours like the content that's posted on those other Pages, chances are that your fans will like that same type of content. Consider posting similar types of content, and see what happens.

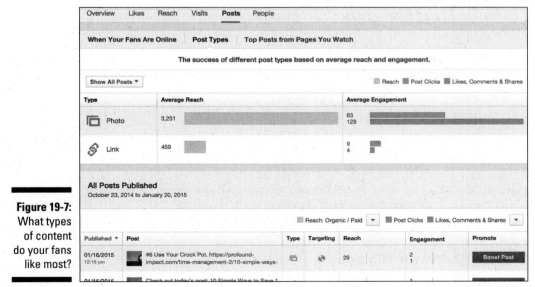

Figure 19-7: What types of content do your fans like most?

Figure used with permission of Julie Gray

People

The final link is the People link. Just like the Posts link, this link has three additional links below it. When you click the People link, you land on the Your Fans page. Next to the Your Fans page are the People Reached page and the People Engaged page.

The Your Fans link gives you demographic information about the people who like your Page. You see gender and age breakdowns, as well as the countries and cities where your fans are and the languages they speak.

Clicking the People Reached link shows you that same demographic information presented in relation to how your content reached these different groups. Perhaps 65 percent of your fans are female, but you reached only 40 percent of them. In other words, only 40 percent of your female fans saw your content. Age ranges, countries, cities, and languages are broken down in a similar way, although age ranges are presented as a percentage, whereas countries, cities, and languages are presented as a specific number of people.

The last link below People is People Engaged. This information is presented the same way as the People Reached data, but the numbers are specific to how many people interacted with your content.

Twitter growth metrics

Twitter Analytics is fairly young, having been rolled out to users in mid-2014. Don't let its youth fool you, though; you can do a lot with the information you glean from its numbers. In fact, Twitter Analytics is the place to go to measure and track the success of your Twitter strategy.

To see your Twitter Analytics, follow these steps:

1. **Log in to your Twitter account.**

   Your Twitter profile appears.

2. **Click your profile photo in the top-right corner of the page, and choose Analytics from the drop-down menu.**

   You're taken to your Tweet Activity home page.

Tweet Activity page

Twitter Analytics is broken into two categories: Tweets and Followers. Links to these categories are on the top menu bar. When you log in to Twitter Analytics, you land on the Tweet Activity page, shown in Figure 19-8.

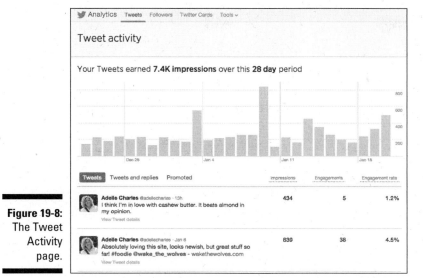

Figure used with permission of Adelle Charles

The bar graph in the center of the page shows how many impressions your tweets earned over a 28-day period — in other words, how many people saw your tweets in the past four weeks.

Below the bar chart are a few of your latest tweets, as well as impressions and engagements for each tweet and the engagement rate, which is the number of actions taken on your tweet (such as clicks and retweets) divided by the total number of impressions your tweets earned as a whole. You can sort this list by tweets, tweets and replies, or promoted tweets (ones you paid to promote).

Pay attention to these numbers, because they tell you how many people are interacting with each tweet. In other words, if your Engagement number for one of your tweets is 150, 150 people clicked somewhere in your tweet (links, username, and so on), retweeted it, replied to it, followed you because of it, or favorited it. That's a lot of opportunities for engagement, so pay attention if your numbers rise significantly.

When you click a tweet in your list, you see even more detailed information regarding each type of engagement.

On the right side of the Tweets page are five small, colorful charts showing the engagements for your tweets as a whole during the selected time period (see Figure 19-9). These charts show engagement rate, link clicks, retweets, favorites, and replies.

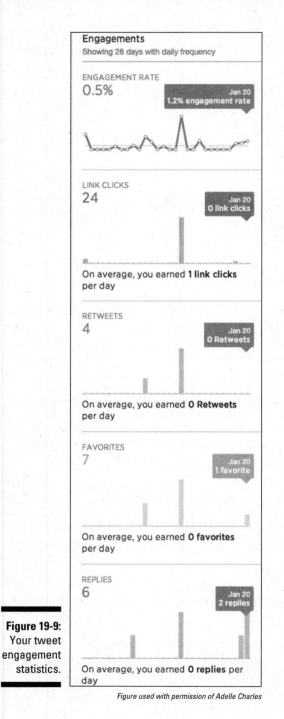

Figure 19-9:
Your tweet
engagement
statistics.

Figure used with permission of Adelle Charles

Use this information to determine what tweets get the most audience interaction. The higher the bar, the more of that type of engagement. Use this information to your advantage when planning your Twitter content strategy. If one of your tweets had a higher number of replies than usual, chances are that your followers had a lot to say about that topic. If another tweet had more link clicks than usual, your tweet text pulled people in and made them want to click to see what you shared.

Followers

The second category that Twitter Analytics offers is Followers (see Figure 19-10). In addition to the total number of followers you have (with changes illustrated in a line graph), you see the top countries and states where your followers live, their genders, their interests, and the other Twitter users your followers tend to follow. Whew. Say that ten times fast.

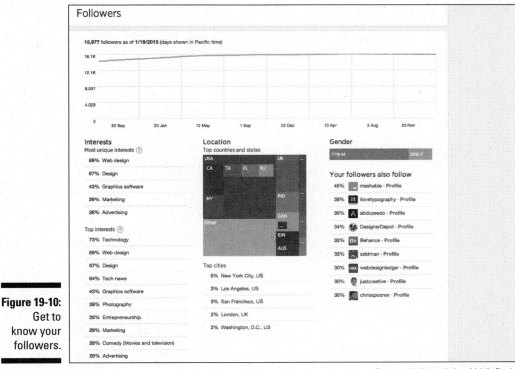

Figure 19-10: Get to know your followers.

Figure used with permission of Adelle Charles

The Location and Gender sections are pretty self-explanatory, but the Interests section is worth a closer look. Interests is broken into Most Unique Interests and Top Interests. The difference between the two is minute. Most Unique Interests are interests of your followers that are unique compared with the interests of all other Twitter users, whereas Top Interests are the topics that show up most among your followers.

This information is helpful for tailoring your content to your audience. Suppose that 69 percent of your followers' interests are related to graphic design and marketing. If you start tweeting links to blog posts about aquariums, chances are that your engagement numbers will be low. To keep your followers around, give them more of what they like.

The other section that deserves a detailed explanation is Your Followers Also Follow. This information is good to have for two reasons:

- It gives you a great opportunity to find new people to follow.

- If a fairly large number of your followers follow a certain account, chances are that they do so because they like the content this other account posts. Head on over to that account's Twitter stream to get an idea of the types of things that person tweets about, and consider modeling your content after it. Think about cultivating a relationship with this tweeter, especially if he's an influencer (see "Influence" earlier in this chapter). You never know — a really great, mutually beneficial relationship can develop.

Part VI
The Part of Tens

Read about ten social media resources worth following at
www.dummies.com/go/socialmediaoptimization.

In this part . . .

- ✔ Understanding ten fundamental rules of social media optimization

- ✔ Finding tools to help you manage your social media profiles

Chapter 20

Ten Rules of Social Media Optimization

*E*veryone loves lists of rules. How many rules are there for social media optimization (SMO)? It depends on whom you ask. I happen to think that ten meaningful rules can be extracted from the body of knowledge on SMO — ten rules with which you can achieve solid results.

I suggest to you that these rules lay a solid foundation for your social media practice and that you can use them as principles for creating an effective practice. The rules can be roughly grouped into three key areas: the approach to your constituents, the management of your practice, and the creation of appropriate content.

Be Authentic

Though these ten rules aren't arranged in any order, this one does belong at the top of the list. The number-one problem I see with social media managers worldwide is a tendency to fall into the trap of losing touch with people and simply parroting the company line. Social media is personal media — at least, it is when it's working well. If you want to create a connection with people, speak to them honestly and openly, from one person to another. You may be representing a powerful, high-profile corporation, but your audience is composed of ordinary human beings. Distance yourself from your competitors by remaining authentic and communicating with people on a personal level. Find a voice that allows you to be yourself, and you'll find the job easier and more rewarding. Always remember: High-impact social campaigns are built one person at a time.

Engage — Don't Broadcast

Broadcasting is one-way communication. Engagement is two-way communication. If someone reaches out to you with a question, a complaint, or a compliment, reply to that person. Embrace feedback, as it means that someone cares enough to take the time to express himself directly to you. If you ignore feedback, you've wasted a huge opportunity. Moreover, don't wait for people to reach out to you. Instead, try to engage them by using any of the following:

- ✔ Questions
- ✔ Surveys
- ✔ Polls
- ✔ Comment threads on articles
- ✔ Other interactive techniques that give people room for expression

The holy grail of social media is engagement. The potential for engagement is what separates this medium from traditional media. All your efforts should be geared toward creating a connection with the audience and encouraging them to interact with you. If you're able to create that connection, the result is goodwill that leaves a lasting positive impression.

Leverage Your Efforts

We're all busy enough, right? Social media management can be a huge time sink. I bet there's not a single person in the business who hasn't frittered away hours wandering about in the caverns of Facebook, YouTube, and Pinterest. It's far too easy to spend a lot of time with little to show for it. Even worse, if you're trying to juggle a large number of accounts, it's easy to burn out. The best way to avoid both of these common problems is to make a concerted effort to leverage your efforts. As the old saying goes: Work smarter, not harder. Some of the best solutions are some of the easiest:

- ✔ Use scheduling tools to create several posts in one session, and let the software publish them for you, either at the times you specify or according to the software's automated scheduling.

- ✔ Use content discovery tools, BuzzSumo (`http://buzzsumo.com`) or Klout (`https://klout.com`) to find new material, saving you hours of research.

- ✔ Use monitoring tools that make it easier for you to assess your efforts.

- ✔ Use cross-posting to automatically publish the same content across multiple channels.

Stay Fresh

You're working in a fast-paced, quickly changing environment. The people who tend to spend time on social media are also people who like new and interesting things. A large percentage of the audience can be characterized as early adopters — people who jump into new technologies without waiting to see whether those technologies are going to go mainstream. You need to be sensitive to the changes going on around you and, like your audience, be willing to try new things.

Don't hesitate to ask people what they're using. It's perfectly acceptable to ask something like this: "Has anyone discovered any cool new social media sites they'd like to share?" You may be surprised by what you find. You never want to miss a chance to gain a competitive advantage by being one of the first to discover an effective new channel. Don't be lulled into complacency by engaging only on the same old channels.

Be Selective

The world of social media includes a ridiculous (and growing) number of options. It seems that new sites and new tools crop up every month. Even though I encourage you to stay fresh by trying some new things, you can't possibly cover every channel or try every tool. You have to be selective. Go with proven winners, and when something new and interesting comes along, don't hesitate to give it a try, but don't sink a bunch of time into it until it proves itself to you.

Moreover, be willing to cut your losses if something isn't generating a return. Your time is better spent on a few effective efforts than on many marginal ones. The added advantage is that decreasing the complexity of your workload significantly reduces management overhead and allows you to be more engaged on the high-touch channels. Don't spread yourself too thin. If you do, all your efforts will suffer, and you're more likely to burn out.

Be Share-Friendly

One of my old bosses used to say, "Turn everyone into a salesman." I like that idea. The same concept can be applied to social media: Turn everyone into a publisher of your content. Fortunately, it is relatively easy to enable people to help publish your content. Social sharing plug-ins for your website are in ready supply; use them. Make it easy for people to share your content with all their friends and thereby turn your audience into your own personal legion of publishers.

Be a Resource

There's so much noise in the market, coming from so many products and brands. All those products and brands are competing for attention. Who will the consumer listen to? The answer is: They listen to the ones they trust. One of the best ways to build trust is to be a reliable resource. Don't simply be there when the customer wants to buy something; be there any time the customer needs something. Sometimes, all that customers need is a bit of guidance or access to good information. It costs you relatively little to provide that information, and the returns you get in goodwill and trust more than offset the expense.

Invest part of your time in creating useful content without a pure commercial agenda. Provide users the information they need to make informed decisions and earn their trust. If you become a trusted resource, you'll find that people will trust you when it comes time to make a purchase as well.

Create Great Content

I've said it before, and I'll say it again: Content is king. Great content inspires. Be a creator of awesome content, and you'll win fans, followers, and lifelong customers. Whether you're working with text, images, or video, be willing to invest in your content creators and enable them to create great content. Content is the lifeblood of your social media efforts. Great content has tremendous potential to become viral content and thereby deliver great rewards. After you find someone who has the ability to produce awesome content, don't let her go — and learn from her.

Know Your Audience

The better you can define your target markets, the more effective you're going to be in efforts to connect with them. Spend time looking at your demographics, and if that data is missing, make an effort to start collecting it. You need to know who you're talking to, as the audience shapes not only the message, but also the selection of the channel and the language used. Certain channels clearly appeal to certain audiences, and audiences do change and evolve. (Is anyone still using Friendster?)

Similarly, the voice you use needs to reflect the language and the sensibilities of your audience. There's no point in talking to a bunch of financial analysts as though they're surfers — and vice versa. The issue is appropriateness, and this is reflected in content selection, in vocabulary, and even in sense of humor. If you get your tone and your voice wrong, at best you're wasting your time; at worst, you have a public relations disaster on your hands.

Plan the Work; Work the Plan

Develop an SMO strategy. Define your objectives, set your goals, and then work the plan. Be aware of the outcomes you're seeking ,and measure against those outcomes. Although a plan alone isn't sufficient for success, failure to have an actionable plan will likely result in inefficiencies and may even result in failure to achieve a measurable effect.

Start with a road map, align your resources with the stages of the plan, and get to work. By following a sensible approach, you set yourself up for success, and you help keep everyone on the same page.

Chapter 21

Ten Tools for Managing Your Social Media Presence

In This Chapter

▶ Finding great tools for managing social media

▶ Understanding how the tools can help you

*I*n this chapter, I list ten of the social media management tools that I find the most helpful. Plenty of tools are on the market, and building the right tool kit is largely a subjective exercise. If you have tools that you love, keep using them. The list in this chapter includes things that I use on a daily basis and others that I've tried and liked but may not rely on. I've tried to avoid overlap, but invariably, some tools include the same features.

I suggest that you try all the following. I tried to select tools that offer free options, though many have more feature-rich commercial versions. I also encourage that you search for new tools periodically. The social media tools market is a very dynamic area, and new tools pop up every month.

Hootsuite

Hootsuite is a social media account management and publishing tool. The tool runs inside your browser, enabling you to stack your various Twitter accounts side by side in columns for easy viewing and management. Hootsuite includes publishing controls and autoscheduling to target the time when you can best reach your followers. Although most people use Hootsuite for Twitter, the tool can also handle Facebook and LinkedIn.

The free version of Hootsuite allows you to manage up to three profiles on a variety of services. In addition to publishing and monitoring tools, the system includes basic reports. Additional features are available to paid subscribers, starting for as little as $8.99 a month. Mobile versions are available for Android and iOS devices.

Learn more at `https://hootsuite.com`.

Quill Engage

Quill Engage isn't directly concerned with social media, but it certainly is helpful. The service connects to your Google Analytics account and emails you weekly and monthly reports on your website's traffic. This tool is a big step up from the automated reporting offered by Google Analytics, as Quill Engage uses artificial intelligence to take all the raw data gathered by Google and convert it to meaningful analysis. The tool is free and a huge time-saver by reducing complex data to actionable intelligence.

Learn more at `https://quillengage.narrativescience.com`.

Buffer

Buffer is a publishing management tool with built-in analytics. It can manage multiple accounts across Twitter, Facebook, Google+, and LinkedIn. The system includes a content discovery function to help you find items to post and helps you discover the optimal time for publishing on each of your channels.

Buffer offers a free plan with limited functionality and premium plans that include extra features starting at $10 a month. Unfortunately, the analytics feature isn't free. Buffer apps are available for both Android and iOS devices. An extension called Bulk Buffer (`https://www.bulkbuffer.com`) helps you upload and schedule large numbers of posts.

Learn more at `https://bufferapp.com`.

Instagress

Instagress automates your Instagram presence in some inventive and possibly even controversial ways. Just sign up, pick a time frame, and set up the campaign; Instagress does all the rest. The Instagress bot finds people, follows people, likes photos, posts comments on photos, and in general acts like a hyperactive "you" for the time period specified. Instagress is a bot, but it's a darn clever bot. There's a fee for using Instagress, but it's very afford-able. Plans start at $0.66 a day.

The system is a bit controversial as Instagram does not approve of auto-mated posting. Some people question how long Instagress will be with us; Instagram may ban or block it. But, for the time being, Instagress is a great way to fast-track the growth of your Instagram account and dramatically raise your profile.

Learn more at `https://instagress.com`.

Facebook Insights

Facebook provides a built-in analytics engine known as Insights. The ana-lytics tool is available free of charge for all Facebook Pages. Insights is a genuinely useful tool and one that Facebook seems committed to improving over time. You can track the success of your posts and your engagement levels, and you can also zero in on fan demographics and the best times to post. There's quite a bit of information inside Facebook Insights, and the tool deserves the small investment of time it takes to figure everything out.

Learn more at `https://www.facebook.com/help/336893449723054/`.

Twitter Analytics

Twitter Analytics is relatively new and may not be familiar to many users. For recently created business accounts, it seems to be turned on by default. For older and personal accounts, you have to set up Twitter Ads to enable Analytics. The setup is a bit confusing, but it's worth the time. The Analytics dashboard is useful and easy to use. Easy-to-decipher graphs show your most engaging tweets, your follower numbers, and much more. If you're also using Twitter Ads for promoting of, the Analytics dashboard provides your reporting engine.

Learn more at `https://analytics.twitter.com/about`.

Klout

Klout combines analysis of user influence with content discovery and pub-lication. You can tie your Klout account to Twitter, Facebook, Google+, LinkedIn, Instagram and Foursquare. The Klout engine assesses your follower count and engagement levels, and gives you a score reflecting your influence. You can also use Klout to discover users to follow and content to publish. The publishing tool allows you to schedule posts and to time them to the optimal viewing hours of your audience. Klout offers all the tools mentioned free of charge.

Learn more at `https://klout.com`.

Circloscope

Few Google+ management tools are available, which is a shame, as Google+ is a powerful tool but often difficult to master. Circloscope helps you manage your circles and discover new users. Multiple tools in Circloscope only works with the Chrome web browser. After you've installed Circloscope, the extension enables you to find and filter users by influence and connections and then add them to your own circles. The discovery tools are quite good. With a bit of cleverness, you can import your LinkedIn and Facebook friends, making Circloscope a great device for expanding your Google+ profile and connections.

Circloscope is a Chrome browser plug-in, and the free version has almost all the features of the pro version. Bulk tools aren't included in the free version, but they aren't necessary.

Download Circloscope from the Chrome Web Store at `https://chrome.google.com/webstore/detail/circloscope/mechgkelogghhgmpmbpofjijifdpppl`.

BuzzSumo

Discovering great content that you can share with your friends and followers is an ongoing challenge for all social media practitioners. Several tools are designed to help you with that task, but I think that one of the best is BuzzSumo. Just type your keywords, and BuzzSumo hunts down content for you. You can filter by date and even by type, such as infographics about WordPress produced in the past 30 days. You can even filter the results by their popularity on Facebook, Twitter, LinkedIn, Pinterest, and Google+, letting you identify the content with the most viral potential.

BuzzSumo also enables to find the most influential users. Simply type your keywords, and the system lists relevant users. You can filter by various criteria and even follow the accounts on Twitter directly from inside BuzzSumo.

The free version includes all the features discussed here. The paid version gives you a few more tools, but for many people, the free version does an admirable job. Paid plans start at $99 a month.

Learn more at `http://buzzsumo.com`.

Tagboard

Tagboard is a hashtag search engine. Use it to find all mentions of a hashtag across multiple social channels, including Twitter, Facebook, Google+, Instagram, YouTube, and Vimeo. It's a wonderful tool not only for discovering content, but also for planning and tracking custom hastags. If you want to use a hashtag for a campaign, start by visiting Tagboard and performing a search to find out whether the hashtag is already in use. When you have your campaign up and running, use Tagboard to track the reach of your tagged posts and see who else has used the tag. You can even set up searches and then link to the search results. Best of all: It's free!

Learn more at `https://tagboard.com`.

Index

• T •

About the Authors

Ric Shreves is the author of more than a dozen books on open source and online technologies, from Linux to content management to SEO. Ric began writing about tech in 1998 and has worked as a columnist for *ComputerWorld Magazine* and for the *Bangkok Post*. Ric began developing websites professionally in 1999 and has built websites for some of the world's largest brands, including BASF, Colgate-Palmolive, Tesco, and many others. An American by birth, Ric has been living in Asia for 20 years. He currently lives in Bali with two cats and two dogs. Ric has a BA and a Juris Doctor from St. Mary's University of San Antonio. This is sixth book for Wiley.

Michelle Krasniak is a freelance copywriter and marketing consultant who specializes in content marketing. She has been writing professionally for more than 15 years and has a passion for helping businesses of all sizes develop content to maximize their social media presence. Michelle co-authored *CityVille for Dummies* and regularly serves as the technical editor on social media and content marketing-related For Dummies books. She currently resides in Minneapolis.

Dedication

This book is dedicated to Ron Shreves, my brother. His selflessness in taking on heavy family responsibly has made a number of good things possible — including this book.

— *Ric Shreves*

I dedicate this book to my family and friends because your love, support, and encouragement throughout the years means more than you'll ever know. I love you all!

— *Michelle Krasniak*

Authors' Acknowledgments

I've written a number of books on technology for a number of publishers. Most tech titles are, quite frankly, a chore to write. The limitations of the subject matter combine with the publisher's own style restrictions to create what is typically very dry instructive text with little room for personality. When I got the chance to get into the For Dummies series, I was thrilled. Finally, a title that lets me play with new technology and write with some vibrancy. I went into this project with a lot of enthusiasm for the idea and never lost it as I went through the process of completing this text. That's not to say I didn't drift and deviate in my work process. Writing a book is always a bit of a roller-coaster ride. This particular ride was made do-able through the combined efforts of my project editor, Charlotte Kughen, and my acquisitions editor, Amy Fandrei. I really mean it when I say this title would never have happened without them. Thank you!

— *Ric Shreves*

I'd like to thank the team at Wiley, especially Acquisitions Editor Amy Fandrei and Project Editor Charlotte Kughen. Thank you for bringing me on board! Much work goes on behind the scenes, so thank you to the rest of the editorial team for all the hard work you put into getting everything into tip-top shape. Finally, a big thanks to my good friends (you know who you are!) who allowed me to occasionally hijack their social media lives in my never-ending quest for information.

— *Michelle Krasniak*

Publisher's Acknowledgments

Acquisitions Editor: Amy Fandrei

Project Editor: Charlotte Kughen

Copy Editor: Kathy Simpson

Technical Editor: Michelle Krasniak

Editorial Assistant: Claire Brock

Sr. Editorial Assistant: Cherie Case

Project Coordinator: Suresh Srinivasan

Cover Image: © iStockphoto.com / popcic